HUGH LANE

To Paul McGuinness, who first proposed Hugh Lane as a subject

HUGH LANE

1875–1915

Robert O'Byrne

THE LILLIPUT PRESS
DUBLIN

First published 2000 by
THE LILLIPUT PRESS LTD
62–63 Sitric Road, Arbour Hill,
Dublin 7, Ireland
www.lilliputpress.ie

A CIP record for this title is available from
The British Library.

1 3 5 7 9 10 8 6 4 2

ISBN 1 901866 55 6

*The Lilliput Press receives financial assistance
from An Chomhairle Ealaíon / The Arts Council of Ireland.*

Set in 10 on 15 Georgia
Printed in Ireland by Betaprint, Clonshaugh, Dublin

CONTENTS

Illustration sections after pages 84 and 148

PREFACE & ACKNOWLEDGMENTS

Little is remembered today of the life of Hugh Lane. He is a presence in every book written on the Irish cultural renaissance of the late nineteenth and early twentieth centuries and he is invariably introduced as Lady Gregory's nephew (whereas for many years she was perfectly happy to be known as his aunt). He is a peripheral character, not a central player, and in the familiar narrative of these years is assigned a handful of appearances that scarcely vary from one book to the next.

Reading of Lane and the work he undertook in Ireland in the first decades of the twentieth century, it seems baffling that his life has not received more attention. There are two explanations for this comparative neglect. One is that, unlike so many other people with whom he was associated – Yeats, Lady Gregory, George Moore, AE – he was not creative in the familiar sense of the word. He was, in effect, an impresario who inspired creativity in others. This has meant his achievements are not always tangible; how is it possible to measure with any degree of precision his influence on artists such as William Orpen, John B. Yeats, Augustus John or Gerald Kelly?

Another reason for the want of work on Lane has been the limitations of the available source material. Until now, almost all information about him will have come from two sources. Lady Gregory wrote a biography of Lane in 1920, five years after his death, primarily because a number of other authors had failed to perform the task to her satisfaction. Twelve years later Thomas Bodkin, who had been a close friend of Lane, also wrote about him. The two books had the same principal purpose: to argue Ireland's right to thirty-nine pictures previously owned by Lane, including valuable examples of Impressionism, whose ownership had been contested between Ireland and Britain since Lane's unexpected death. Bodkin's work had been commissioned for this very purpose by the Irish government of the time. The group of paintings, and the establishment of the Dublin gallery for which they had originally been destined, therefore figure largely in his book, as they do in that written by Lady Gregory. Even more than Bodkin, she felt driven by a sense of obligation to her deceased nephew, as well as duty to Ireland. She was never likely to be an impartial biographer and her book leaves a great deal about Lane's life unexplained.

While familiar with his work in Dublin, Lady Gregory knew far less about her nephew's activities elsewhere. Lane made his living as an art dealer, a profession that imposes a certain degree of discretion on its practitioners; clients may require confidentiality about their purchases, for example, and business rivals (of which Lane had many) can take advantage of any details that are divulged. Bodkin correctly observed that 'Lane could be enigmatic when he chose, and his designs were not always quite apparent to everyone.'[1] The sense of enigma was greatly increased by Lane's inability to communicate his intentions or wishes clearly. His responses were intuitive and he expected to find the same characteristic in others. When this proved not to be the case – a frequent occurrence – his response was bafflement. But he remained a poor communicator, shrank from speaking in public, wrote little other than a handful of catalogue prefaces, and even in the expression of his judgements on art usually lapsed into banality.

In many respects, he was an eccentric man. Although conservative by nature and anxious not to draw attention to himself, he could be indifferent to public opinion. One feature of Lane's character on which contemporaries often remarked was his meanness when spending money on food or drink. As Henry Tonks wrote of Lane after his death, 'He would pay seventy pounds for a box at a charity ball, and have his meal at a coffee stall on the way.'[2] He preferred to walk rather than pay a taxi or bus fare, but could lose hundreds of pounds without a qualm while gambling in Monte Carlo. Lane saw nothing odd in such apparent contradictions. Nor did he seem to feel the necessity to reveal anything of an inner, emotional life. He wrote an enormous number of letters, but in all his extant correspondence there is no reference to personal feelings. Certainly, he could express anger or disappointment when his work failed to go as planned, or delight on occasions when success was achieved. But these emotions concerned his professional activities, not his private life. Of the latter he made no mention.

The temptation is to view such an absence as being due to reticence or the necessity for concealment and to believe that he had some alternative hidden life. An article about Lane in the *Irish Times* in 1995 proposed that 'folk memory in Dublin has privately held that his inborn inclinations were similar to Wilde's or Casement's'.[3] This judgement, presumably, is based on Lane's devotion to art, his somewhat effeminate manner and his bachelor status. Today, it seems impossible to imagine that not everyone is sexually active, or at least conscious of sexual opportunity. Lane's inclinations may have been homosexual. 'Folk memory' aside, however, there is no firm evidence of this. His name was never linked with that of any other man and his close male friends, such as William Orpen, Grant Richards and Alec Martin, were married and indisputably heterosexual. Any hypothesis as to Lane's sexuality must quickly lapse into speculation.

What cannot be disputed is the force of his personality and its appeal to both sexes. He knew, and was held in high regard by, a great many people, but somehow remained slightly aloof, or disengaged, from them all. He seems to have reserved his most intense emotions for inanimate objects. Art was his greatest, if not only, passion; as Tonks commented, Lane had 'an almost morbid desire to surround himself with the most beautiful objects possible'.[4] The occasion on which he appeared most distraught was when he was threatened with the sale of his private collection due to financial necessity. 'I suppose that it is always what one cares for most that gives us most trouble and anxiety,' he wrote to Lady Gregory at the time. 'In my case it is the probable losing of all my pictures.'[5] A three-page document describing Lane, sadly unsigned, comments: 'His interest in art was everything, it filled his life completely – human beings hardly counted.'[6] Perhaps the clearest proof of Lane's priorities comes from his will. Although he knew that the person to whom he was closest, his sister Ruth Shine, had very little money on which to live, he left her only a relatively small bequest and the bulk of his estate went to create a picture-buying fund for the National Gallery of Ireland. Art and its dissemination always took precedence over people.

Lane's inarticulateness meant that he could express his love of art only through action. This helps to explain why, despite constant setbacks, he was so driven to accomplish his ambitions; he needed to demonstrate his devotion to and, ideally, convince others of the merits of what he loved. His failure to appreciate the importance of language as a means of persuasion often led to disappointment. This was especially the case in Ireland, where verbal dexterity has always been held in high regard and where the visual arts have never received as much support as literature. It is a cliché to claim that the Irish are visually illiterate, but one borne out by Lane's efforts to encourage greater appreciation of art in Dublin and Belfast. These attempts failed more often than not, and yet he never gave up the struggle.

His loyalty to Ireland was strange and unexpected. Perhaps, as George Moore proposed, Lane was following Lady Gregory's example and therefore felt he must always 'be doing something for Ireland'.[7] Equally important, Ireland offered him opportunities that would not have been available to an ambitious young man in Britain. But undoubtedly there was also a personal fascination with Ireland and a genuine desire for its betterment. In her memoirs, Daisy, Countess of Fingall, who knew Lane well, wrote of many men, mostly politicians, who came from London to try to improve conditions in Ireland. She regularly advised them not to become too engaged by the country because in her estimation Ireland sucked its admirers dry of all energy. 'You should not give the Irish anything that they do not ask for,' remarked her husband.[8] Lane should certainly have heeded that advice before he embarked on his Irish schemes; usually uninvited, they were largely thankless and frequently unsuccessful. Of course he eventually became aware that this was the customary outcome. While considering the idea of applying for the directorship of the National Gallery of Ireland, he told Dermod O'Brien (a rival for the position) that he realized 'how little Dublin cares for work which may cost one one's life blood'.⁹ Even his one indisputable achievement, the foundation of a modern art gallery in Dublin, did not live up to his expectations. Not only were purpose-built premises never found during his lifetime but, more importantly, the collection failed to make the impact he intended. In successive catalogue prefaces, Lane always argued that only the presence in Ireland of a representative selection of international contemporary art could ensure that the country developed its own distinctive school of painters. In fact, there is nothing to show that when a group of recognizably Irish artists, such as Paul Henry and Seán Keating, emerged in the first decades of the twentieth century they had in any way been influenced by, or were even necessarily aware of, Dublin's Municipal Gallery of Modern Art.

Of course, Ireland was never Lane's only sphere of activity. His career as a dealer was based in London, where he was familiar with most of the leading artists and curators of the period. His social life too centred at least as much on England as Ireland. Then there was his work in, and for, another country offering opportunities to the ambitious, South Africa. Looking at how much he achieved, and in so short a space of time, it becomes clear that Lane was a man who felt impelled to accomplish certain tasks regardless of obstacles placed in his way.

After his premature death, and even during his lifetime, Hugh Lane was something of a blank slate onto which more articulate members of the creative élite in Ireland and Britain could project their own aspirations. Until now, therefore, most of what has been said and written about him has been refracted through other mythologies. The intention of this book is to examine Lane's life on its own terms, and to relocate him closer to the centre of cultural life, particularly in Ireland, during the period in which he attempted to increase public appreciation of visual art.

The author wishes to thank the following people and institutions for their kindness and assistance: Brendan Barrington; Fr Roger Bush; Jillian Carman; Kit Orpen Casey; Fionnuala Croke; Barbara Dawson; Bríd Doyle; Roy Foster; Kathy Gilfillan; Vivienne Guinness; Christina Kennedy; Ruth Kermode; Noel Kissane; Bernard Meehan; Gareth O'Connor; Brendan O'Donoghue; James Pethica; Susanna Segnit; Michael Stevenson; David

Thistlethwaite; and the respective staffs of the National Library of Ireland, the library of the National Gallery of Ireland, the Hugh Lane Municipal Gallery of Modern Art, and the Berg Collection at the New York Public Library. Finally, acknowledgment is due to the Board of Trinity College Dublin for permission to quote from Thomas Bodkin's papers, and to the Council of Trustees, National Library of Ireland, for permission to quote from various sources in their possession.

1
CHILDHOOD

While in Dublin for the annual Season in 1885, George Moore addressed himself to the Lord Lieutenant's State Steward. Moore explained that he was writing a novel, which he would call *A Drama in Muslin*, dealing with the social and political power wielded by the viceregal authorities. He therefore wished to be invited to an official dinner party in order to make sure that what he wrote was accurate. The invitation, however, was not forthcoming, perhaps because Moore had boasted to the State Steward that his books were extensively read. So too was the account of his application's refusal which Moore subsequently wrote for a nationalist newspaper, the *Freeman's Journal*.

The dinner which he had so hoped to attend was just one of a series of social events that took place each year between early February and mid-March. The Dublin Season was always a short affair, allowing those participants with sufficient income and inclination to move on to London where a longer programme of balls, receptions and other entertainments was available. In Dublin, all attention and activity centred on the Castle. Here the Lord Lieutenant and his entourage – not just the State Steward but also the Chamberlain, the Gentleman Usher, the Comptroller, the Master of the Horse and assorted ADCs and Gentlemen-in-Waiting – took up residence in the State Apartments for the six-week duration of the Season, temporarily forsaking more comfortable quarters in the Phoenix Park. The highlights of the social programme were a brace each of levees (attended by men only), balls and Drawing Rooms. It was at the last of these, which began at half-past ten in the evening, that Irish débutantes formally came out by being presented to the Lord Lieutenant. Customarily dressed in white satin with a regulation train of three yards, each girl would be brought into the Throne Room and there kissed on both cheeks by His Excellency before taking a handful of steps backwards and exiting with whatever dignity she had managed to retain. A buffet supper was then served in the Castle's adjacent Picture Gallery.

This was the ceremony in which Adelaide Persse participated when she made her court début in late February 1861. At twenty-one, she was the same age as Alice Barton, the heroine of *A Drama in Muslin,* and therefore somewhat older than most débutantes. But within her own family she was one of the few members to enjoy this privilege: her younger sister Augusta had to do without a Dublin season when she reached marriageable age.

The Persses were members of that now-vanished class, the landed gentry. Family tradition claimed filiation with the Percys of Northumberland and indicated that a forbear had been settled in Ireland during the Cromwellian period. Since the latter part of the seventeenth century, they had lived in a house called Roxborough, five miles from Loughrea in County Galway and set in an estate of some six thousand acres. Adelaide Persse's father Dudley differed little from either his predecessors or his peers except perhaps in fecundity; with the help of two wives, he oversaw a household of sixteen children, which explains why he could not afford to send all of them to Dublin for the Season. Frances, his second spouse and Adelaide's mother, had been pretty and frivolous when young; but in middle-age, like *A Drama's* Ladies Cullen, she spent much of her time attempting to convert Roxborough's Catholic tenantry to Protestantism, and her older daughter Elizabeth, having married a neighbour Walter Shawe-Taylor, opened a proselytizing school at Castle Taylor. The Persses' excessive interest in the salvation of local souls was later cited as an explanation for why Roxborough was burnt down in 1922.

Adelaide Persse was also to turn to religion but this trait had yet to show itself when she went to Dublin to be presented at the viceregal court. She had been considered the family beauty and therefore expected to make a good match. As a rule, Mrs Persse discouraged money being spent on dresses since the end of the world might be imminent, but an exception was made in the case of her best-looking child. The cost of a season in Dublin was justified by the thought of its probable outcome. However, following the St Patrick's Ball which officially closed the Castle's – and thus the capital's – annual festivities, Adelaide Persse returned to Galway without having met her match. There had been admirers but none of these proposed marriage, perhaps because, despite being beautiful, she was shy and nervous in company. The following year saw the same scenario and so, it appeared, she was destined to remain unwed. She had fallen in love with a cousin but was forbidden by her mother even to consider the possibility of an engagement.[1]

Instead, like other members of her family, she began to occupy herself with matters spiritual, and this may be how she came to meet James Lane, a young divinity student at Trinity College, Dublin. For more than a century, Lane's family were affluent merchants in Cork. His grandfather had been mayor of the city some thirty years earlier, one of three ancestors to hold this office (seven had been elected as high sheriff of Cork). His father, also called James, qualified as a solicitor before establishing a legal practice that continued until late in the twentieth century, when this branch of the family died out. However, his eldest son showed little interest in law and after schooling at Winchester College in Hampshire, the younger James Lane went to Dublin in 1864 intending to become a clergyman. But first he became engaged to Adelaide Persse, whose family immediately made plain their disapproval. Unlike many troublesome Irish engagements, religious difference was not a problem in this instance. Not only was James Lane a divinity student, but one of his great-uncles had built a Church of Ireland chapel-of-ease at his own expense.

At Roxborough, it was later remembered, the news of Adelaide Persse's proposed engagement was received as though a death had occurred. The family's old nurse announced that she always mistrusted names like Street, Field or Lane because they tended to be given to foundlings. For the Persses, there were more fundamental reasons for discouraging the proposed marriage. A young cleric, after all, was unlikely to enjoy a substantial income. Furthermore, the Lanes, as a brief glance at Burke's invaluable guide could show, were not landed gentry; they were tradesmen and one of them owned a brewery in Cork. And finally, Adelaide Persse was more than six years her fiancé's senior.[2]

Despite all objections raised, she and James Lane proved intractable in their determination and they were therefore instructed by their respective families to stay apart for the next three years. They were not to meet and only permitted to write to each other once annually. James Lane continued with his studies and Adelaide Persse returned to County Galway. Here, she bided her time and took part in whatever local amusements were available, such as amateur theatricals at other houses like Lismany near Ballinasloe.

Her future husband, meanwhile, moved to Emmanuel College, Cambridge, where he took his degree in 1869, the same year he was made a deacon. Twelve months later, he became a Church of England priest and finally received permission from her parents to marry Adelaide Persse. But, as an indication of their continued disapproval, they did not allow the ceremony to take place in the church on Roxborough's demesne and another nearby chapel had to be used instead.

Following their marriage, James and Adelaide Lane moved to Kingston-upon-Hull in Yorkshire, where James was a curate in the parish of St Mary's. There they remained for three years before he was transferred south to St Andrew's, Walcott, Bath, in 1873. It was here that Adelaide had her first surviving child, Alfred, two girls having died almost immediately after birth. In 1874 another boy, Harold, was born. The following winter she was pregnant again and temporarily living in Ireland. James Lane's recently deceased aunt, Eliza Lane, had left him a property called Ballybrack in Douglas, a village two miles from Cork city where she had subscribed to the building of a new church.

Though only constructed a few decades earlier, Ballybrack House was full of family pictures and furniture, and Adelaide Lane sorted through these items while waiting for the birth of her child. He arrived on 9 November 1875 and was christened Hugh Percy. Soon afterwards, the family returned to Bath and Hugh Lane never again spent any time in Cork until, with a tragic irony, he died almost within sight of the place where he had been born.

Aside from occasional holidays abroad, James Lane's clerical responsibilities were to keep him in England for the rest of his life. In 1876 he was moved again, to Stonehouse East near Plymouth in Devon, but within twelve months had at last been given his own parish. Although its residents might dispute this description, Redruth in Cornwall is not an especially prepossessing part of the county and was even less attractive a proposition in the nineteenth century when the town was at the very heart of the English copper-mining industry, which accounted for two-thirds of global production. The surrounding landscape was scarred with some 350 pits and their associated buildings, remains of which can still be seen today. Mining only began to fail towards the end of the century when cheaper sources of copper were discovered elsewhere around the world, but for much of James Lane's time in the area it was the chief source of employment. If Cornwall had any attraction for Adelaide Lane, it was that her younger sister Gertrude had married a local man, Edmund Beauchamp of Trevince; unfortunately, Gertrude Beauchamp had died in 1876 leaving three young daughters.

A local report at the time of James Lane's appointment estimated the living of Redruth to be worth around £900 annually – in fact, the annual income was only a little more than half that amount – and described its new rector as being an 'evangelical but broad churchman'.[3] Although the population of Redruth and its surrounding district numbered in the region of 40,000, the great majority of these people were Methodist, Wesley having preached here with great success on a number of occasions from 1762 onwards. Nonetheless, James Lane decided to undertake the building of a new church, St Andrew's, the foundation stone of which was laid in July 1883. Consecration took place in November of the following year although much still remained to be done. Funds for the project were always short; an appeal collecting book from 1885 announces that while almost £5,000 had been raised from parishioners, local efforts were now exhausted and a further £700 still needed.[4] Work on St Andrew's was not completed until the mid-1930s.

Meanwhile, the Lane family continued to grow. A fourth son, Ambrose, was born in 1878 and followed by a girl, Ruth, two years later. Adelaide Lane gave birth to her youngest child, Eustace, in 1884. By then, she was already spending much of her time apart from James Lane. The marriage had proven to be unhappy almost from the start. Many years later, Adelaide's sister Augusta would blame the couple's separation during their engagement for the troubles that followed. Instead of having an opportunity to discover whether their personalities were naturally suited to one another, they had been kept apart. The marriage, she argued, had been based on nothing more than a shared determination to thwart parental wishes. In order to produce Hugh Lane, two lives had been spoiled.[5]

Their characters were certainly very different. Whereas Adelaide Lane was self-effacing and socially reserved, her husband was expansive and accustomed to getting his own way. They soon found out how few interests they shared. He loved to read, for example, unlike his wife. She had, after all, grown up at Roxborough, a household in which sporting pursuits always took precedence over those of the intellect, particularly as Mrs Persse forbade her children to read novels before they were eighteen. In an attempt to please her fiancé during their long engagement, Adelaide Persse had once sent him a poem she copied from a book. James Lane thought this her own work and it was only a few days after the marriage that he discovered the truth. She told one of her sisters of the disappointment this caused him and added that 'things never went very well with us after that'.[6] Their early years together also proved trying to Adelaide, who had moved from the comforts of a large country estate to living in a northern English city on a curate's meagre salary. Travelling back from a visit to stay with the Archbishop of York and his wife, the Lanes sat in a second-class railway carriage and discovered their companions were the servants who had waited on them at table the night before. It was a harsh way to learn the merits of personal humility. Adelaide Lane found it easier to practise the tenets of her religion from Roxborough, where her family had considerable social status, than she did as the wife of a minor clergyman.

Soon after the family moved to Cornwall, she began to travel, staying in a variety of towns along the south coast of England and sometimes going as far afield as the Channel Islands and even Paris, where young Hugh may have spent a year with his mother. Plymouth, Portsmouth,

Jersey all provided temporary homes for her during these years, after which she would come back to Redruth and her duties as the rector's wife. In the parish, she presided over a variety of charity bazaars and her children were mentioned in local newspapers as helping in whatever way they could to raise funds for good causes. Master Hugh P. Lane would play the piano while his younger sister Ruth participated in fancy-dress parades. But much of the time they were moving from place to place with their mother as, financially supported by her own family back in Ireland, she regularly left James Lane and Redruth. As a result of her restlessness, none of the young Lanes ever benefited from much formal schooling, although some of the elder brothers studied in Heidelberg. Thomas Bodkin later suggested that Hugh Lane's limited education had left him with a handicap when it came to being persuasive in either speech or print.[7] However, even a cursory glance at his subsequent career shows this not to have been wholly true: Lane's conversation was distinguished by an irresistible charm. Nonetheless he always felt at a disadvantage. When proposing himself for the directorship of the National Gallery of Ireland in 1914, he admitted his academic skills were almost nonexistent and observed that the only subject for which he had ever acquired much aptitude was history.[8] But he also managed to study music, always a comfort for the rest of his life, and to learn rudimentary French during visits to France with his mother. Poor health meant he was unable to spend time studying in Heidelberg, unlike his elder brothers; in the diary kept on his first visit to Germany, he wrote that being unable to speak or understand the native language was a drawback.

Adelaide Lane was never the easiest of wives but she was always an attentive mother; her sister Augusta thought that, had such a career been possible at the time, she would have made an excellent nurse.[9] Of all her children, she was particularly close to Hugh during these years as he was less healthy than his siblings and more in need of special attention. His father was liable to grow irritated and impatient with the delicate boy who, unlike his heartier brothers and many cousins, showed no interest in playing outdoors. Instead, he would remain inside looking after plants, dressing up dolls or making decorations. William Orpen said that during Lane's childhood, 'his chief joy was needlework, and beautiful things he did, which he kept near him always'.[10] When brought over to Roxborough, he never went shooting or hunting ferrets but spent his time looking at the Persse family paintings and miniatures and examining old ornaments.

These early years do not seem to have been a particularly happy time for Lane and later accounts of his life make few references to them. In adulthood, he appears to have spoken little or not at all to friends about his youth. He kept almost no souvenirs from the period beyond a handful of press cuttings. Nor after leaving Cornwall in his late teens did he ever revisit the area, even though his father continued to live there. It is almost as though he had made a decision to erase the past. Discovering which aspects of his character were already evident during Lane's youth is therefore almost impossible, although surviving photographs show that from an early age he possessed a love of fancy dress. Not yet five, he can be seen on a swing in Paris, decked out in dark velvet with heavy lace collar and cuffs. Five years later in Truro, he was photographed dressed as a Chinese mandarin, while at the age of fourteen his choice of costume is that of a mid-eighteenth-century gentleman. Like his mother, he read little but his highly attuned visual sense was soon apparent. Therefore, while he was in his mid-teens and living in Plymouth, Adelaide Lane arranged for him to take lessons with an elderly woman who cleaned and restored pictures. Called Mrs Hopkins, her pride was considerably greater than her income and so she refused to accept any money for the skills she taught the boy. Instead, Adelaide Lane would give her an occasional bottle of port wine and some biscuits, but this recompense was insufficient: Ruth Lane would later remember that Mrs Hopkins eventually died of starvation.[11]

Once more on her travels, in the early 1890s Adelaide Lane took the decision to seek a formal separation from her husband. Such a step was highly unusual for a clergyman's wife, and this may explain why the process took so long. She did not achieve her ambition until the end of 1893 and only then thanks to the involvement of her sister Augusta. The latter both undertook to intercede with James Lane's solicitor and underwrote Adelaide Lane's substantial costs. As the marriage disintegrated, it seems that the rector had sought sympathy from someone other than his wife; while nothing untoward necessarily took place, Adelaide Lane had gained possession of letters to her husband from another woman. These she handed back only in return for her dowry of £2,000. A legal agreement was signed in December and Adelaide Lane parted from her husband for the last time.[12] They appear never to have met again and James Lane had little thereafter to do with his children except, curiously, Hugh, who had so irritated him when younger. In 1907, for example, the son arranged for his father to be painted by William Orpen. By then, Hugh Lane had long since established himself in the career begun around the same time as his parents formally separated.

2
THE APPRENTICE DEALER

Augusta Persse, unlike her elder sister Adelaide, had never been expected to find a husband. But in 1880, at the age of twenty-seven, she married a County Galway landowner, Sir William Gregory, a widower thirty-five years her senior. The marriage was a success in part because Augusta Gregory assumed the role of pupil to her husband, who was able to give his bride all the educational stimulation she had lacked at Roxborough. Sir William's varied career had drawn to a close by the time he married for the second time, but he remained active in both political and cultural circles and continued to travel extensively. In London, among his other duties, he had been chairman of a committee appointed to oversee the reform of the British Museum and was a Trustee of the National Gallery, to which he bequeathed a number of paintings. He and his wife therefore knew many artists. Some of these remained close to Lady Gregory after her husband's death in March 1892; among the most important friends from these years was the Irish-born painter and Director of the National Gallery, Sir Frederic Burton.

Augusta Gregory also saw a considerable amount of the peripatetic Adelaide Lane, to whom she gave both moral and financial support; she paid for young Eustace Lane's education when his mother could not afford to do so. Around the time of the Lanes' legal separation, their son Hugh reached the age of eighteen and it became necessary for him to find some kind of professional occupation. With scarcely any schooling, he was unfit for most jobs but his interest in art was thought to hold promise. Lady Gregory's assistance was once more requested. She asked advice from another old friend of her husband, Sir John Charles Robinson, then Keeper of the Queen's Pictures, and he, in turn, put Hugh Lane in contact with Martin Colnaghi, a London art dealer who gave the young man a job in his gallery at the salary of a pound a week.

Hugh Lane's entry into the art world could scarcely have occurred at a more propitious moment. It coincided with a rapid growth in both supply of and demand for old master paintings. Until the closing decades of the nineteenth century the market for these pictures had remained relatively static simply because the number of fine examples coming up for sale had been limited. That situation now began to change radically, for several reasons. Among the most important of these was the declining value of land during the last quarter of the century, as cheap imports of grain from the Americas caused prices in Britain to fall by almost 50 per cent. Landowners suddenly found the value of their holdings enormously diminished and they needed to discover other means of generating revenue. In this, they were helped by recent legislative changes: the Settled Land Act of 1882 (and its successor two years later) permitted owners of heirlooms to override even the strictest of wills and dispose of their assets in a way previously impossible. The result was a spate of auctions during Lane's youth in which the contents of country houses were sold, the earliest of which were the Hamilton Palace sale of 1882, the Stowe sale of 1884 and the Blenheim sale of 1886. Thereafter, scarcely a year passed without another great collection going under the hammer and with many individual works of art being discreetly removed from the walls of a grandee's home and offered to a dealer. The situation was further aggravated after death duties were introduced by a Liberal government in 1894, which only increased the pressure on owners to dispose of artworks in their possession.

Bad as their predicament was in England, Scotland and Wales, the plight of landowners in Ireland was infinitely worse, not just because their estates had always made smaller returns but also because this was the era of the land wars, during which many tenants refused to pay the rents demanded. Combined with agricultural depression and accumulated mortgages on their estates, the result was that Irish landlords often made barely any money at all from their holdings. When George Moore inherited his County Mayo estate in 1870, for example, although it was supposedly worth £4,000 a year, after all debts were serviced, he received an annual income of only £500. Many landlords in Ireland were forced by their mortgage holders to sell up entirely, as was the case in 1881 with Lord Fermoy who, forever short of cash, was later to sell a number of family paintings to Hugh Lane. In Ireland, as elsewhere, the most obvious solution to the pressing want of ready money was to sell off valuable possessions either in a single glorious auction or, more commonly, one by one as need demanded.

It was a feature of the landowning classes of the late nineteenth century that they rarely displayed any great interest in the art collections so lovingly assembled by their predecessors except when the works in question could be transformed into cash. The experience of Helen, Countess of Radnor was typical of the period: when she had asked her father-in-law about the origins of his family's exceptional collection of old masters, he told her he had no idea where any of them came from and did not believe anyone else knew. The inference was that nobody should care very much about such matters.[1] Even if severely devalued, land still remained the ultimate symbol of wealth and was cherished as such. It was the last possession to be sold, whereas moveable treasures were far more frequently put on the market, particularly since the price they made was increasing even as that fetched by land was in decline. In the decades immediately preceding the First World War, landed families regularly offered heirlooms for sale. Between 1886 and 1902, the second Earl of Dudley, who was to be Ireland's Lord Lieutenant during Lane's first years in Dublin, sold paintings, jewels and other treasures worth almost a quarter of a million pounds and he was regarded as a wealthy peer. Less affluent aristocrats, such as the Marquess of Anglesey, had to sell the entire contents of their homes.

Thankfully for such people, their desire to sell works of art was matched by the wish to buy them on the part of a new class of collector. These individuals were almost never British, the majority of them being American and South African, although there was also a small group of

Germans who bought not for themselves but for state institutions. The late nineteenth and early twentieth centuries were the period in which the concept of art as investment began to be widely understood. In 1891, for example, the *Art Journal* was advising readers on the difference in financial returns between fine art and stocks and shares, while the September 1903 issue of the *Connoisseur* carried a feature on 'Collecting as an Investment'.[2] In August 1905 the *Burlington* magazine could write that attending art auctions had become 'a society craze' before going on to warn potential bidders of how 'grotesquely extravagant prices' were being paid for 'rubbish'.[3] But a great many genuinely valuable art works were also being offered for sale at this time, and whereas a number of other European countries passed laws to ensure important pieces could not be exported, Britain continued to allow her treasures to leave. Only private initiatives such as the creation of the National Art Collections Fund in 1903 ensured that certain important old masters were saved for the state. However, once started, the emptying of the nation's great houses was impossible to stop; in 1909 and 1910, more than £1 million worth of art left Britain. Among the most notorious transactions of these years was the sale to American collector P.A.B. Widener of Rembrandt's *The Mill* by the Marquess of Lansdowne, who owned large estates in Ireland.

The plight of landowners forced by changing circumstances to sell family heirlooms was widely publicized even if it excited relatively little public sympathy. Among the fictional depictions of aristocratic impoverishment and its consequences was Henry James's *The Outcry* (1911), in which Lord Theign must sell a portrait by Sir Joshua Reynolds to an American collector in order to raise essential funds. At the time of the book's publication, many readers believed the novelist had based the character of Hugh Crimble, an art devotee, on Hugh Lane. James, after all, had been a friend of Lady Gregory for almost thirty years and during the last decade of his life he became devoted to another of her many nephews, Dudley Jocelyn Persse. Lane was not Crimble, however: his aunt only introduced him to Henry James after *The Outcry* had been written.

For much of the nineteenth century, two firms of art dealers had been pre-eminent in London: Agnew's and Colnaghi's. The number of dealers now grew in proportion to the amount of business being offered. However, the profession only very gradually acquired the respectability it was to enjoy for much of the twentieth century. When Hugh Lane began his career, art dealing was not a well-ordered business and its practitioners were looked upon with suspicion. Of course a great deal of money could be – and was – made by the most skilful players. The Bostonian collector Isabella Stewart Gardner, for example, was to pay £1,500 in 1900 for Giotto's *The Presentation in the Temple*, which had been sold at an English country house auction eight years earlier for £1. The substantial profits dealers enjoyed did little to help their popularity; but their reputation suffered also because so many of them were Jewish in an age when anti-Semitism was still widespread, if not always overt, in British society. Dealers like Duveen, Kleinberger and Wertheimer – all Jewish – came to the fore and made themselves extremely wealthy through the sale of artworks that had usually been in the possession of the same family for centuries. When Maud Gonne wished to aggravate W.B. Yeats in 1913, she sneeringly dismissed his friend Lane as acting like a 'Jew picture dealer', adding that since he had lived in that world, it was to be expected he would adopt Jewish habits of mind and conduct.[4] And even Lady Gregory was not immune to such prejudice, telling her nephew in 1911 that he should travel to New York and take for himself some of the enormous profits being made on picture sales there by Jews.[5] In the biography she wrote of him she also used the term 'Hook noses' when referring to other dealers with whom her nephew was in competition.[6] Soon after she had helped Lane establish himself in London, her friend Sir Arthur Birch wrote expressing the wish that she might find something else for her nephew to do as dealing was too difficult a business and he possessed too nice a disposition.[7] Evidently, this was no profession for a gentleman.

Martin Colnaghi, to whom Lady Gregory secured an introduction for Lane, was one of the most successful dealers of his generation and was to exert a lasting influence over his young employee, even if the period in which they worked together was brief. His grandfather had started the original firm of Colnaghi's (which still continues to operate in London) but, following the example of his father, Martin Colnaghi had established an independent business in 1860. By the time Hugh Lane joined him in

1893, he was dealing from premises called the Marlborough Gallery at 53 Pall Mall, where he showed both old masters and examples of more recent work such as the Barbizon school. Colnaghi believed the best way to learn about art was not by reading books but through examining work, and this was just one of the many lessons he passed on to his staff. He was particularly knowledgeable about Flemish and Dutch pictures of the sixteenth and seventeenth centuries. These were also to be among Lane's own greatest areas of expertise. Colnaghi claimed to have handled one hundred works by Frans Hals at prices varying from £5 to £100, but, as will be seen, his judgement was by no means infallible. One of his greatest coups was buying a Raphael from the Earl of Ashburnham for £17,000; the American collector J.P. Morgan later paid £80,000 for this picture. When he died in June 1908 at the age of eighty-six, Colnaghi left a number of paintings to the National Gallery in London, as well as the residue of his fortune to establish a purchasing fund for the same institution.

Martin Colnaghi was already in his seventies when he took on Hugh Lane, a boy of eighteen, as an apprentice dealer. At first the two seemed to take to each other, but relations very quickly deteriorated, and barely six months after taking up his position Lane was being asked to leave. Lady Gregory was to suggest a number of reasons for this unfortunate outcome: her nephew's handwriting, she argued, was almost illegible due to a childhood injury (her own script, however, as anyone who has attempted to read her voluminous correspondence can testify, is infinitely worse); Lane's manners were too courtly and smooth for his employer's tastes; the young dealer wanted to know too much too fast.[8] But her diaries from the time suggest that Lane was also inclined to give himself airs unsuited to someone occupying a very junior position. In early summer 1894, she wrote that although she had taken her nephew out to lunch on several occasions, what she described as his second-rate fashionable talk and vulgarity of mind always irritated her.[9] But he did confide one amusing story to her which demonstrated that even the most experienced of dealers could be deceived. His one ally in the Marlborough Gallery was its manager, John Caroline, a lifelong friend remembered in Lane's will. Caroline painted from memory a picture he had once seen by Frans Hals and was persuaded by Lane to put this into a public auction as an example of the Dutch artist's work. There it was bought by Martin Colnaghi, who brought the picture back in triumph to the gallery; although he eventually realized he had acquired a fake, he never learned who was behind the deception.[10] A letter from Lady Gregory to Adelaide Lane shows that she tried to arrange a reconciliation between her nephew and Colnaghi who, she was told by Humphrey Ward, art critic of *The Times* and husband of one of the period's most popular novelists, actually thought well of his young employee but preferred to present a gruff and unwelcoming façade.[11]

Lane stayed with Colnaghi no more than a year before starting to buy and sell pictures in his own name. By September 1895 he had made enough for himself to take a holiday travelling through Holland, Germany and Belgium. For the first week, spent in Antwerp and Brussels, he was accompanied by his mother, but then continued his travels alone for just over a fortnight more. The trip cost him £55, of which £20 had been borrowed, and he kept details of every item of expenditure in a diary which also reports all the towns and galleries visited.[12] Still not yet twenty, Lane was an earnest and conscientious traveller, not especially imaginative in the choice of places seen or his descriptions of these. He made a point of examining, and recording, every old master painting on show in churches and museums, evidently following Colnaghi's precept that first-hand experience of art was the best possible teacher. But his judgements are often banal, testifying both to his youth and to Thomas Bodkin's later memory of Lane as inarticulate on the subject of art. So Rubens's *The Raising of the Cross* in Antwerp Cathedral is summarized as 'a lesson in anatomy and colour, but not very pleasing', and Cologne Cathedral is dismissed as 'fine but not very interesting'. That he passionately loved painting was never in doubt; he simply lacked a facility for communicating his enthusiasm.

As much space in the diary is devoted to information about his overnight accomodation and meals as the art galleries and museums explored. Lane's limited budget meant he could not afford any extravagance; rather than pay for a porter, he carried his own luggage from railway stations and would diligently hunt in each town for the cheapest hotel. The price of every cup of tea and every museum ticket is noted and

his daily outgoings precisely added up. He could not afford any amusements other than those provided free, such as brass bands playing in public parks, and a lot of time when picture galleries or churches were closed
he spent wandering aimlessly along shuttered streets. His descriptions of
the cities in which he stayed are just as concise as those of the pictures he
inspected. Antwerp was 'the dullest place' and Aix La Chapelle 'a very
large town'; Utrecht was more expansively described as 'quaint rather
like an Irish town with a smell of peat which they use here'. In Amster-
dam, as a treat, he went to the opera to hear Gounod's *Faust* and, through
a misunderstanding at the box office, paid four shillings for his ticket,
leaving him with just £3 for the remainder of his time abroad.

The frugality Lane practised on this holiday became a lifelong habit
and one of the most noted aspects of his character. William Orpen called
him 'the meanest man to himself I have ever known. No matter how tired
he was, if he had time he would walk to save a penny bus fare.' He particularly disliked spending money on food and forever remained a devotee of cafés where inexpensive meals were served. Unfortunately, as any
friend accompanying him to dinner or lunch in such establishments discovered, very cheap food was often barely edible, but Lane appeared
indifferent to this drawback. When he took Edwin Lutyens to a restaurant
in Chelsea where three rather meagre courses cost just eighteen pence, he
lavished praise on the establishment's excellent value. A still-hungry
Lutyens politely concurred, then suggested that since it really was so
good, they should immediately order the meal again.[13] Lane's refusal to
spend more than was absolutely necessary became something of a mania.
Motoring in Sussex with Thomas Bodkin, he insisted they return to a
town already visited because a cheaper tea could be found there than anywhere else.[14] As Grant Richards reported, Lane would make 'the effect of
any good meal that came his way, or that he gave – for he was very hos-
pitable – last over into the next day'.[15]

Lady Gregory, among others, believed her nephew's lack of interest in
good nutrition eventually damaged his health irreparably. Her letters to
him contain an abundance of exhortations to eat more – and better. However, her arguments in this matter may have been weakened by personal
example, because her own diaries show she too tended to suffer from ill-

ness induced by poor diet. On one occasion, she was instructed by her doctor to pay more attention to, and spend more money on, her food.[16] Lane was perfectly happy to survive on tea and bread, along with plentiful supplies of the equally low-grade and low-price cigarettes he habitually smoked. The South African architect Joseph Solomon, in a memoir written after Lane's death, remembered his friend had told him how, when he was still a young dealer, he would go without meals for several days in order to save money for the purchase of a picture or sculpture. Extravagant in many matters, he believed everyone should practise the same parsimony where food was concerned. According to Solomon, Lane always regarded expenditure on lunches and dinners as 'waste', reprimanded those who indulged themselves and regularly pronounced that 'young artists should only depend upon a good dinner when they were invited out'.[17] Grant Richards recalled that he was often berated by Lane for not buying works of art: 'If you would only spend on pictures the money you pour down your throat month after month, year after year, in the shape of food and drink, you could have as many pictures as I have!'[18] However, he had a very sweet tooth and could never resist cakes, which would be sent to him as presents by many of the older women with whom he was friendly. Typically, an invitation he received to dinner in June 1910 included the promise of plenty of sweet treats, although his hostess warned she would not be able to reverse the menu's usual running order so as to begin at the end.[19]

Lane's solitary travels of September 1895 testify to his loneliness at the time. He was, after all, still in his teens, working alone in London with very little money and almost no friends. He lived in a single room in Bayswater and would go to bed early at night because he could only afford half a candle which burned for just two hours. He later told Joseph Solomon that he had been very unhappy during these years, when almost his only regular social contacts came through Lady Gregory. She would eventually feel ashamed of her dismissal of him at that time as an aggravating snob and remember only his poverty and determination to better himself. On weekends, having nothing else to do and no funds to spend on entertainment, he would walk for miles out of London to visit Bicknell Collin, who had once been his father's curate. Otherwise, much of Lane's time was spent haunting the National Gallery and temporary exhibitions in the city where he could study paintings and add to his store of knowledge.

By 1896, barely twenty-one years of age, he felt sufficiently certain of his expertise to go into partnership with an established dealer, E. Trevelyan Turner, who like Martin Colnaghi had premises on Pall Mall, called the Carlton Gallery. Here he was engaged as buyer of old masters to be offered to the public. For a share of the business, Turner requested an investment of £800 which Lane had to borrow from his mother, together with the contribution to the gallery's stock of a number of pictures he had collected. Once more, although initially all was well, the arrangement soon soured. In a statement written more than a decade later when suing Turner over another matter, Lane explained that he discovered the gallery's senior partner had been spending money paying off private debts, having misrepresented his financial position. Over the next few months, the younger man found not only his own investment being squandered, but his pictures being sold without him receiving any recompense and, eventually, his salary not being paid. His statement noted that Lane had to take Turner to court in order to recoup the money he was owed.[20] This was probably the occasion he described much later to Thomas Bodkin when, dissatisfied with his barrister's performance, Lane requested leave to act for himself and was initially refused permission by the judge because his youthful face made him look like a minor. Finally allowed to do so, he pleaded his own case and won. Bodkin dated from this period his dislike of all lawyers and reluctance to have anything more to do with them than was absolutely necessary. In 1914, Lane wrote to his aunt describing the profession as being not only immoral but also, rather oddly, illegal.[21] But this attitude towards the law may have been a family trait as, writing to him ten years earlier, Lady Gregory was equally virulent about lawyers, insisting that they always made mistakes.[22]

His unfortunate experience with Turner and the Carlton Gallery decided Lane to open his own establishment, which he did in a small room at 2 Pall Mall Place in February 1898. Here he sat on his own each day, only able to buy new stock when he had sold some of what he already possessed. Lady Gregory tells a story illustrating the problems he encountered as a single, small trader. Taking a break from the premises to meet some cousins, he discovered on his return that he had missed London's Lord Mayor, who had called by with the likely intention of buying a picture.[23] Probably because his apprenticeship had not been a success, he never again worked with another dealer but looked after all his own business for the rest of his career. This arrangement would have its disadvantages, particularly as he became more successful. Despite the suggestion of friends, he refused to hire a secretary and replied to all correspondence himself; this might mean writing dozens of letters daily.

If Lane was suspicious of working with others, he had good reason. An American journalist, Carl Snyder, who spent time examining the London art market in 1903/4, concluded after seeing a number of dealers that the entire business was crooked and that any information members of the profession gave out was worthless. He cited a number of instances of corruption within the trade, including the venality of art critics who, while supposedly objective in their opinions, could be bribed to produce favourable reviews.[24] This situation was exacerbated because many of the most distinguished writers on art such as Bernard Berenson and Robert Langton Douglas – the latter eventually to become Director of the National Gallery of Ireland after Lane's death – were also dealing in old masters and therefore not likely to be disinterested in their approach to the subject. One obvious result of this divided loyalty was that many works were intentionally misattributed so as to increase their value. Forgeries and pictures that had undergone extensive over-painting also regularly came onto the market during these years.

That dealers were, as a rule, lacking in scruples when conducting their business was shown by Snyder in his description of a 'knock-out'. Early in his solo career, Lane discovered the same practice and was so shocked that he regularly told the story of his experience to friends. The 'knock-out' was a common ploy of London dealers who, having seen a picture they all wanted, would agree among themselves who should buy it by meeting before the auction and making private bids. Whoever offered the top price would then attend the sale and, since he faced no competition, usually manage to buy the lot for a relatively small sum. He then called together his fellow conspirators and divided between them the difference between the price he had been willing to pay and whatever the picture had actually cost him. This happened to Lane when he went to a country house auction and spotted a Frans Hals for sale. Other dealers had noticed the same picture and so he found himself invited to a local public house where the knock-out was held. Since he did not submit the highest bid, Lane eventually found himself several hundred pounds richer, without having had to spend any money at all. However, he would insist, he never engaged in practices of this kind again.[25]

3
SUCCESS

In June 1901, the National Portrait Gallery in London acquired a painting of Edward VI by the sixteenth-century Dutch artist William Scrots.
This anamorphic portrait of the English boy king is so exaggeratedly distorted that its subject can only be clearly seen if the work is held at a particular angle. For this reason, when the picture came up for sale in
London a year earlier, it had been categorised as a portrait of a girl 'in
eccentric attitude'.[1] But its purchaser on this occasion had taken the trouble to examine Scrots's painting closely and had noted there were rings
on one side so that, when pulled outwards from the wall, the necessary
angle of view could be obtained. In addition, the reverse was stamped
with a crown and initials showing that the picture had once been in the
collection of Charles I. So, despite the sneers of everyone else at the auction, Hugh Lane had bought the work for £8. He then sold it to the
National Portrait Gallery for £100.

Lane's success as a dealer throughout his career was dependent on his
ability to spot what others had overlooked. He very quickly developed a
reputation for having an exceptionally astute eye and, as a result of this
talent, for making considerable amounts of money from his transactions.
In 1918, the painter Dermod O'Brien claimed that by the time Lane was
twenty-one, he already had £23,000 to his credit in the bank.[2] This seems
unlikely, as at that age the youthful dealer still had to borrow money from
his mother in order to become a partner at the Carlton Gallery. But he

was soon enjoying a substantial income and a few years later was able to tell Lady Gregory that it was a poor year in which he did not make £10,000 for himself.[3]

Lane certainly took very little time to create both a name and a collection of paintings for sale that other members of his profession were to envy. He made his first will in August 1898, just six months after establishing himself in Pall Mall Place. When this document was drawn up, he already owned a couple of canvases – works by the seventeenth-century Dutch artist Aelbert Cuyp and the eighteenth-century English landscapist Richard Wilson – that he judged good enough to bequeath to the National Gallery in London. The bulk of the rest of his estate he left to Adelaide Lane.[4] The quality of his stock was such that he began to be asked to lend pictures to temporary exhibitions, such as that celebrating the monarchs of Great Britain which opened at the Royal Academy in December 1901; this included three paintings owned by Lane.[5]

Dermod O'Brien remembered Lane paying only £300 at a Christie's sale for a painting by Gainsborough, the attribution of which was questioned at the time. Once taken away and cleaned, the work's true value became apparent and Lane was able to realise much more from its subsequent sale.[6] Although his own attempts to paint proved disastrous, the training he received as a teenager in picture cleaning and restoration was extremely useful once he began to act as a dealer. Again at Christie's, in the autumn of 1911 he bought for £756 a portrait presumed to be by Sir Thomas Lawrence, not least because the female sitter's clothing so clearly belonged to the early nineteenth century. But Lane's eye told him that Lawrence was not the artist and when he brought the work home, he started to clean the canvas himself. Soon the Regency costume was rubbed away to reveal that the original picture had been painted several decades earlier but was probably then altered on the instructions of its owner when fashions changed; George Romney's portrait of Mrs Edward Taylor is now in the National Gallery of Ireland, bequeathed by Lane.[7]

Lady Gregory gives many more instances of Lane's judgement in assessing the real value of overlooked artworks: a Rembrandt he spotted neglected above a door mantel in the house of friends and bought for £1,000; a Velazquez picked up for just £200 at Christie's because the canvas was dirty and overpainted; the reattribution to the Dutch seventeenth-century landscape artist Aert van der Neer of a canvas in Cape Town's art gallery until then believed to be by Jan Both.[8] Because of such successes, Alec Martin of Christie's was to describe Lane as the finest judge of a picture he had ever met and Sir Frederic Burton told Lady Gregory, 'I have never in all my life been able to have the same courage in my opinion as that young man'.[9] After Lane's death, Henry Tonks wrote of him in *The Burlington* that he possessed an extraordinary power 'which seemed like a natural gift' of detecting a good picture amidst the dross. He invariably managed to see through overpainting and, according to Tonks, 'the happiest moments of his life were when he was superintending or actually doing himself the removal of paint'.[10] The writer believed his friend's exceptional memory of what he had seen before was of obvious assistance when looking at paintings, but he also noted that, having made up his mind, Lane refused afterwards to be swayed by the opinions of anyone else, which was to prove a hazard on a number of occasions. It was obviously not helpful that the dealer was relatively inarticulate when arguing a painting's merits; he tended to appear stubborn rather than authoritative.

Lane's success in his profession depended upon maintaining an irreproachable reputation as an expert in the judgement of old masters. However, like Martin Colnaghi, he relied primarily on instinct – and personal experience – rather than academic research when making his assessment on any work's merits. The decades during which he operated were a period when art scholarship underwent enormous advances thanks to the studies of Wilhelm von Bode, Giovanni Morelli, Bernard Berenson and Robert Langton Douglas, among others. Early in Lane's career, in February 1895, Berenson had published an essay in response to an exhibition of Venetian masters then being held at London's New Gallery; this irrefutably proved that the majority of the pictures on display, all from private English collections, were misattributed and of little inherent worth. The essay caused a furore and helped to ensure that in future vendors and buyers alike were much more cautious when assigning the names of artists to pictures being offered for sale. In October 1893 Berenson observed in his notebook that until recently any accurate comparison of pictures had been out of the question and hence systematic assessment of an old master's oeuvre almost impossible.[11] From this period on, however, academic connoisseurship started to be the norm. Lane's methods were therefore somewhat anachronistic. His want of schooling meant he would never be able to compete with intellectual authority of the kind enjoyed by Berenson *et al.* and had to rely instead on his own innate judgement. But the problem remained that while he knew himself to be right in his attributions, he could not explain why he had made them. When others were able to argue on the grounds of technical details and signature elements in a picture, he was obliged to fall back on such statements as 'If a painting is beautiful, it is certain it was not painted by a second-rate man'.[12] As a defence of his opinions, this could never have been terribly convincing. In March 1900 Lane gave his aunt a small canvas he had bought at Christie's as being a work by Poussin.[13] This attribution was questioned by another art expert on specific technical grounds. Lane's response was very simple: 'That yellow tree is Poussin.' But was it? After all, of the four works he donated or bequeathed to the National Gallery of Ireland as being by Poussin, only two are now attributed as such. Lane was by no means the only dealer whose judgement could be open to question and he operated in an age when scholarly attribution was just beginning to be given serious attention. Nonetheless, his lack of academic training would leave him vulnerable whenever opportunities arose to question assessments he had made.

As if to compensate for this weakness, he continued to travel extensively in Europe whenever the opportunity arose and to use these journeys to visit as many galleries as possible, thereby widening his knowledge of different schools of art. A diary he kept in September 1899 describes his five-week route through Italy and Switzerland. Comparison with its predecessor of four years earlier shows Lane to be considerably wealthier and more sophisticated than before. He was less preoccupied with the price of his meals and accommodation. But his descriptive powers remained as weak as ever, with St Peter's Basilica in Rome meriting no more than 'not very interesting' while the local English church where he went to Sunday services is regarded as 'a handsome building'. Michelangelo's Sistine Chapel *Last Judgement* 'is monotonous is colour and in bad condition' although he thought the building's ceiling 'very decorative and much more pleasing'. Michelangelo was obviously not to Lane's taste; his sculpture of Moses in San Pietro in Vincoli 'rather startles one with its very heavy limbs' and his Medici tombs in Florence contained 'repulsively nude figures for a church'. Lane was a meticulous but not especially imaginative tourist, enjoying the Colosseum as 'the most attractive ruin in Rome as well as the most imposing' and worrying about the threat of catching fever while walking through 'the most disgusting slums' to see Naples's churches. The distaste for Michelangelo's nudes and fear for his health in Naples suggests a certain prudishness and reserve on Lane's part. He was a very sensible young man, who conscientiously undertook to examine the principal attractions in all of Italy's most important cities; sensual pleasure in those attractions is never mentioned in his diaries. Nor, indeed, are the Italians. Like one of the more respectable characters in E.M. Forster's novels, such as *A Room with a View* or *Where Angels Fear to Tread* (both published within the next decade), Lane did not mix more than was necessary with the local population but socialized instead with other British tourists. In Venice, for example, he spent much of his time with one of Lady Gregory's closest friends, Enid, Lady Layard, who owned a palazzo in the city. While there, he also bought a pair of eighteenth-century Guardi school pictures he reckoned would pay for the cost of his entire holiday. His dealer's instincts awoke again in Basle, where he had time to visit bric-à-brac shops and picked up four works including a portrait of a child by the seventeenth-century French artist Charles Lebrun for £4.10s.[14]

Now in his mid-twenties, Lane's appearance was to remain almost unchanged for the rest of his life. Standing just under six feet tall, his figure was slight and willowy, staying so because of his lack of interest in food. But this slimness may also have been due in part to the restless nervous energy remarked upon by anyone who met him; one observer said he entered a room like a breeze. W.B. Yeats commented that for Lane life was all bars against which he beat himself, and that he could never experience tranquillity because he was incapable of feeling satisfaction with what he had done, leaving him in a state of 'perpetual exasperation'.[15] He found it difficult to remain still and tended to dart about in an unsettled – and unsettling – fashion. Although he loved sleep, he suffered from insomnia and would often be exhausted after a night in which he was unable to rest. He spoke softly, his voice light and high. Charming and persuasive in private, in more numerous company shyness and a self-conscious awareness of his educational shortcomings meant that he usually followed rather than led conversation. Thomas Bodkin would write that 'although he had a slightly nervous manner, he was never ill-at-ease'.[16]

The febrile side of Lane's character was evident in his large brown eyes, which, like the rest of him, never stayed still for long. Under heavy lids, they were perhaps the most arresting aspect of his face, in which angularity was the other dominant quality. While the chin was a little weak, both his ears and nose were large; he used to joke that the only reason Sargent agreed to undertake his portrait was because the painter had a weakness for big ears. Until the last years of his life, when he grew a full beard, he had a moustache, the ends of which were usually waxed. In his youth he wore his hair parted in the middle, but later, as it became steadily thinner, he brushed what remained straight back. He was vain about his appearance and took trouble to be turned out impeccably on all occasions, happy to spend on suits what he would not on food. However, his extremely thin figure meant clothes could hang from him unless intentionally cut close to the body. As a young man in the 1890s, he adopted a dandyish approach to dress, favouring boldly checked waistcoats and jackets. His style became more sober with age as the need to secure attention diminished and he grew more confident of achieving his aims. But he never lost the air of extreme tidiness that had marked his person from the start. It was typical of his attention to detail that the tie and tiepin he wore would be chosen to harmonize with each other.

Lane's restlessness of spirit helps to explain why he had few interests outside art; nothing else ever managed to engage him in the same way. Although he never lost his interest in music and had a particular fondness for composers of the romantic school such as Chopin, he treated piano playing primarily as a method of relaxation whenever he found himself to be under excessive stress. Books held no interest for him; almost the only ones he possessed were monographs on old masters. 'Nothing but press cuttings', was how he summarized his reading habits to Joseph Solomon.[17] Books required that he be sedentary and his feeble education had not encouraged any great interest in them; he could always read a picture more quickly than a book. And other distractions could also be found to take up his time: the arrangement of furniture – his own or that of other people – and of flowers; the pursuit of gifts for friends; the organizing of social engagements, particularly tea parties which were to be his favourite form of entertaining.

By 1900, Lane had a substantial enough fortune that he could afford to work less hard, or not at all for a few years, provided he curbed any tendency to extravagance. He wrote to friends telling them that he intended to give up his premises in Pall Mall Place, taking comfortable chambers first at 43 Duke Street and later 93 Jermyn Street, from both of which he dealt in a more discreet but just as profitable fashion. In October 1900, *The Times*'s Humphrey Ward wrote to pay Lane for a picture he had bought and to congratulate the dealer on his move, as 'you are too good to sit in a stuffy little shop'. All the same, Ward asked Lane to let him know if he discovered a chef d'ouevre or two, thereby showing he did not really expect his correspondent to give up dealing altogether, even temporarily.[18]

Lane now found that he could spend more time with his family, almost all of whom were living in Ireland. Following the death of her mother in March 1896, Adelaide Lane had been left a legacy allowing her to buy a house in Dublin at 51 Dartmouth Square, where she was to remain until her own death thirteen years later. The majority of her children settled there too, as the state of persistent ill-health into which she quickly settled required their constant attention. Her sister Augusta's letters to Adelaide are replete with somewhat formulaic expressions of regret for the latter's illnesses, as well as descriptions of fruit and meat she was sending to Dartmouth Square. These give the impression that the rector's former wife was as short of funds – and as reliant on the more affluent members of her own family – as ever. Perhaps this is why, in the years that followed, although her son Hugh was frequently in Dublin, he never stayed with his fractious parent but always in rooms at the United Services Club on St Stephen's Green. After their exceptional closeness while he was young, Lane and his mother grew apart. She felt the philanthropy he came to practise should be directed towards members of his own family and not impoverished artists. He, on the other hand, was ambitious and looked beyond the constraints of the Lane household. Having been left alone in London at the age of eighteen, he had, of necessity, developed a sense of independence. His mother was written out of a new will he made in 1907; she, in turn, was to leave nothing to him. Their period of intimacy was over and a succession of other women would take the role of his surrogate mother.

The rest of Adelaide Lane's children retained closer ties with their mother, perhaps through lack of choice. None of them showed the same initiative or flair as Hugh and their subsequent careers could never be described as glorious. While they were not to share his interest in art or the good fortune this brought, except for Ruth they were all to be plagued by the same poor health as he. By 1900 the eldest child, Alfred, had followed the example of so many other well-bred but impoverished young men and departed for the colonies; in his case, South Africa where he joined the Cape Mounted Rifles. Here was a life distinguished only by his manner of leaving it; seemingly he was savaged to death by a pack of lions in the bush although his body was never found and only in 1911 did the probate of his will go through, his sister Ruth declaring that to the best of her knowledge he was dead. Harold Lane fared little better. After many years of vacillation over his future during which the possibility of a career in the colonial civil service was considered, he eventually decided to emigrate to South Africa in 1904. Before then, Ambrose Lane had begun to study law with the intention of becoming a solicitor and his sister Ruth had trained in horticultural design at Dublin's Botanic Gardens, one of the first women in Ireland to do so. Around the same time as her brother Harold left for South Africa and a year before her marriage, she went to work at Glynde, the Sussex home of Dublin-born Viscount Wolseley, whose wife Louisa liked to hire 'lady gardeners'. The youngest of the Lanes, Eustace, eventually found himself left alone to mind his mother, who in July 1907 was being congratulated by Augusta Gregory on having a son who was such a skilful nurse, presumably not an occupation he relished.[19]

Hugh Lane understandably wanted the rest of his family to enjoy the same social advantages he had created for himself and told his mother that Ruth should be presented at court. In February 1902 she made her début at Dublin Castle, where she was presented to the Lord Lieutenant by the Countess of Westmeath. Lady Gregory exasperatedly noted these aspirations in her diary; she continued to find such instances of snobbery irritating, as she did Lane's inclination to boast of his success as a dealer.[20] But he was, after all, still a very young man and, having had to establish himself in the London art world with almost no help or capital, the temptation to let others know of his achievements must have been irresistible. Maturity was to bring greater self-confidence and, in turn, more discretion when talking of his business affairs. However, while sometimes annoyed by Lane's habit of informing her of his latest triumphs in the salesrooms, Lady Gregory also began to enjoy the benefits of these. In March 1900, after she had been unable to afford the price of a painting by Simeon Solomon at Christie's, Lane bought for her at the same auction the little canvas supposedly by Poussin. It represented Homer or, as she preferred to imagine, Raftery the blind poet of Connaught who had died in the mid-1830s and whose work she was then collecting and translating into English.

This gift marked something of a turning point in the relations between Lane and Lady Gregory, who thereafter looked on her nephew as an ally and friend, rather than just a youthful relative who had to be entertained to lunch periodically. Writing to thank him for the picture and self-effacingly insisting she had done nothing to deserve such a beautiful object, she observed: 'I don't know whether to scold or thank you most!'[21] That confusion was to remain a feature of their dealings thereafter, as Lady Gregory alternated between acting like Lane's sister and his mother. The maternal impulse in her was certainly very strong, and he was by no means the only younger man to benefit from this. Being a blood relative and no longer close to his own mother, he responded instinctively to his aunt's concern over his well-being. Soon she would be sending him letters plangent with anxiety that he had not been eating enough or taking sufficient care of his health. She loved to fuss over each of her charges and Lane responded enthusiastically to such attention, regularly replying to these enquiries with detailed accounts of his current ailments.

Lady Gregory was by no means the only woman to behave like a mother towards Lane, but relations with her nephew at times were similar to those between siblings. Despite an age difference between them of twenty-three years, she often behaved as though younger and he as though older, a feature of their respective temperaments that was beneficial to the burgeoning friendship. In times of tribulation – and there were to be many – each knew the other was always prepared to provide support and reassurance. But in their correspondence, there is also on her part a vivacity and sometimes even a suggestion of flirtatiousness unexpected in letters between aunt and nephew. She would give him tasks to undertake on her behalf: finding a piece of jewellery, perhaps, or recommending a good dressmaker. He responded to such requests with alacrity, writing to her in August 1907 after she had asked him to track down a diamond setting for an old sapphire she possessed that this was precisely the kind of commission he liked and that he had spent an entire day happily pottering around shops looking at jewellery.[22] She was forever trying to gain his approval for her efforts to present a smart appearance, describing in February 1910 how she had blossomed out in a toque she had wanted him to see since he was sure to have admired it.[23]

This intimacy was still ahead of them when Lane sent his aunt the Poussin picture in 1900. But his gesture meant that before the end of the year, she was considering the possibility of her son Robert, whose interests were proving to be more artistic than academic, joining her nephew in the picture-dealing business.[24] Robert Gregory eventually chose to become a painter but in the meantime, Lane had come to stay with his aunt at her home Coole Park. It was a visit that had momentous results, although these were by no means immediately apparent.

The Lady Gregory hitherto known to Lane was very different from the one he discovered in County Galway. Since her widowhood eight years earlier, she had continued to spend a certain amount of time annually in London socializing with the friends met during her marriage. But alongside this, she began to develop what might almost be classified as a second, although by no means secondary, life in which Ireland and its cultural development took precedence. In the mid-1890s, she had been introduced to W.B. Yeats and, following his lead, started to study Irish folklore and mythology. In 1897, together with Yeats and Edward Martyn, she had begun to imagine the creation of a national theatre which, as the Irish Literary Theatre, opened in May 1899. During these years, Lady

Gregory moved from holding the unionist views typical of her class to being a proto-nationalist capable of exclaiming on one occasion, 'I defy anyone to study Irish History without getting a dislike and distrust of England!'[25] Meeting her in London, Lane was little aware of such sentiments, or of the circle his aunt now gathered around her at Coole. There she scarcely mixed with the local gentry or even with members of her extensive family, but instead invited to stay the poets and playwrights whose company she had come to prefer.

These were Lane's fellow guests when he arrived at Coole in September 1900, and he was taken aback by the discovery. In the days before his appearance, Lady Gregory and the other members of her house party, including W.B. Yeats and Douglas Hyde, had been attending the *feis* in Galway and holding a commemorative ceremony at Raftery's grave in Killeenin.[26] It is indicative of how far she had abandoned her old way of life that, on the day she first managed to identify the blind poet's tomb, she should have encountered the local hunt on her way home and later wondered whether any of those she met would even have known of Raftery's name.[27] Probably none, and neither would Hugh Lane, had she not brought it to his attention. For her self-consciously urbane nephew, the company Lady Gregory now kept was a trial and a disappointment. With a bluntness that occasionally characterized his conversation, he told Lucy Hyde that his aunt had lost her position in the county 'by entertaining people like your husband'.[28] In reaching this verdict, he was merely reflecting the views of contemporary Anglo-Irish society; after Douglas Hyde's first visit to her home, some neighbours told Lady Gregory that no one who spoke Irish, as he did, could be a gentleman.[29] Presumably Lane held the same opinion even though Hyde, like himself, was the son of a clergyman. Certainly, having no interest in Irish folklore and being neither a writer nor a reader, he was soon bored; the company at Coole lacked social polish and was, moreover, too industrious for a man on holiday, with everyone else retiring to their rooms in the morning to work.

If Lady Gregory's guests failed to impress Lane, nor did he greatly impress them with his talk of smart London life and salesroom successes. Forgetting his own foppish youth, Yeats was later to remember only Lane's excessively dapper appearance, out of place in a house where everyone else took a more casual approach to dress. The young dealer's urban clothes and smooth manners, along with the boastfulness still characteristic of his conversation in company, had precisely the opposite effect from that intended. Still worse, whenever talk at Coole turned to literature – a subject of overwhelming interest to everyone else – he was unable to participate. And even his taste in pictures seemed suspect; when Yeats tried to discuss the merits of an artist with him, Lane offered no measured criticism of the paintings but responded only that they would fetch very little at Christie's.[30] It was, therefore, with relief on both sides that after a few days he left Coole, the likelihood of another visit seemingly remote.

4

THE DISCOVERY OF IRELAND

John Butler Yeats, a painter who could create portraits as effectively with his pen as with his brush, once described Hugh Lane as 'an artist in social life'.[1] That artistry was rather lost on Lady Gregory's house guests at Coole in September 1900, although they were later to change their minds about Lane, just as he would his own about them. For the moment, however, he preferred to exert the charm he possessed in abundance on a society more to his taste: that gathered around Dublin's viceregal court. Here he mixed with a group of people who, in addition to friendship with him, shared a number of other characteristics: they were usually several decades older than he; had inherited rather than made their money; and were in possession of a title.

Typical in this respect were Ponsonby William Moore, ninth Earl of Drogheda, and his wife Anne. The same age as Lane's father, he had inherited the earldom, together with the family seat Moore Abbey in Monasterevin, Co. Kildare, from a distant cousin. The Droghedas' enormous gothicized eighteenth-century home was to become one of the young art dealer's favourite retreats; despite its reputation for extreme coldness, he was even to spend one Christmas there. The couple were not artistically minded, but they enjoyed music and Lord Drogheda could be persuaded without much difficulty to sing at parties. Lady Drogheda and her daughter Beatrice were devoted to Lane and often asked his advice about items they wanted to buy on expeditions to Dublin, where they stayed at Power's Hotel on Kildare Street. Lord Drogheda was to be one of the founding members of the committee established by Lane to campaign for a modern art gallery in Dublin.

Another was Dermot Bourke, seventh Earl of Mayo, who with his wife Geraldine lived in considerably greater comfort than the Droghedas at Palmerstown in Straffan, Co. Kildare. The house had been largely rebuilt in Queen Anne style by public subscription in memory of the earl's father after the latter's assassination in 1872 while viceroy of India. Thanks to this refurbishment, Palmerstown offered guests such luxuries as an abundance of bathrooms and water-closets, then otherwise still something of a rarity in Irish country houses. Although the earl had been a lieutenant in the Grenadier Guards, he was much more cultivated than most former military men. In 1891, he had founded the County Kildare Archaeological Society and four years later he became chairman – and driving force – of the committee that organized the first exhibition of the Arts and Crafts Society of Ireland; the secretary of this body was Richard Caulfield Orpen, who was to become another of Hugh Lane's most loyal supporters. Geraldine Mayo showed a number of items she had made at the exhibition and her own organizational abilities had been put to the test in 1894 when she raised funds to regenerate the Royal Irish School of Art Needlework in Dublin. Her husband was to be president of the Arts and Crafts Society for many years and to oversee subsequent exhibitions of Irish work at home and abroad. While Lord Mayo's interest in promoting modern art in Ireland was to be expected, he made it clear to Lane that his services were offered not with the expectation of success 'but because you work hard & do something which many Irishmen do not, they talk'.[2]

Less easy to explain is the enthusiastic advocacy of another retired army officer, Lieutenant Colonel William Hutcheson Pöe. In the mid-1880s, he had participated in a number of campaigns in Egypt, losing his right leg during the last of these. Returning to Ireland, he married an heiress, Mary Domville, and settled at Heywood, a house his wife had inherited in what is now County Laois. Hutcheson Pöe was a relentless improver of his property, the gardens of which were redesigned in 1906 by Edwin Lutyens, who retained memories of Heywood's owner sitting in a chair and supervising the workmen employed on the site, his wooden leg stretched out before him. The men responded by going on strike, so, as Lutyens told Lane in October 1910, 'things go slow'.[3] Hutcheson Pöe also oversaw Heywood's internal redecoration and bought a number of pictures for the house on the advice of Lane, who persuaded the colonel and his wife to sit for their portraits; he to the sculptor John Tweed, she to the painter J.J. Shannon. An indefatigable campaigner on behalf of his friend's schemes – 'No man has worked more disinterestedly or more unselfishly in the cause of art than Lane', he declared in 1907, '& no man is more deserving of every honour that the people of Ireland, & especially the citizens of Dublin, can pay him'[4] – Hutcheson Pöe could be irascible, but not as much as another wealthy landlord to whom he introduced the dealer in 1905.

Windham Wyndham-Quin, fourth Earl of Dunraven, first met Lane when he asked the latter to advise him on the pictures in his family home, Adare Manor in County Limerick. This was a common request to which Lane usually responded assiduously – it could, after all, lead to future purchases for him should the owner decide to sell – but Dunraven's aristocratic hauteur led to a corresponding frostiness on the part of the art expert. Soon the earl was complaining to Hutcheson Pöe that Lane had written him a 'shirty' letter saying he was not a picture hanger.[5]

The difficulty eventually passed – the Adare pictures were duly inspected and valued – and Dunraven proved to be helpful in drumming up further aid for Lane, but the incident illustrated how precarious the support of the wealthy would always be. This would be shown again by the most important of members of the Dublin Castle set in the first years of the century, the Lord Lieutenant William Ward, second Earl of Dudley, and his wife Rachel, one of the great beauties of the Edwardian era. The Dudleys were both young and rich, spending over £50,000 of their own money in making sure the viceregal court during their tenure was a social success. Although he had disposed of a substantial part of his father's art collections, the earl was no philistine and he, together with his wife, offered to help Lane in his efforts to establish a modern art gallery in Dublin; specifically, Dudley promised a contribution of £250. The money was never forthcoming. By June 1908, the former Lord Lieutenant was writing to Lord Mayo complaining that members of the gallery commit-

tee were harassing him for the contribution which he now had no intention of giving.[6] Fortunately, his friend the dashing George Wyndham,
Chief Secretary for Ireland for much of the same period, was more unwa-
vering in his commitment to the modern art scheme and would eventually donate to the gallery a bronze bust Rodin had made of him.

Lane found Dublin society sufficiently congenial to return to the city
on a regular basis. While visiting in 1901, he attended the exhibition that
first excited his interest in contemporary Irish art. The show had been
arranged by Sarah Purser, a painter whose own organizational abilities
were as considerable as her artistic skills. By then in her early fifties, Miss
Purser, as she was invariably known, had been showing her work since
before Lane was born. She had decided to study art after her father's business had failed and she was obliged to earn a living; having spent some
time in Paris, where her friends included the Impressionist painter
Berthe Morisot, she returned home and began to find work as a portraitist.

For almost half a century Sarah Purser was a regular exhibitor at the
Royal Hibernian Academy, and it was as a result of what she perceived to
be a slight by this institution that she independently undertook to
arrange a show in October 1901. The slight was not to herself – Miss
Purser's forceful personality was never troubled by such matters – but to
two other artists whose work she admired: Nathaniel Hone and John
Butler Yeats. The former was seventy and no longer much troubled either
to paint or show work, but Yeats, although just eight years Hone's junior,
continued to produce pictures from financial necessity. Sarah Purser
believed neither painter had received due recognition from the RHA,
which early in 1901 had rejected pictures offered to its annual exhibition
by Yeats. At her own expense, she therefore undertook to provide both
Yeats and Hone with a show, held in the rooms of the Royal Society of
Antiquaries at 6 St Stephen's Green. Opening on 21 October and running
for two weeks, the exhibition contained twenty-eight landscapes by Hone
and forty-forty pictures, predominantly portraits, by Yeats. Among the
many reviews of the show, that written by George Russell for the *Irish
Statesman* expressed a wish that it would catch the attention of 'those
who would like to believe in the existence in Ireland of a genuine art'.[7]

This comment soon found a response after Lane visited the St Stephen's Green rooms and was so impressed with what he saw that he not only bought a number of pictures by each artist but engaged Yeats to undertake a series of paintings for him.

Whatever about Hone, it seems almost impossible that Lane, through his aunt Augusta, would not have been familiar with the work of John Butler Yeats. As Lady Gregory's friendship with W.B. Yeats grew in the mid-1890s, she had come to know the other members of his family and in particular his charming but feckless father. Realizing the persistent hopelessness of John B. Yeats's finances, in June 1898 she had commissioned from him a series of portrait sketches to make what she called a 'gallery of my best countrymen';[8] these included members of her own circle such as Douglas Hyde, George Russell, Edward Martyn, Horace Plunkett, John Millington Synge and eventually Lane himself. Lady Gregory was also an enthusiastic supporter of John B. Yeats's painter son Jack, buying work at a number of his exhibitions from February 1899 onwards and chivvying friends such as the New York collector John Quinn to do likewise. Indeed, she seems to have been more enthusiastic about Jack Yeats's work than was her nephew. The younger Yeats regularly wrote to Lane seeking support; by December 1910 he had abandoned polite requests and instead issued the bald instruction 'you really ought to buy some of my pictures'.[9] This approach was no more successful than any other and it was only at the 1912 RHA annual exhibition that Lane purchased a Jack Yeats picture, *Maggie Man*, which he subsequently presented to the Municipal Gallery. His interest in the artist, despite close friendship with W.B. Yeats, was to remain limited.

John Butler Yeats, on the other hand, he found endlessly engaging, and why not? The painter was a conversational sprite, amusing, voluble and consistently able to suggest that somehow the problems besetting him were not of his making. Despite his years, he forever retained a childlike optimisim. Enchanted, Lane paid for Yeats to set up studio at 7 St Stephen's Green and engaged him to paint a series of portraits of notable Irishmen, together with a number of English politicians associated with Ireland, such as the Earl of Dudley and George Wyndham. Other subjects, suggested but not necessarily executed, included George Moore,

Douglas Hyde, Horace Plunkett, Edward Dowden and J.M. Synge. Lane intended that these canvases be donated to an Irish national portrait gallery whenever it was established. The price of each picture was to be a modest £10, but the venture eventually cost its originator much more because John B. Yeats, as his children had long since discovered, was forever in need of money. Even after telling his son W.B. in May 1904 of the marvellous new opportunities now open to him thanks to the portrait series, he concluded by asking for a loan.[10] In his many letters to Lane, there are two leitmotifs: a plea for further funds and an assurance that the artist intends to forsake his slack habits and tirelessly devote himself to work. In November 1903, he wrote to say how flattered he was by the dealer's good opinion and that he would do any number of portraits for him; the following June, he suggested Lane must have 'a fairy purse' as it always seemed to produce money on demand. Exactly two years later, by which time financial support from this source was no longer quite as forthcoming as had once been the case, he could still gush thanks for yet another donation, winningly observing: 'I think to help must be a Persse hallmark – & accomplishment – your aunt always knows how to help'.[11] Inevitably, as anyone with more experience of John B. Yeats could have forseen, not all the portraits commissioned by Lane were completed and other painters had to be drafted in to help complete the series. A letter from Walter Osborne, then the most fashionable portrait painter in Dublin, suggests Lane may have entertained ideas of inviting this artist to undertake some work, but perhaps he was discouraged by the much higher prices expected: Osborne's list starts at £80 for a head and rises to £300 for a full-length portrait.[12]

However, the engagement with John B. Yeats, which only ended in 1907 when the artist moved to New York (after Lane, Sarah Purser and others had collected money for him to visit Italy), was certainly not a failure and it confirmed the art dealer in a role he was to play for the rest of his life: that of lordly patron. W.B. Yeats was by no means the only person to view Lane as representing a noble tradition of patronage while most of his contemporaries opted instead for the values of a self-interested bourgeoisie. The observation was acutely made, even if not entirely accurate, since it was coloured by the poet's own romantic vision of someone he had come to admire. Still, there were no obvious advantages for Lane in either commissioning work from John B. Yeats or remaining loyal to him long after the artist had proven to be maddeningly unreliable. Had Lane abandoned the idea of acting as a patron after this first undertaking, he could scarcely have been blamed for doing so. Instead, the same loyalty was to be shown to a number of other painters, even if none of them was quite so undisciplined. Among J.B. Yeats's successors were William Orpen, Augustus John and Gerald Kelly, and only the last of these showed unremitting appreciation for what was done on his behalf. In the late 1940s, Kelly told Lane's sister Ruth that without her brother's encouragement 'I should probably never have become a painter at all'.[13] His portrait of the dealer, painted in the last year of Lane's life, is now in Cork's Crawford Art Gallery. 'You don't know how nicely and lavishly you praise,' Kelly wrote to Lane in November 1907. 'It is very pleasing to hear, and one is forced to the opinion that you have great taste!'[14] Inviting Kelly to tea, he would bring him over to other guests and insist they sit to the young artist for a portrait. The dealer may never have been able to paint, but he showed himself to be a shrewd judge of other people's talent, John B. Yeats noting how 'he did want to have things his own way, even in painting'.[15] Artists learned to respect Lane's judgement; Walter Sickert, for example, would only submit a work of his to Dublin's Municipal Gallery on condition that its founder told him frankly whether the picture came up to expectations.[16]

Although Lane met John B. Yeats late in this painter's career, in most other instances where he acted as a patron, he did so at a time when the artist was young and such support was most beneficial. Not only would he commission work himself but he encouraged wealthy friends and acquaintances to do likewise. The outcome was that soon young artists were inviting him to their studios and asking for advice about their work. A young Dublin painter called John Currie, whose studio Lane visited in September 1907, afterwards wrote to him: 'I would like to do really good work and if you would favour me by letting me know of any noticeable improvement, I would be sincerely gratified'.[17] When Joseph Solomon came to stay with Lane in London in 1911, he noticed how many artists were helped by the dealer, sometimes with the gift from his collection of valuable old frames, on other occasions with a useful introduction to someone who might commission a picture.[18]

So, far from being discouraged by his involvement with John B. Yeats, Lane was stimulated into fresh activity and began to entertain notions of helping to revive Irish art from what he, like so many of his contemporaries, believed to be a moribund condition. George Russell's remarks at the time of the Yeats/Hone exhibition in St Stephen's Green indicate that faith in the ability of the country's artists was not necessarily widespread. The most common perception, and with good reason, was that only a handful of painters could manage to make a living in Ireland. Around the same period as his *Irish Statesman* notice, Russell had plaintively written to Lady Gregory that, due to the limited supply of commissions, Dublin could support no more than one portraitist – and that was Osborne.[19] Other artists, he argued, unless fortunate enough to possess independent means (which was the case with Hone), had to eke out their income through alternative means, such as teaching the next generation of impoverished painters. Unquestionably there were many fine Irish painters during this period. The problem was that so few of them remained in Ireland. Either, like John Lavery, they moved to London where much more work, and support, was to be found, or, like Roderic O'Conor, they chose the more sympathetic cultural climate of France; these had been the two most popular options for Irish artists since the mid-nineteenth century. Their native country accordingly remained a relatively barren place and it was this condition that Lane aspired to change when he embarked on his scheme of developing a robust Irish 'school' of art.

Understandably, he first turned for endorsement to the institution charged with encouraging art in Ireland, the Royal Hibernian Academy. Founded by Royal Charter in 1823, the RHA had never flourished in the same way as its older London counterpart. Again, the primary problem was neglect from the local population; during the 1830s, for example, no work was sold for four successive seasons from the academy's annual show and even when there were purchases, these could be pitifully small – a mere thirty shillings' worth in 1838. At the start of the twentieth century, conditions were little better than they had been seventy years earlier.

Reviewing the annual show in 1900, *The Studio* dismissively commented: 'Few of the pictures displayed each year on the walls of the RHA reach the level of mediocrity.'[20] In the face of such criticism, annual attendance figures dropped to fewer than 8,000 visitors. All sorts of reasons were proffered to explain the RHA's want of success. One of the most popular – and illogical – was that the academy was situated in the wrong place: a handsome building designed and built by the architect Francis Johnston at his own expense on Lower Abbey Street in 1826. The premises were described by Thomas Bodkin as 'dingy, dull and uninviting' as well as being in 'the worst possible position, a dirty commercial side street'.[21] If only, ran this argument, a more fashionable location – preferably south of the river Liffey – could be found, then potential art lovers would flock to the RHA and buy what they saw there. But inadequate funding was also a problem: the RHA received an annual government grant of just £300. Early in the new century, the Academicians led by their president Sir Thomas Drew began to campaign for a public enquiry into why the organization had come to receive so much less financial assistance than equivalent institutions in Scotland which enjoyed yearly funding of at least £2,000. The Lord Lieutenant had already commissioned a report on the institution in 1901, but four years later an official committee was established to examine the work of both the RHA and the other body in Dublin that offered classes to aspiring artists, the Metropolitan School of Art. The results of the inquiry were inconclusive and the RHA remained as impoverished and unfashionably located as ever, the latter problem only being resolved when its building was entirely destroyed in 1916 during the Easter Rising.

In the meantime, however, Lane decided on a more practical course of action, organizing a winter exhibition of old master paintings in the RHA's premises. Events of this kind had been held for a number of years at London's Royal Academy and were among that institution's most popular shows. Lane correctly reckoned that the same success could be achieved in Dublin. In early October 1902, therefore, he approached Sir Thomas Drew and offered to arrange an old master exhibition, the works on show coming from Irish country houses. The initial response to this proposal was cautious, not least because there were fears that expenses incurred would not be met by door receipts. But Lane was impossible to refuse, particularly when he promised to cover any deficit personally and he eventually received permission to go ahead with the show.

In retrospect, Lane's professional life has come to look like a sequence of impulsive decisions. It was as well that his success as a dealer over the previous few years now allowed him the opportunity to be a gentleman of leisure, even if he never acted in a leisurely manner. The old master show was scheduled to open at the RHA on 15 December, although Lane only heard on 24 October that he could go ahead with the event. He had less than eight weeks to organize everything, including the loan of enough paintings, none of which had yet been secured. His first step was to write to the Irish newspapers explaining the nature of his intentions which, if successful, 'would do much to revive an interest in art and would eventually encourage modern painting in Ireland'.[22] He then went on to ask that owners of suitable works might loan them for the show. Press response to Lane's project was enthusiastic, the *Irish Times* noting that the show would be not only of interest to both the general public and art students but immensely beneficial for the RHA.[23] The *Evening Herald* remarked that 'At a time when so much is being done for the revival of Irish literature, old Irish music and Irish industries, it would be strange, indeed, if the interests of national art should be altogether forgotten'.[24]

Lane now embarked on an intensive campaign of letter writing and travel, calling to as many houses as he could in order to inspect their pictures and entice the owners into lending them for his exhibition. Inevitably, he met a warmer response in some parts of the country than others, but it is an indication of his persuasive charm that a young man still almost entirely unknown in Ireland should have been able to prise valuable heirlooms, if only temporarily, from the walls of so many country houses. The eventual list of lenders included Lords Mayo, Drogheda, Massy, Inchiquin, Bangor, Ely, Ardilaun, Fingall and even the Duke of Leinster. Portraits dominated the show, in which work by eighteenth- and early nineteenth-century English artists such as Romney, Reynolds, Gainsborough, Hoppner and Lawrence was to the fore. On the day of the opening, the *Irish Times*, which had provided its readers with regular bulletins of the exhibition's progress over the preceding weeks, was stirred to declare that 'This is the most interesting artistic event in the recent history of Ireland'.[25] It was certainly the most fashionable, with a large number of women holding lunch parties in Dublin before proceeding with their guests to the RHA for the three o'clock arrival of the Earl of Dudley, who performed the official opening.

That the exhibition attracted larger crowds than any other in the academy's recent history was due not only to the quality of the pictures on display but equally to the sequence of social events Lane now co-ordinated. Several of his friends gave 'At Home' tea parties in the RHA's galleries, the first one hosted by Lady Drogheda. On these occasions, guests – who still had to pay their shilling admission, which sometimes caused embarrassment when they arrived at the academy without their purses – would be entertained while they drifted through the show by army bands, or even Lord Drogheda's singing. Attendance figures were so impressive that the Academicians decided to keep the exhibition running for several weeks longer than had originally been planned, right up to the beginning of the official season. Sir Thomas Drew also used the show's success to launch yet another campaign for improvement in the RHA's official funding, publishing a document in late January 1903 which called for a new location, new charter and more money for the RHA, although he also wanted the Academy to maintain its autonomy.

Lane's show eventually closed on 5 February 1903 but was evoked a month later by the Dudleys' first state ball of the year in Dublin Castle, when the dress code was based on old master paintings and most women came wearing costume inspired by Romney or Reynolds. The latter painter had been responsible for the one element of discord during the show's otherwise harmonious course. Just before the opening, two members of the honorary executive committee Lane had assembled, Walter Osborne and W.G. Strickland, chose to resign their positions because they questioned his attribution of a portrait to Reynolds, insisting the work was a copy. To make matters worse, they wrote to the national press about their resignation, thereby forcing the exhibition's organizer to make a public statement as well. Lane's reputation as a competent judge of old masters – and therefore as a creditable dealer – was at risk and, as he stated in his letter on the dispute sent to the *Irish Times*, 'I could not allow myself to be thought capable of making so glaring a mistake as taking a "copy" to be an original'.[26] In support of his case, he undertook extensive research on the picture's provenance and asked members of the London art world including Humphrey Ward and the dealer Morland Agnew to confirm his Reynolds attribution. The crisis passed, but this was by no means the only time his judgement was to be publicly questioned.

In some quarters, the incident raised another query about Lane's motives in organizing the show. Why would an art dealer based on the other side of the Irish Sea want to see what old master paintings were owned by impoverished members of the Irish aristocracy? Could his intentions be entirely honourable in undertaking the project, or was he using this opportunity to discover almost unknown work which might sooner or later come onto the market? In *Vale*, his 1914 book of memoirs, George Moore quotes Sir Thornley Stoker describing Lane as 'a London picture-dealer who had come to Ireland to see what he could pick up'.[27] Working without pay, he was assiduous in his task, and so gained access to a great many houses that would probably not have been open to him had he approached their owners in the guise of a potential purchaser of the contents. And some of the pictures he first saw while collecting for the RHA show did eventually pass into his hands after he had announced that, were they to come up for sale, he would be interested in acquiring them. He was defended by supporters against charges of self-interest, but the suspicion his seemingly altruistic behaviour first attracted in 1902 was never to leave him.

Lane now showed a keen interest in being awarded an official position. He was appointed to the board of the National Gallery of Ireland in September 1903, and thereafter he applied for many professional posts and even, on one occasion, proposed that a job be created just for him. In May 1904 he drafted a long letter to Lord Dudley outlining all that he had already achieved on behalf of Irish art but explaining that he was hampered by his youth and a want of any formal role. He therefore asked if the Lord Lieutenant might talk to the King about creating a position for Lane in Ireland, perhaps along the lines of surveyor of pictures at the viceregal and Chief Secretary's lodges, as 'my work would be greatly assisted and at the same time I could be of some real service'.[28] Nothing came of this ambition, nor of Lane's hopes to win the directorship of the Walker Art Gallery in Liverpool when that position became vacant in the autumn of 1903. Applying for the post, he explained to the chairman of the gallery's board that he was 'anxious for every opportunity of doing useful work'.[29] He lobbied hard and had friends such as the English artist Henry Scott Tuke and the dealer Robbie Ross canvas on his behalf; the former perceptively remarked to Lane that were he to be appointed to the directorship, 'you will really only use it as a stepping stone to higher things'.[30]

Ross, meanwhile, discovered in the course of his enquiries that another candidate was almost certain to be given the Walker Art Gallery directorship but encouraged Lane 'to drive along and get what backers you can'.[31] His list of references included the earls of Mayo and Drogheda along with Humphrey Ward and Sir Thomas Drew, but he was once again unsuccessful. Undaunted, he wrote to another well-connected friend and relation by marriage, Lord Gough, a career diplomat then acting as British Resident at the Courts of Saxony and Coburg. Lane informed him that when recently passing through Darmstadt, he had gone to view the civic collection of pictures and found these in terrible disorder with many works misattributed. He therefore asked Lord Gough whom he might contact about undertaking a thorough reorganization of the entire Darmstadt Gallery, which he was prepared to do without pay.[32] Once more nothing came of the proposal, but Lane's efforts to secure a job for himself were not yet exhausted. Even as he became steadily wealthier by dealing in old masters, he continued to long for the recognition bestowed by officialdom. Lane obviously found his own professional success insufficient; he needed to have his expertise confirmed by a formal appointment. Being a dealer would never be as satisfying to him as being the director of a state gallery or museum. The one brought him money, the other honour, and it was the second of these which mattered more to him. Many of the tasks he was to undertake in the years ahead, often at considerable personal cost, can be explained by this persistent desire to find himself an official job.

5
THE IMPACT OF IMPRESSIONISM

Buoyed by the success of his old masters exhibition, Lane immediately started to consider arranging a similar event for winter 1903. He would have been encouraged by the RHA's president, Sir Thomas Drew, who had already written asking whether he could persuade some of the current stars of the London art world, such as John Singer Sargent and Laurence Alma-Taddema, to lend works to Dublin.[1] However, in July 1903 Drew wrote again, this time advising Lane that the academy's rooms were already promised for a winter show;[2] the previous April, Walter Osborne had unexpectedly died of pneumonia aged only forty-three and the RHA had decided to honour his memory with a retrospective exhibition in December. Lane had been greatly shocked by the painter's death, telling Sarah Purser he regarded Osborne as one of Ireland's few geniuses and someone from whom he had hoped for still better work. 'You will be recognized as his heir (artistically)', he informed her.[3] At the RHA show in December 1903, he paid £60 for three paintings by Osborne: *Fishmarket*, *Mother and Child*, and *Teatime*. Lane presented the three to the Municipal Gallery in 1912.

Because of the Osborne show, he did not go ahead with another project at the RHA even though Drew offered him a single room there; already, there were signs that the academicians were beginning to resent this outsider who managed to gain more publicity for his schemes than they were able to do for their own. After all, the previous winter he had

proven that many of the reasons they regularly invoked for poor attendance at their exhibitions had no validity. The fundamental problem was
not the location of the RHA or the inadquacy of its annual grant from government, but the quality of the work exhibited within the rooms. Lane
also knew what he had achieved with his show. Responding to Drew's
July letter, he made it quite clear that, were he to become involved in
preparing another exhibition for the RHA, he would not accept 'any interference at all except of course from you'. He also insisted he would have
to be considered as director of, and entirely responsible for, any future
shows he organized at the academy.[4]

The RHA proving a disappointment, he turned his attention elsewhere
and at the beginning of 1904 a seemingly ideal opportunity arose. The
World's Fair was being held in the United States at St Louis from April
until November and Lane decided, although a British art exhibition
would take place, that Ireland ought to be independently represented at
this event. He persuaded the organization then responsible for the country's official art activities, the Department of Agriculture and Technical
Instruction, where Lady Gregory's ally Horace Plunkett was vice-presi-
dent, to give him the task of selecting and dispatching to St Louis a representative selection of Irish pictures. It was late January by the time
approval had been given, and work for the show would have to leave Ireland by mid-March. Once again, time was short but this did not impede
Lane's ambitions. The Irish exhibition he planned was to have four sections: a collection of paintings showing Ireland's greatest artists from the
eighteenth century to the present; a series of historical portraits of important Irish men and women; a display of the country's miniaturists; and
some paintings showing notable Irish beauties. For the last of these, an
octagonal panelled room was to be constructed. Appealing publicly for
help in a letter to the press on 22 January, Lane explained the St Louis
show would be 'the first real opportunity we have had of proving to the
world the artistic talent that Irishmen possess and which has led them
with very little encouragement to produce great works'.[5] Because of the
intended exhibition's scope, he had simultaneously to look for assistance
from two different sources: owners of old masters and living artists. With
the former group, the distinction between Lane the dealer and Lane the

exhibition organizer was often unclear; letters requesting loans of paintings might contain the suggestion that if these were likely to be for sale,
he would be happy to buy or find a purchaser. However, many owners of
such work were far less supportive of his proposal than they had been in
1902, simply because they did not relish the idea of their paintings being
dispatched across the Atlantic for six months. Horace Plunkett, who had
interceded on Lane's behalf with the Duke of Devonshire, owner of a large
collection of Irish art at Lismore Castle in County Waterford, wrote to say
His Grace would not lend anything as 'he draws the line at exhibitions in
this country'.[6] The Marquess of Waterford, the Earl of Cavan, Lord Bangor and even the National Gallery of Ireland's director Sir Walter Armstrong also declined Lane's request, as did King Edward VII, who felt he
had already done enough for art and for St Louis by sending pictures
from the royal collection to the British section.[7]

There was a more positive response from the artists to whom he
wrote. Some were initially reluctant, or even hostile to the proposal, such
as John Lavery who in early February wrote from Berlin that even his
patriotism would not induce him to take part in an event arranged 'in
such unseemly haste'. Within ten days of that letter, however, he was
observing that although he still could not imagine how a good show could
be pulled together in the short time available, nevertheless thanks to
Lane's 'kind and enthusiastic invitation' he would send the best possible
selection of his pictures to St Louis. A week later, he was even suggesting
other places where good Irish pictures might be found for the exhibition.[8]
Lavery succumbed to Lane's charm, effective even by letter, as did many
of the other artists approached. The promise of loans was also secured
from a number of English and Scottish public galleries which owned good
Irish pictures. While not, perhaps, as spectacular a collection as Lane
might have hoped, the eventual line-up for the St Louis show looked
impressive, particularly when it was understood how quickly the task had
been accomplished.

Then, just before the pictures were due to depart for the United States,
the entire project was cancelled. A number of serious fires in Baltimore
and other American cities had led to steep rises in insurance rates and an
insistance that paintings in St Louis be displayed only in secure buildings.

Unable to meet these demands, the Department of Agriculture and Technical Instruction announced that the Irish exhibition would not go ahead after all. Despite Lady Gregory's pleading with Horace Plunkett for a reprieve, Lane was instructed to return all borrowed pictures to their original owners. If he was indignant at this peremptory behaviour, his friends were even more so. Writing to John Quinn in New York about the affair, W.B. Yeats insisted that the fault lay with T.P. Gill, the department's secretary, and James Reardon, who was Ireland's representative at the St Louis fair. Yeats's fury might have been fanned by disappointment at the opportunity missed by his brother Jack, who had a number of pictures in the cancelled show, as well as irritation with Reardon, whom he accused of trying to throw together a troupe of Irish players to perform the writer's plays in St Louis.[9]

Lane may have been disappointed but he refused to be daunted by this setback and at once began work on an alternative opportunity of showing Irish art to a wider audience. By 15 April, the *Irish Times* was able to report that London had responded to a request from Dublin for an exhibition to be held in the Guildhall Art Gallery.[10] Lane already knew this venue well; its director Alfred Temple had organized highly successful loan exhibitions for the past fourteen years, borrowing two Lane-owned paintings in April 1902 for a show of eighteenth-century French and English art.[11] The previous spring, the gallery had devoted its rooms to an exhibition of early and contemporary Dutch pictures, but nothing had been planned for 1904 until Lane approached Temple with a proposal that he take what was originally intended for St Louis. Called 'An Exhibition of Works by Irish Painters', the show opened at the Guildhall on 30 May after a month which cost its organizer not only considerable effort but also a great deal of money; Lane later reckoned he had spent more than £1,000 ensuring the event went ahead to his satisfaction. But he had, by now, become sufficiently engaged with Ireland to feel this expenditure was justified, writing to the Earl of Dudley that the undertaking would be 'the means of forming an "Irish school" and of attracting the necessary attention to 'the neglected state of art culture in Ireland'.[13] Featuring 465 exhibits, the show ran for eight weeks and attracted just over 73,000 visitors; while the latter figure was little more than half that achieved by the Dutch show of 1903 (and nowhere near the 305,000-plus visitors to a Spanish show at the Guildhall in 1901), it was still gratifying for all participants, especially those who would hardly have expected their work to be shown in London on this occasion. Included were examples of work by both living and dead artists, among the latter being George Barret, Thomas Danby, Adam Buck, Hugh Douglas Hamilton and William Mulready. Lane was now so keen to advance the cause of Irish art that his interpretation of who was eligible to represent the country became somewhat elastic.

In his prefatory note to the catalogue, having first introduced the idea that Irish birth and blood were almost interchangeable, he suggested that 'There is something of common race instinct in the work of all original Irish writers of today, and it can hardly be absent in the sister art'.[14] Witnessing the success at this time of the country's literary movement, he clearly felt it could be extended to the visual arts but then recognized there might not yet be a sufficient number of practitioners whose work he cared to promote. A generous definition of who could qualify for inclusion was therefore essential. 'Have written to make Boyle Irish'[15] reads a note from this time in Lane's hand. The approach was not necessarily helpful to his cause, as it tended to cause widespread confusion over the nature of not just Irish painting but Irishness. Lavery had to persuade him not to include Whistler, 'his connection with Ireland being so very remote not to say doubtful',[16] but other Americans of Irish ancestry who did feature included J.J. Shannon and Mark Fisher. Many of the Guildhall show's reviewers commented on the number of artists featured who had not hitherto been popularly regarded as Irish, with one critic describing the display as an amalgamation of the Glasgow school and the New English Art Club.[17] The consensus was that, while Lane had gathered a fascinating collection of artists, they had few, if any, common characteristics. Gerald Kelly, like Lane the son of a clergyman, and Ambrose McEvoy were both English, C.H. Shannon could only muster grandparents who were part-Irish, and even Lavery, although born in Belfast, was then customarily regarded as a representative of contemporary Scottish art. Nathaniel Hone and Walter Osborne were indisputably Irish, as was William Orpen, but the last of these felt obliged to inform Lane that

Augustus John, also intended for inclusion in the Guildhall, was actually Welsh.[18]

Distant cousins, Orpen and Lane had first come into contact with each other the previous year when the painter wrote asking for advice about holding an exhibition of his work in Dublin in July 1903.[19] When the St Louis exhibition was being organized, Orpen had featured among the participants, and at the Guildhall he showed eight oils and five water-colours, these being among the most critically appreciated works of the entire event. Thereafter he and Lane became close friends and by mid-July he was writing his thanks to the dealer for the loan of old master paintings which he felt sure were doing him 'much good'.[20] Superficially, the two men had little other than a love of art in common. Three years younger and very much shorter than Lane, Orpen was convinced of his own ugliness, although he was evidently attractive to women. He could be as infuriatingly disordered as John B. Yeats and even more demanding; he quickly grew accustomed to expecting commissions from among Lane's wide social circle and, whenever business was slack, would write looking for work. He had little of the neatness of person that distin-guished Lane, nor his sense of orderliness, but he could be just as charm-ing and it must have been this quality more than any other that allowed him to take liberties no one else would have risked. Only he, for example, would have presumed to give Lane the nickname Petticoat, a play on the dealer's profession and the London street where second-hand goods have traditionally been sold; before long, he was addressing his letters to 'Dear Petticoat', or even 'Petti'. Orpen also had an abundance of one quality lacking in Lane's personality: pragmatism. Having grown up in Ireland, he viewed the place in a far less romantic fashion than his friend and understood that talk was often more highly valued than action among his fellow countrymen. In their correspondence, he teased Lane for his seem-ingly naïve enthusiasms and, despite his metropolitan sophistication, for a want of worldly wisdom, at least where Ireland was concerned.

In his memoirs, *Stories of Old Ireland and Myself*, Orpen described Lane as being 'a force one could not withstand. He used us all like little puppets, and we loved him and worked for him gladly.'[21] Lane used Orpen to continue the portrait series of notable Irishmen left incomplete by

John B. Yeats and still for just £10 each. Among his subjects were William O'Brien, Michael Davitt, Timothy Healy, Nathaniel Hone and the Chief Secretary, Augustine Birrell. In 1904 Lane even persuaded both Orpen and Yeats to paint his sister Ruth at the same time, and almost in competition with one another – an experience neither artist much enjoyed. As with the older painter, so Lane naturally fell into the role of patron in his dealings with Orpen, but in return he benefited from being introduced to many young artists whose work, and persons, he would otherwise probably not have known.

Until this time the contemporary English art world had remained almost entirely alien to his experience. After leaving Dublin, Orpen had attended London's Slade School of Fine Art, where his teachers included Philip Wilson Steer and Henry Tonks, and Augustus John had been a fellow student. All three men, perceived as radicals by their more conservative contemporaries in Edwardian England, were to become well known to Lane along with many of the painters Orpen met through exhibiting with the New English Art Club. This organization had been established in 1886 by a group of artists who felt neglected by the Royal Academy and inspired by what they believed were more enlightened circumstances in France. Orpen showed work at the NEAC for the first time in 1899, the year in which he went on a painting holiday in Normandy with Charles Conder, Augustus John and William Rothenstein, whose sister-in-law Grace Knewstub he married two years later. These were among the closest members of his circle and, as such, they too came to know Lane.

In future, there would be two strands to Lane's professional life, one focused on the past and another preoccupied with the present. His awareness of recent developments in European art increased substantially thanks to a holiday he took with Orpen in September 1904. They travelled first to Paris and, despite having little more than twenty-four hours in the city, managed to see not only the Louvre and Luxembourg museums but also the pictures being offered for sale by the dealer Paul Durand-Ruel. His family business, based since 1869 on the Rue Le Peletier, had promoted Impressionist painting long before that school had achieved anything other than notoriety. Durand-Ruel met both Monet and Pissarro in 1870 when they were all in London because of the Franco-Prussian war.

He carried a stock of their work, as well as that of Renoir, Degas, Puvis de Chavannes and Alfred Stevens, just as his father had supported contemporary artists and his sons were to be advocates of Bonnard, Redon and Gauguin.

Orpen was already familiar with the principal Impressionist painters but he liked to claim that Lane had never seen their work until this visit to Paris. However, the modern French school was by no means unknown, either in England or Ireland. Durand-Ruel had held a number of Impressionist exhibitions in London, Monet showed twenty of his paintings at the city's Goupil Galleries in 1889, and four years later, Degas's *Absinthe Drinker* had been seen at the Grafton Gallery, leading to animated arguments in favour of Impressionism, with George Moore one of its principal advocates. Moore had originally planned to become a painter and with this intention had left his native County Mayo in April 1873, taking himself and his valet to Paris. After three years he discovered painting was not, after all, his métier but by then he had become acquainted with a number of artists, including Manet who made several portrait sketches of him and, when questioned about these replied: 'Is it my fault that Moore has the look of a broken egg-yolk?'[22] The future novelist also came to know with varying degrees of intimacy Degas, Monet, Pissarro and Renoir. He was to write extensively about them all and if he somewhat exaggerrated their friendship with him, he was nonetheless responsible, through his magazine articles and his 1893 book of essays *Modern Painting*, for increasing awareness of Impressionism in the English-speaking world. In January 1886 he brought his cousin Edward Martyn (who was also Lady Gregory's neighbour in County Galway) to Paris, persuading him to buy two Degas pastels and an oil by Monet. Now all in the collection of the National Gallery of Ireland, to which they were left by Martyn on his death, the three pictures were shown in Dublin as part of an exhibition of modern art organized in April 1899 by a committee including the indefatigable Sarah Purser, Walter Osborne, Walter Armstrong and W.G. Strickland. The spur for this event had been a letter written the previous autumn to the Dublin *Daily Express* by George Russell, who argued that the lack of what he called 'national' art was due to so few good paintings being seen in Irish exhibitions.[23] The eighty-eight works on show

covered most of the principal trends in art during the previous half century thanks to the presence of Martyn's Degas and Monet pictures, a
Manet which Moore agreed to lend and canvases by, among others,
Whistler, Steer, Corot and Courbet. Although well received – the *Irish
Times* pronounced that there was not a single picture 'which is not fully
deserving of attention'[24] – the exhibition failed to have the effect desired
by Russell. In its immediate aftermath, no new school of Irish art came
into being and nor did local painters begin to work in an Impressionistic
manner. However, like similar events in London, the show had at least
alerted anyone interested to what was happening in contemporary art
elsewhere in Europe.

According to Orpen, however, only when Lane passed through Paris in
1904 did he discover Impressionism, asking the painter when they were
on Durand-Ruel's premises: 'What is that? A Manet?'[25] If this was really
the case, then Lane learned quickly, because he was soon able to judge the
quality of modern French painting for himself and not rely on anyone else
for opinions. But a complete ignorance of Impressionism before this date
seems improbable; more likely, until he looked at the pictures in the company of an informed enthusiast, they had failed to inspire much interest.
As a boy, he had already announced that he 'preferred the old painters to
the new'[26] and he would always insist old masters were the only area in
which he possessed any expertise. His taste at the time of this holiday
with Orpen was still evolving, and some of the works included in the
recently closed Guildhall exhibition, such as *Victory of Faith* by St George
Hare – an Irish painter who specialized in titillating nudes, of which this
was a perfect example – show that Lane's critical judgement was sometimes flawed. He possessed an unexpected streak of popularism. George
Moore once complained that Lane had told him, were he to become director of the National Gallery, he would attempt to attract the widest possible audience 'by the purchase of popular pictures'.[27] And when a gallery of
modern art was proposed for Dublin in 1906, he argued that, in order to
ensure the venue would appeal to all classes, 'one room might be set aside
for loan pictures of a more popular order'.[28] It may be that, like John B.
Yeats, he believed exposure to any art, even if not of the first rank, might
in time lead to an improvement in taste. Certainly his own personal taste

was eclectic. During the early years of the twentieth century Lane was as likely to buy a painting by Manet as one by the minor Pre-Raphaelite Simeon Solomon, five of whose pictures he owned.

Still, for much of his lifetime Lane remained one of the few collectors in Britain or Ireland who acquired Impressionist pictures. In February 1908, Durand-Ruel, who had been bringing examples of late-nineteenth-century French art to London for the past three decades, wrote to Lane that, despite setbacks, 'I always believe that I will see a movement take shape in favour of modern painting'.[29] During the same month, the English art critic D.S. MacColl recalled in the *Saturday Review* how three years earlier Durand-Ruel had organized a very substantial show of Impressionist painting at London's Grafton Gallery. Among the pictures on offer at the time were Manet's portrait of Eva Gonzales and his *Le Concert aux Tuileries* as well as *Vétheuil: Sunshine and Snow* by Monet. Despite the efforts of another English writer, Frank Rutter, to raise funds for the purchase of at least one of these paintings for the state, only the price of a small Boudin could be managed. In the meantime, as MacColl observed, these particular examples of Manet's and Monet's art had been bought by Lane; 'the freelance with knowledge and courage and no great amount of money did in a year or so what official buyers will now find it difficult to do at all'.[30] By no means the only collector of Impressionism outside France, Lane was certainly one of the first and the best-known. When Theodore Duret was looking in September 1909 for illustrations from British collections for an English edition of his book *Manet and the Impressionists*, he informed Lane: 'You are the only collector, after repeated inquiries, whose name has been given to me as owning pictures of that kind.'[31] Lane's publicly expressed admiration for modern French painting helped to ensure it found a wider audience, particularly after these works were put on display at the Dublin gallery. But Impressionism was slow to win approval. As late as November 1912, a pseudonymous writer to the *Irish Times* was warning: 'Ireland must not be misled regarding this matter of Impressionism as if it were the only true method.'[32]

Impressionism never would be the only method for Lane, but in 1904 it was a thrilling discovery, if all too briefly enjoyed because he and Orpen soon left Paris for Madrid, where the greater part of their holiday together was spent. The painter quickly discovered his new friend was not the ideal travelling companion. As he wrote to Grace Orpen, Lane tended to tire easily and could not be persuaded to get out of bed early in the morning.[33] He also did not care for the same amusements as Orpen; the latter sent his wife a drawing and a description of Lane sitting in a café looking thoroughly discomfited when approached by a Spanish dancer who proceded to chuck him under the chin.[34] According to Orpen, Lane 'looked on it as a wicked waste to spend a peseta on a dance hall; and such things also rather shocked him, I think'. The prudishness of character which made him unable to enjoy the sensuality of Michelangelo's nudes in Florence was now seen by Orpen. Lane's obsession with saving money eventually infuriated the artist, who remembered that every day during lunch in a cheap restaurant, he 'would pocket some bread and fruit there for his dinner. He never dined all the time we were in Madrid.' Petty disagreements meant that by the time the two separated – Lane going on to Rome while Orpen intended to return to London after a few more days in Spain – their friendship seemed to have cooled. However, when Orpen went back to his hotel, he found concealed inside his bed one of Lane's visiting cards and two terracotta statuettes representing Adam and Eve. Made by the seventeenth-century painter and sculptor Alonso Cano, these figures had been seen and coveted in a Madrid antique shop but, priced at 150 pesetas for the pair, were outside Orpen's budget. Unknown to him, Lane had bought the figures and on his departure left them behind as a present. It was a typical gesture; although he had fought with Orpen over expenditure on food and other unnecessary extravagances – as he perceived them – gifts for friends were never subject to the same strictures.

Generosity of spirit may explain why, at the end of his visit to Rome, Lane once more began to occupy himself with the prospect of another exhibition in Ireland. Given the rebuffs he was to face over the next ten years, finding any reason other than blind loyalty for his continued engagement with the country becomes a difficult task. After all, he had been neither born nor raised in Ireland, and until 1900 his association with the island was negligible. Yet, very rapidly, Irish art and its promotion came to be Lane's keenest interest, almost the driving force of his life. In April 1905 he drew up a fresh will, overriding that made seven years earlier. The later document no longer leaves any works to the National Gallery in London but requests instead that its Dublin counterpart be offered the best old master pictures in his personal collection. Aside from a few minor legacies to friends and family, the remainder of his estate was to be sold, so that a 'Lane Fund' could be created. He intended money from this source to be used for the purchase of work for the modern art museum he hoped to see established in Ireland. Nothing was left to his mother, even though she was still alive when this second will was drawn up.[35]

Why was Lane so devoted to Ireland? Lady Gregory liked to declare he had been converted to the cause of Irish nationalism by the discovery that the dirty windows of the Viceregal Lodge in Dublin 'could not be cleaned without long pondered leave from London'.[36] But Lane's interest in politics was always negligible and he was certainly not a nationalist as that term was commonly understood at the time. In *Vale*, George Moore gave a more likely explanation for the dealer's persistent association with Ireland, recording a probably aprocryphal conversation in which Lane is asked why he went to so much trouble for his adoptive country. 'Well you see,' is the response, 'I am Lady Gregory's nephew, and must be doing something for Ireland.'[37] Seeing all that his aunt and her circle had managed to achieve for Irish theatre in a relatively short time, he felt inspired to attempt something similar in his own area of expertise. In her biography of Lane, Lady Gregory attributed Ireland's sudden literary flowering to a release of the country's collective imagination from political preoccupations after the downfall and death of Parnell in 1891.[38] It was a simplistic piece of reasoning, but one with some merit, not least because so convincing to Lady Gregory and her contemporaries. She remembered how when she, Yeats and Martyn had first considered the notion of an Irish national theatre in 1897, 'things seemed to grow possible'.[39] And if things were possible in one art form, why not in another? The country's late-nineteenth-century literary renaissance seemed to occur with such unexpected rapidity that Lane was by no means the only well-intentioned observer to believe the same creative force could be unleashed among painters and sculptors. This personal longing to do 'something for Ireland' was widespread, manifesting itself in Lane as a drive to create a modern Irish school of painting. A similar urge had led Horace Plunkett to promote the concept of agricultural co-operation. When Lady Gregory wished to explain the literary activities in which she and others were engaged, she said: 'We work to add dignity to Ireland.'[40] The same impulse, typical of his class and era, also motivated Lane. He wanted to add to the dignity of Irish art and to have its merits internationally acknowledged. But in his case, this desire to work for Ireland was further accentuated by an abiding interest in acquiring an official position of some kind, an ambition easier to achieve in Dublin than in London. While the latter city, because of its importance in the international art market, remained Lane's base for his activities as a dealer, projects of greatest personal interest to him took place elsewhere. Immediately after coming back from Italy in October 1904, he thought he was about to embark on his finest project yet for Ireland.

6

THE STAATS FORBES COLLECTION

The principal location for Hugh Lane's activities as an impresario of the visual arts suffered from many disadvantages. During his lifetime, while London had the good fortune to be one of Europe's richest cities, Dublin was among the very poorest. The first would remain his home, even while the second constantly engaged, stimulated and tormented him. The economic poverty of Ireland's capital meant opportunities for decisive action there would always be more limited than might have been the case in London. That city, of course, was just as culturally conservative as its Irish counterpart, so it may not have permitted Lane any greater success. But the endless struggle to raise funds for his schemes that he faced in Dublin might have been avoided because London at least had an abundance of wealthy citizens, some of whom were willing to assist various philanthropic and cultural causes.

By the late nineteenth century, evidence of Dublin's poverty had become unmistakable and its causes much discussed. An investigation by the Royal Commission on Sewerage and Drainage in 1879 showed that 70 per cent of the city's inhabitants lived in 30 per cent of its houses, predominantly in single-room tenements over 2,000 of which, according to the same commision's report, were unfit for human habitation. The 1901 census revealed that a quarter of Dublin's population now lived in a single room, of which over half were occupied by three or more people.[1] When Alice Barton, the heroine of Moore's *A Drama in Muslin*, is driven to a ball in Dublin Castle, she must confront the reality of urban life, as the poor of the streets gather to peer into carriages waiting to deposit their scented cargos at the viceregal party. Alice's mother wishes the poor would not stare so intently, commenting: 'One would think they were a lot of hungry children looking into a sweetmeat shop.'[2] It was an apt analogy; for the majority of Dubliners, hunger and destitution were their customary experience and the pleasures of a ball as unlikely as a bag of sweets.

Under circumstances of such widespread deprivation, the money available from the public purse for cultural initiatives was liable to be limited. In addition, private patrons would prove to be scarce. As Lord Mayo explained to Lane in December 1906, Dublin had long since become 'narrow, provincial & even parochial' and her few affluent citizens were only interested in acquiring honours from London. 'People who have money there do not care one jot about art', he wrote, explaining 'they want peerages or baronetcies'.[3] But Lane would not allow himself to be deflected from his purpose. Within a month of the earl's remarks, he was quoting George Bernard Shaw's maxim that 'It is the part of the rich to provide luxuries for the poor; they will find the necessaries for themselves.'[4] He was to discover that, in this instance, the Dublin rich were not especially willing to meet their responsibilities.

This discovery was made soon after he returned from Rome in the autumn of 1904 and began working on his next scheme for the development of art in Ireland. Its origins lay in a collection assembled by the Scottish entrepreneur James Staats Forbes, who had died at the age of eighty-one the previous April. An engineer by training, Staats Forbes had been responsible for the construction of many railway lines in Britain but art was always his greatest passion. He particularly appreciated the work of John Constable and of the Barbizon school, the group of French landscape painters who had been based around a village in the forest of Fontainebleau and were in many respects precursors of the Impressionists. His private interest was clearly obsessive; at the time of his death, Staats Forbes owned no fewer than four thousand pictures, including 150 works by Jean Francois Millet and 160 by Jean-Baptiste Corot.

The executors of his will now intended to offer the entire collection for sale, but before this could occur they were approached by Lane with a proposal. He may have learned of their plans through William Orpen, who had painted a portrait of the railway magnate in 1901. Hearing of the executors' intentions while preparations for the Guildhall exhibition were underway, Lane suggested that a selection of the pictures be shown in Dublin, where he hoped the response would be so enthusiastic that they would be bought by philanthropic-minded individuals and donated to the city. It was a typical instance of enthusiasm stifling any rational analysis, but by no means as extreme as his first idea. Lane had initially thought of assembling a small committee to buy all four thousand works for the price of at least £220,000 demanded by Staats Forbes's executors; the group would then sell half the collection for £150,000 – 'not a difficult task as every dealer and collector would be glad to obtain even one picture' – and somehow find funds to pay the balance of £70,000 so that the other two thousand pictures might remain in Ireland and in public ownership.[5] Relinquishing this notion, he settled instead for a representative group of the very finest work being offered for sale in Dublin and eventually narrowed the number down to 160. According to Lane, 'competent persons' had declared that the pictures, wherever they were shown, should attract between 20,000 and 30,000 art lovers annually, 'so that it would be an untold benefit to a city such as Dublin'.[6] In case the selection of Staats Forbes's collection was considered insufficiently attractive, he made use of his new acquaintance with Durand-Ruel to borrow a number of Impressionist paintings from the Paris dealer and then, for good measure, added to the intended exhibition's list of work some pictures he personally owned.

Looking for a suitable venue in Dublin, he once again approached the RHA, which was initially sympathetic to the project. In mid-October, the academicians agreed that he could hold the show on their premises either during November and December or after their own annual exhibition the following spring, these being the only periods available. With his usual precipitation, Lane chose the earlier option and the Staats Forbes exhibition was opened by Dublin's Lord Mayor on 21st November. Included were fourteen paintings by Constable and twelve by Corot, sixteen Millet drawings, as well as work by Daubigny, Diaz, Courbet, Bastien-Lepage, Fantin-Latour and Whistler. In addition, Durand-Ruel had lent three

Monets, two Manets, and a Puvis de Chavannes. The Academy's President, Sir Thomas Drew, took advantage of the occasion to make yet another appeal for his institution to receive greater official support, remarking how 'the culture and advancement of living art in Ireland has suffered a disregard and discouragement up the present from those who represent the State'.[7]

Even before the exhibition was seen, Lane's supporters had been working to ensure neglect of this kind no longer occurred. An editorial in the *Irish Times* declared that 'the exhibition which opens today in the rooms of the RHA marks an epoch in artistic education in Ireland ... without the inspiring examples of the great contemporary art of Europe, it is almost impossible for our native students to rise out of the slough in which they have been for so many years'.[8] Writing in the Dublin *Daily Express* on the same day, John B. Yeats wondered whether the city's population would awaken to the need for art, and remarked: 'Mr Hugh Lane, being a person of great activity, ardent for national progress, believes that they will make this discovery.'[9] However, the public chose to awaken at a leisurely pace because, while the show drew substantial attendances – aided once more by a succession of sociable tea parties and other entertainments arranged by Lane's friends, such as the ever-musical Droghedas – picture sales were slow. Discussing the exhibition in the *Saturday Evening Review* in early December, the English critic D.S. MacColl remarked that while the collection of work was better than anything yet seen in London, when it came to finding money for the pictures' purchase, 'the sum required would daunt anyone less sanguine than Mr Lane in a country so poor as Ireland'.[10]

That sum was estimated to be in the region of £36,000, but Lane was not the only one who refused to be daunted by the task. A group of Irish writers, including Lady Gregory, W.B. Yeats, Douglas Hyde, Edith Somerville and Violet Martin (under her *nom de plume* Martin Ross) now issued a circular appealing for support to secure the Staats Forbes paintings for Ireland.[11] Yeats, who claimed to be visiting the show almost daily, went to work among English journalists of his acquaintance, persuading them to give generous coverage to the show, while Lane wrote to Irish friends asking them to pay for at least one of the less expensive pictures.

Both the *Irish Times* and the *Freeman's Journal*, spurred by their readers, started subscription lists. To encourage potential purchasers further,
a lecture series was organized at the RHA, beginning with George Moore
who on 8 December chose to share his 'Personal Reminiscences of Modern Painters'. Despite his reservations about speaking in public, he had
been flattered by Lane into acquiescence, having been told 'you are the
only one in Dublin to have actually known these painters'.[12] Moore's
memories were less well received than either lecturer or organizer might
have hoped, although since the evening's chairman Count Markievicz
chose to address his audience in French, it ought to have been apparent
that applause would not be easily won. Sketched by John B. Yeats as he
spoke, Moore proceded to deliver a sequence of self-conscious aphorisms
such as the conceits that 'well-mannered people cannot think sincerely'
and 'an artist should be almost unaware of any moral codes to succeed'.
His doctrine for the night was 'Be not ashamed of anything but being
ashamed', which can hardly have helped his – or Lane's – cause.[13] The following day, the *Daily Express* crushingly commented that 'It is a good
thing that no one takes Mr George Moore seriously' as otherwise the project he was supposed to be aiding would have suffered a setback.[14]

But the picture-buying campaign faced more serious problems than
poor public speakers. Not everyone necessarily found the works on display of great artistic merit. A letter signed simply 'Philistine' appeared in
the *Daily Express* on the same day as Moore's lecture. The writer asked
whether there was any evidence 'that loan collections of pictures help in
any way our resident artists', before going on to recall the 1899 exhibition
in Dublin and dismiss 'the collection of grotesque specimens of the works
of cranks and faddists of the modern impressionist school'.[15] The relatively high prices being asked for the paintings – £1,250 for Corot's *Avi-
gnon, Palais des Papes*, £600 for a Monet view of Waterloo Bridge, £500
for Constable's *Cornfield* – were also questioned. In the *Irish Times* on 21
December, a correspondent called 'Viator' (Lane's opponents often took
refuge behind pseudonyms), having established his credentials as a judge
of art by claiming 'long experience of modern pictures and prices',
announced that in the exhibition at the RHA 'there is not one picture of
first-rate importance – some are not even second-rate in subject and

treatment'. He then suggested that were the entire group of Staats Forbes paintings to be offered for sale at auction, they would hardly fetch as much as £3,000, let alone the £36,000 being asked.[16] Viator may have been Lieutenant-Colonel George Plunkett, then Director of the National Museum and a man implacably opposed to contemporary art; at the opening of the Guildhall show, he had announced to Lady Gregory that he hoped never to see a picture hung in Dublin 'until the artist has been dead a hundred years'.[17] But he was not alone in his estimation of the pictures' worth. A special report on the show in the *Evening Herald* on 2 January 1905 was particularly critical of the French paintings, accusing them of two specific, if contradictory, defects: 'false sentimentalism and realism often of a grossly sensual kind'.[18] Arthur Severn, an English painter married to a cousin and ward of the late John Ruskin, came to stay in Dublin early in 1905 and began an intense correspondence in Irish newspapers when he wrote to the *Irish Times* that the prices of the Staats Forbes paintings were too high;[19] letters were exchanged in the press on this subject for at least a month without any satisfactory resolution.

Elsewhere, now-customary questions were quite being asked about the precise nature of Lane's involvement in the undertaking. He was, after all, an art dealer and had brought the pictures from London to Dublin, where they were being offered for sale. Might he be taking a commission from any works which found a buyer? As he reported to one of the Staats Forbes executors, 'It is quite openly said that the Forbes pictures are mine and that I am making my fortune from the transaction.'[20] His supporters were indignant at the very suggestion, insisting Lane's motives were entirely altruistic. But they knew his character better than the general public, and too little effort was made to understand, and respond to, the latter's concerns. Instead, these were dismissed by Yeats, Lady Gregory and others as the machinations of a hostile group led by disgruntled members of the RHA. Relations with the Academy had been strained for some time as the institution felt itself used for Lane's schemes without enjoying any obvious benefit from these. Lane had argued that his only concern was for the future of Irish art but then presented a large exhibition of foreign paintings at the RHA, inviting patriotic art lovers to buy them rather than the academicians' own work. As a means of promoting the development of painting in Ireland, his method was too oblique for their understanding.

Nevertheless, when open hostilities broke out, they were instigated by Lane and his followers, and not by the RHA. It had been made clear to him when he first asked for the loan of the Academy galleries that these could be given either in the last months of 1904 or in 1905 after the annual spring exhibition. He had taken the former but now, in the hope of securing further sales, wanted the exhibition to run longer than had originally been planned. Unfortunately, the galleries were long since promised for January 1905 to another organization, the Decorators' Guild of Great Britain, which booked the space every three years. This commitment had always been understood, but was interpreted as a calculated slight by members of Lane's coterie. In early December, George Moore wrote indignantly to the *Daily Express* alleging that it was a 'matter of public notoriety' that the only reason the academicians refused to alter their arrangements was because the present exhibition contained so many better pictures than would their own spring show.[21] W.B. Yeats, who relished a public spat, soon joined in and told the same newspaper's readers that 'the paper hangers', as he chose to describe the Decorators' Guild, could have been persuaded to forgo their contract had the RHA wished them to do so.[22]

The Academy, through its secretary Stephen Catterson Smith, responded to these accusations in tones of self-righteous indignation. One of Smith's letters to the press early in the new year made a point of stressing that although held on the RHA's premises, the exhibition 'was not under its auspices, as may not be generally known, nor had its members any part in its selection'. He continued with the suggestion that, should any readers wish to help the cause of Irish art, 'their contributions should be conditional on a more deliberative procedure than has been advocated by some writers in the press'.[23] Two days later, the RHA issued a statement drawn up by Sir Thomas Drew saying Lane's exhibition contained 'pictures which would not in any respect be acceptable ... in a pleasing or popular gallery'.[24] Thereafter the Academy would have no more to do with Lane, and although he participated in the official enquiry held in autumn 1905 to examine the activities of the RHA, he simply used this opportunity to press for the establishment of a museum of modern art in Dublin. So single-minded was he on the subject that eventually the commission's chairman Lord Windsor had to tell him, 'I can quite sympathise with your object, but I am afraid it does not come within the scope of our inquiry'.[25] It was not until another of his long-standing allies, the painter Dermod O'Brien, was elected as the Academy's President in 1910 that he once more associated with the RHA.

Obliged to remove the pictures from those premises at the end of December 1904, Lane needed to find an alternative exhibition space. He asked the Staats Forbes executors if they would allow him to retain a smaller number of the paintings in the new year and, having received their permission, he whittled down the 160 borrowed works to eighty-two. Although offered a room in the National Gallery of Ireland by his fellow board members, he chose instead to exhibit the remaining paintings in the rotunda of the National Museum, a strange decision given the clear hostility of this institution's director. Plunkett made Lane's job difficult in a number of ways, not least by leaving large display cases in front of many walls and so restricting the space for showing pictures. But the decision had been taken to use this venue and on 18 January 1905 the exhibition was reopened in the museum.

As before, the Staats Forbes pictures were supplemented by a number of others such as Edward Martyn's Degas and Monet, as well as a further example of the latter's work lent by Durand-Ruel, who also sent Pissarro's *Printemps, Vue de Louveciennes*; this last was bought by Lane for £500. By now less than £4,000 had been promised for purchases and a further £15,000-£20,000 was still needed, so fresh appeals for financial assistance were made. Within a fortnight, help came and in its wake more – and less manageable – publicity than Lane could have imagined. Lady Dudley, wife of the Lord Lieutenant, had from the start of Lane's activities in Ireland been one of his most loyal supporters. On 22 January she brought a large party of friends to see the show and promised to buy a picture. The Chief Secretary, George Wyndham, went even further by commiting himself specifically to the purchase of Constable's *Near Arundel* for £38. At the start of the following month, the Dudleys persuaded the Prince of Wales (later King George V) and his wife, who were then visiting Ireland, to call into the museum and see the pictures, their guides being the Earl of Mayo, newly created a Knight of St Patrick, and Lane. Although hardly renowned for his artistic interests, the Prince had been sufficiently impressed by the exhibition to write to Lord Dudley on 11 February after his return to London offering £1,000 to buy two works by Constable and two by Corot; the Princess of Wales would present another Constable to the collection Lane intended to retain in Ireland.

The donations were widely reported and praised but a fortnight after the Prince's letter the *Illustrated London News* published a photograph showing a painting that bore an uncanny resemblance to one of the pictures he had given, under the headline 'Is it a Corot? The challenged authority of one of the Prince of Wales' gifts to the Dublin Gallery'.[26] The Corot in question, *Peasants by a Lake*, was a small landscape, believed to have been one of the very first works painted by the artist, and a favourite of Staats Forbes who had kept it on an easel in his bedroom. Lord Mayo had agreed to buy the picture, but in view of the Prince's interest, he agreed to pay instead for another canvas, Fantin Latour's *Venus and Cupid*. Although *Peasants by a Lake* was not typical of Corot's style, until now there had been no doubt cast over its attribution. However, the *Illustrated London News* revealed that a correspondent in Budapest had noticed striking similarities between the French picture and one painted by a Hungarian artist called Geza Meszoly, who had been much influenced by the Barbizon school. The story was quickly picked up by Irish newspapers and soon developed into an unmanageable controversy thanks to the association between the supposed Corot and the Prince of Wales. It was a matter of enormous embarassment to Lane, not least because already fraught relations with the Staats Forbes executors now became damaged beyond repair. Some of the latter's number had not wanted to permit any pictures from the collection to remain in Dublin once the RHA exhibition closed. Nor were they particularly happy when Lane pleaded not only for more time to raise funds, but also asked for sums being asked for various items to be lowered. The executors, he was told, 'cannot see their way to accept any reduction whatever on the prices for which the several works have been issued as they have strong grounds for the belief that, sold individually, nearly all the works would fetch higher prices than those quoted to you'.[27] Once the disputed Corot's merits became a matter of public debate, they demanded the return of all paintings not yet purchased, 'as the estate is only suffering by their further retention in Dublin'.[28]

Lane's cause was not helped by the behaviour of some people supposed to be among his supporters. George Moore, for example, gave an interview on the subject to the *Evening Mail* in which he airily declared that 'all public galleries are full of forgeries'.[29] Other friends insisted on treating the affair as though it were a vendetta, with William Orpen – despite personal doubts about the picture's attribution – loyally writing to the Dublin papers against a 'crusade of calumny directed against Mr Lane (for this has become a personal matter, deny it who will)'.[30] Not only was Lane's reputation as a judge of painting once more called into question, but his entire scheme for buying the Staats Forbes collection risked being discredited if allegations that the picture on show in Dublin was a fake could be proven true. Although the Meszoly landscape, *The Fishermen's Rest at Lake Balaton* on display in Budapest's National Museum, was considerably larger than the Corot, the resemblance between the two was otherwise undeniable.

Supporters rallied round him. 'Do not believe all the rot & gossip you hear,' advised Lord Mayo, 'if you do, you will have sleepless nights'.[31] But when his authority as an art expert was challenged, Lane had to respond. His first response was to discredit the Hungarian work, condescendingly dismissing Meszoly as 'an artist hitherto practically unknown in western Europe'[32] whose work he had never seen. He insisted the Corot attribution had been meticulously checked and invited a number of recognized authorities to confirm the work was authentic. However, his cause suffered somewhat when it transpired that one of the people consulted, Thomas Wallis, had first sold the picture to Staats Forbes, and two of the others, Martin Colnaghi and Lockett Agnew, were both dealers who would have a clear interest in ensuring that paintings handled by members of their profession were free of any suspicion. In late May, Imre Szalay, Director of the Hungarian National Gallery, wrote to the Irish press insisting 'our picture ... is a genuine Meszoly' painted between 1875 and 1877 at the request of the state and with a clearly documented history.[33]

Lane continued to receive some backing in the press, particularly from the *Irish Times*, but other newspapers were now less keen to support him, especially after many of the other pictures from Staats Forbes's collection went on show at London's Grafton Gallery at the start of May. Several English art critics denounced this exhibition for being full of 'shams', with the authenticity of many Constable canvases particularly questioned.[34] In early June, the *Evening Mail* announced that 'Dublin has had a providential escape', before going on to argue that poor sales of the paintings Lane had assembled could now be explained: 'No legitimate appraisal of the collection had been made, and art lovers very properly declined to buy a pig in a poke.'[35] Whatever about the merits of any other Staats Forbes pictures offered for sale, today this assessment seems true of the little landscape then attributed to Corot and now in the collection of the Municipal Gallery in Dublin. Bela Lazar, an art expert who travelled from Budapest to Dublin in 1905, concluded that the French picture was not an original, but his verdict remained largely unknown outside Hungary. After hovering in a critical limbo for more than seventy years, the work was finally confirmed as a copy of the Meszoly, probably painted when the latter was on show at the Paris World Exhibition of 1880. On this occasion, at least, Lane's famed judgement had proven incorrect.[36]

Meanwhile, in Dublin throughout spring and well into summer 1905, controversy over the Corot's attribution continued, in part because it permitted such irresistible opportunities for different factions to engage in point-scoring. One cartoon published at the time showed Hamlet standing before the painting and rhetorically asking, 'To Corot? or not to Corot?'[37] At the end of March, Lane announced to the press that £6,000 worth of pictures had been bought and the other works were now being returned to the Staats Forbes executors.[38] Those retained he placed on show by themselves. Lieutenant Colonel Plunkett, although he had permitted Lane to hang the pictures in the National Museum, now decided to make plain where his own loyalties lay. On the doors leading into the exhibition, he had framed photographs of both the Meszoly and Corot pictures screwed to the wall so that visitors could compare the two works for themselves. Lady Gregory wrote angrily to her nephew that she had seen Plunkett deliberately steering visitors to the museum away from the paintings and in the direction of the two photographs. What could be done to salvage the situation? The Prince of Wales prevaricated over accepting the London experts' verdict and eventually Lane proposed that he pay for another picture, *Village and Roadway* by Henri Harpignies, while the disputed Corot be bought by supporters in Dublin.

One supporter, however, refused to let the matter drop. In late August, Lane's cousin Captain John Shawe-Taylor, who had just returned from his honeymoon in Austria and Hungary (which included a visit to Budapest's National Gallery), called into the museum. Having explained to the policeman on duty that he wished to make a protest against the obstructive behaviour of the institution's officials, Shawe-Taylor unscrewed the two photographs and carried them out of the building.[39] The action could have had unpleasant consequences, so Lane immediately carried his cousin off to lunch with the Dudleys at the Viceregal Lodge, where a full confession was made and a promise given that no official action would be taken against the offender. The bold captain's action was later commemorated by satirical writer Susan Mitchell, whose 1908 book *Aids to the Immortality of Certain Persons in Ireland* included 'The Ballad of Shawe Taylor and Hugh Lane'. Having described the photographs' removal, she went on to give an imaginary list of witnesses to the event:

> A.E. was there with his long hair,
> And Orpen, R.H.A.,
> Sir Thomas Drew was in a stew,
> And looked the other way,
> But Martyn, who left the stage
> To play the patriot's part,
> Called for Hungarian policy
> In everything but art!
>
> And John B. Yeats stood near the gates
> With mischief in his gaze,
> While W.B. the poet, he
> Pondered a telling phrase,

You'll find it in the *Freeman*
After a day or so
And Moore was there – the same who is
High Sheriff for Mayo.[40]

John Shawe-Taylor, whose proselytizing mother Elizabeth had been a sister of Adelaide Lane and Lady Gregory, was in many respects typical of the people who rallied around his art-dealing cousin. Until his early death in June 1911, he wrote regularly to Lane, calling him 'dear Charlie' and urging him not to be discouraged in his enterprises because, as he wrote in February 1906, 'the victory is to those like yourself who undaunted by apathy and opposition stick to their guns'.[41] Invalided out of the British army during the Boer War, Shawe-Taylor possessed substantial reserves of energy and imagination, but few outlets for these. In late 1902, observing the still-unresolved problems between landlords – of which he was one – and their tenants, he proposed convening a series of meetings to find a solution. The Irish Land Conference permitted members of his class to negotiate a settlement with representatives of the Nationalist party, and the results were embodied in George Wyndham's Land Act of 1903, which offered generous financial incentives for landlords to sell and tenants to buy property. Lane numbered many friends among the land conference's participants, not least his brother Ambrose, then a law student, who acted as secretary at meetings; in May 1903 he and the Earl of Mayo published a well-received twenty-four-page handbook called *The Outlook in Ireland: The Irish Land Question*. Other members of the conference's committee included the Earl of Dunraven (who was also George Wyndham's cousin) and Colonel Hutcheson Pöe.

These men were representative of a very specific stratum in Irish society, members of the Ascendency class but keenly interested in the welfare of their country and, unlike many of their peers, not rabidly unionist in outlook, so allowing them to reach agreement with nationalists. In August 1904, for example, on the basis of the Land Conference's success, Lord Dunraven set up the Irish Reform Association; among its leading participants were, once more, Hutcheson Pöe as well as Sir Algernon Coote. The latter was premier baronet of Ireland and yet another of

Lane's friends drawn from the same relatively narrow social circle. Like Horace Plunkett and Lady Gregory, the members of this group were aristocratic in background (and all too often in manner as well) but did not wish to stand aloof from Ireland. They wanted to play as active a part in the country's cultural and political evolution as their forbears had done. They were motivated by a sense of duty and a dread of marginalization. The problem, as most of them eventually discovered, was that their country increasingly could find no role for them to play. The 1903 Land Conference was almost the last occasion on which this group found an opportunity to have their views heard and, even more importantly, acted upon. Thereafter, they were pushed out of politics, failing to secure seats at successive elections because the moderate unionism they espoused was regarded as too weak by the majority of their class and too strong by the majority of the country. Mainstream unionists thought them traitors tainted by nationalism, while nationalists considered them inescapably bound to their own class. Lord Dunraven's Irish Reform Association, for example, never had more than thirty members. And despite all John Shawe-Taylor had done for Ireland, his younger brother Frank was to be ambushed and shot dead by the IRA in March 1920; no matter how personally well-intentioned, he had still been a landlord. The people who rallied around Lane were therefore almost the least effective of all in Ireland, because they could rely only on themselves for support. As was to become clear, their energy and enthusiasm was not enough to ensure the success of any undertaking in which they became involved. Lane obviously had to take help where he found it, but his knowledge of factionalism in Irish society remained weak. He had not grown up in Ireland and London would always remain his home; these were serious handicaps. He once claimed his movement to encourage the development of modern art was 'unique in Irish history, all classes and ranks joining without distinction of politics and creed in helping it on'.[42]

This remark suggests either disingenuousness or naïveté. Questions of politics and religion were inescapable in early-twentieth-century Ireland and they tainted every undertaking in the country, even those associated with cultural development. W.B. Yeats was aware of this fact when he wrote to his friend, the English journalist Clement Shorter, in December

1904 that Lord Drogheda had been urged not to associate with the modern art movement in Dublin because of its connections with 'rebellious people'. Yeats continued in the same letter that the 'political question' was giving a lot of trouble at the time.[43] Lane was certainly not entirely ignorant of politics in Ireland; on one occasion he advised Yeats not to take issue on his behalf because, as the poet wrote, he found association 'with us Nationalists' injurious to his schemes in some quarters. 'Many of his rich friends', Yeats wrote to Lady Gregory, 'are saying that they will not help him now that he is part of the movement'.[44] Lane was nothing of the kind, of course, but his inability to appreciate sufficiently the central role politics would come to play in Ireland over the next decade eventually proved a more serious mistake than his failure to spot a fake Corot.

7
A MODERN ART GALLERY FOR IRELAND

According to Lady Gregory, even as a small child in the nursery Hugh Lane had begun formulating his ambition to create 'a wonderful gallery of pictures'.[1] The desire to encourage public access to great works of art had become widespread throughout Europe during the nineteenth century, when many museums were established. Lane's scheme to set up a new gallery in Dublin was therefore by no means unusual for the period. But where he differed from like-minded philanthropists was that he also acted as an art dealer. The potential for conflict he attempted to resolve by insisting repeatedly that while he bought and sold old master paintings, he collected contemporary art (although he gave examples of both to public galleries in Ireland and Britain). Lane once told James Duncan, husband of one of the founders of the United Arts Club in Dublin, Ellen Duncan, that while buying pictures was a pleasure, 'selling is the very devil. I never sell a picture till I am driven to it.' However, Duncan remembered, Lane also insisted that he never minded giving away paintings to galleries or museums because 'It is as much mine as ever, I still possess it, I can see it when I like and everyone else can see it too, so there's no waste in the matter. I hate waste.'[2]

This support for the development of public collections echoed that of his first employer, Martin Colnaghi, who would also leave a substantial legacy to a national institution. But Lane differed from Colnaghi in two respects: Ireland, not England, became his concern; and he was increasingly preoccupied with living artists. And even when old masters held his attention, he usually had Irish interests at heart. In November 1905 Velazquez's *Rokeby Venus* came on the market and he argued that the picture should be bought for Dublin instead of London because 'we are possibly more impressionable to the influence of such a masterpiece than a community for years sated with good things'.[3] Despite his best efforts to convince the members of the National Art Collections Fund that Ireland deserved the picture, in the end the *Rokeby Venus* went to London's National Gallery.

Lane first started to formulate clearly his ideas for a gallery of modern art in Dublin while organizing the Guildhall exhibition of summer 1904. It was a natural development of the theory he had already articulated that only through generous exposure to the best examples of contemporary work could Irish artists hope for self-improvement. Insularity was the enemy of new talent. Writing to the *Irish Times* in January 1903 he suggested, 'With opportunities of support and encouragement, we may produce a school of painting equal in importance and in profit to any in the world'.[4] That support and encouragement, he believed, could best be provided by the establishment of a museum where a collection of modern works could be shown. 'A gallery of Irish and modern art in Dublin', he explained in his preface to the Guildhall show catalogue, 'would create a standard of taste and a feeling of the relative importance of painters. This would encourage the purchase of pictures, for people will not purchase where they do not know.'[5] The interest in purchasers was inevitable in someone who made his living buying and selling art, but Lane was also reflecting a fairly widespread awareness that contemporary artists could best be helped by finding a market interested in supporting their work. Speaking at the Winchester School of Art in March 1911, for example, Robert Ross, then art critic of the *Morning Post*, proposed that schools for buyers were more necessary than schools for artists.[6]

But obviously Lane was also concerned with the aesthetic well-being of artists, and in the same Guildhall catalogue he suggested the reason they would benefit from a gallery of modern art was that 'it is one's contemporaries that teach one the most. They are busy with the same problems of expression as oneself, for almost every artist expresses the soul of his own age.'[7] Barely a week after the exhibition opened in London, he issued his first manifesto in favour of a modern art gallery, decrying the fact that 'There is not in Ireland one accessible collection or masterpiece of modern or contemporary art'.[8] This document, which looked for the provision of a suitable building in Dublin, was signed not just by Lane but also the RHA's Sir Thomas Drew (still an ally, although not for much longer), the Earls of Drogheda and Mayo, and Colonel Hutcheson Pöe.

Once the Staats Forbes pictures were exhibited, Lane's proposal started to receive more widespread encouragement. When this show opened in late November 1904, the *Irish Times* felt moved to declare that the foundation of a gallery of modern art 'is an event of no small importance'.[9] The pictures offered for sale were therefore to be bought for inclusion in the intended gallery's collection. At the same time, artists in both England and Ireland were invited to present examples of their work to the project. A document distributed to prospective donors indicated that the gallery was 'to be opened at the Royal Hibernian Academy, Lower Abbey Street, Dublin', and invited the artist in question to list the pictures being offered before confirming 'I am prepared to present the above work to form part of the nucleus in the collection of modern art for Dublin'.[10] Lane now set up a committee to campaign for the project's successful conclusion. Most of its members were also subscribers to the scheme, including Colonel Hutcheson Pöe who offered £1,000, Lords Mayo and Drogheda who gave £100 each, Lady Gregory (£50), and Sir Josslyn Gore-Booth (£10). The sister of the last mentioned, Constance, Countess Markievicz, was another supporter of the project, subscribing £5 and five shillings and helping to form a 'Ladies' Picture League', of which she became co-secretary with Mrs Noel Guinness. At the time, Constance Markievicz was a painter and still a welcome guest of the Dudleys in Dublin Castle, but an interest in rebellious causes, which would soon draw her to the nationalist movement, meant that, for a while at least, she was one of Lane's champions. Other familiar names on the list of supporters included W.B. Yeats, the Earl of Dunraven, George Russell, Dermod O'Brien and Nathaniel Hone, as well as the M.P. and leader of the Irish Nationalist Party, John Redmond.

In early December 1904 the committee members issued their first letter of appeal. While acknowledging that 'the task of creating a modern art gallery in Dublin, except by long and slow degrees, might seem to be enormous and well nigh impossible', they insisted the undertaking had been 'rendered unexpectedly easy of fulfillment' thanks to the presence in the capital of the Staats Forbes pictures. If bought for Ireland, they explained, these could form an ideal nucleus for the proposed museum's collection.[11] Lecturers at the exhibition, such as John B. Yeats and the National Gallery of Ireland's director, Sir Walter Armstrong, also made a point of urging the necessity of a modern art gallery. While the people of Ireland were encouraged to give what they could afford to a purchasing fund, Lady Gregory made an appeal for assistance to the United States and was rewarded in mid-February when President Roosevelt, an admirer of her writings, sent a cheque for $25. When the Staats Forbes paintings moved to the National Museum in January 1905, a fresh appeal brochure was issued by the now firmly established Modern Art Gallery Committee.

Inevitably there were carping voices wishing to be heard, among them that of George Moore. His attitude towards Lane alternated between encouragement and opposition. After living in Paris and London for many years, in 1901 Moore had moved to Dublin, taking a house on Upper Ely Place. His behaviour thereafter seems to have been primarily governed by a sense of grievance that the rest of the city was insufficiently grateful for his presence. In relation to Lane, he probably also felt considerable resentment at seeing his self-assigned role as the champion of modern art usurped so thoroughly by a younger man. What else can be the explanation for the extraordinarily hostile letter he wrote to the Dublin *Daily Express* in late June 1903 when a gallery of modern art for Dublin had barely been proposed? Nothing, he claimed, could be 'more certain than that, far from helping art, this Irish picture gallery will lower and hinder it'. The only beneficiaries from the scheme, he argued, would be those who profited from 'a huge misapplication of public money'. He sneered at the women who had hosted tea parties at Lane's exhibitions (whiling away time 'until they meet suitable matches at the Castle balls') and insisted that the recently deceased Walter Osborne 'used to speak to me with terror of Mr Lane's project'.[12] No wonder John B. Yeats, responding to this outburst in the same newspaper a few days later, decided Moore 'seems to breathe most freely when, like a fish, he swims against the stream'.[13]

Other opponents could not be dismissed so easily. In 1918 Dermod O'Brien attempted to explain the hostility his old friend aroused by saying Lane had been 'one of those personalities so abnormal in his passion for the beautiful, in whom unlimited generosity amounted almost to a mania, that all his life he was apt to be misunderstood and his motives queried by that huge majority of us who think first of self'.[14] It was always the accusation of self-interest that Lane had to face, but his supporters were also expected to justify themselves. A correspondent who chose to sign himself 'Peter de Hooch' wrote to the *Evening Herald* on 31 December 1904 saying the modern art gallery proposal did not represent popular opinion 'but is rather the nursed enthusiasm of a coterie'.[15] This was a charge that could be denied but never successfully refuted. An effective response was hindered by the simple truth that the campaign for a gallery of modern art had only begun after Lane's arrival in Ireland; it was his concept and had been taken up by his circle of friends. Even more problematic, the pictures being proposed for inclusion in the gallery represented his taste and judgement.

Friends of Lane were quite happy with this state of affairs. They insisted that the best way to form a representative collection of contemporary art was to leave the task to a discerning individual – such as Lane. To support their argument, they pointed to the disaster of the Chantrey Bequest, a fund established in London in the mid-nineteenth century by a Royal Academician to purchase British works of art. The bequest was soon being used to buy paintings shown by members of, and in, the Royal Academy. When displayed in public at the Tate Gallery from 1897 onwards, the collection had drawn critical damnation. A fear that the projected Dublin gallery would become another Chantrey Bequest, filled with second-rate pictures bought by a committee, was widely expressed, not least by the ever-changeable Moore. Lane's 'coterie', however, responded that if Lane, the originator of the project, assumed responsibility for developing a collection, high standards would be maintained. Interviewed on the subject of modern art galleries in New York in 1914, he suggested the director of such an institution 'should not be an artist, but a man of broad art culture and taste, and he should not be hampered by a Board of Trustees, for such Boards never agree on any artistic subject'. He went on to propose that the hypothetical director should be given 'full power' but only for a term of five years in case he proved unequal to the task. Following the same line of argument, in December 1906 W.B. Yeats had insisted that 'committees make bad galleries, they lack the incentive to unresting labour and they have no real taste'.[17] Less than two years later, writing in *The Academy*, Frank Rutter postulated that in municipal art galleries, the executive and purchasing power ought to be entrusted to one man.[18]

Dublin's modern art gallery inspired a decade of correspondence in Irish newspapers. The amount of press coverage Lane managed to attract for his projects, even if sometimes hostile, shows what an accomplished publicist he could be. He retained the services of several clippings agencies and instructed his sister Ruth to paste into scrapbooks every reference to him in chronological sequence. Those that still survive show just how important a device the national press was in encouraging support for his schemes and, less advantageously for Lane, in assisting public debate on them. From the 1902 old masters exhibition at the RHA until his death, his name was rarely out of the Irish newspapers, but his work also received intermittent coverage around the world. He actively sought attention from the press and happily agreed to features such as a 'Celebrities at Home' series carried in *The World* magazine in late 1909.[19] Both as an art dealer and as the initiator of contemporary art exhibitions, he needed as much publicity as possible and would, therefore, cultivate members of the press if this appeared necessary. An English journalist called Harold Begbie, who interviewed Lane for the *Morning Post*, was subsequently sent, by way of thanks, a portrait by Sir Joshua Reynolds. While the dealer was always known as a generous man, this 'most noble gift', as Begbie called it in his own subsequent letter of appreciation, could be interpreted as little more than a bribe.[20] However, exposure to Lane's charm usually sufficed to ensure he achieved what he wanted in dealing with the press. At the time of the old masters show in the RHA galleries, he called on the acting editor of the *Freeman's Journal*, Matthias M'Donnell Bodkin, a barrister and former Nationalist M.P. who, while a fine writer, knew little and cared less about the visual arts. Lane, however, managed to persuade Bodkin to publish a long and complimentary feature on the exhibition. When he returned to the newspaper's offices to thank the editor for his kind assistance, he endeared himself so much that Bodkin eventually invited him back to the family home on Upper Mount Street for dinner that night. There Lane first met his host's fifteen-year-old son Thomas, on Christmas holiday from Clongowes College. The latter was immediately captivated by the charm of his parent's new friend and became a life-long admirer.

Although he followed his father's example and studied law, Thomas Bodkin's principal interests were artistic and he eventually became Director of the National Gallery of Ireland, as well as the author of a government-commissioned report which led to the establishment in 1951 of the Irish Arts Council. He was the first of a succession of younger men who were to be protégés of Lane, their tastes carefully nurtured by him and their careers subjected to much scrutiny and advice. Writing to Dermod O'Brien soon after the death of his mentor, Bodkin said of Lane: 'He always encouraged and guided me, bringing me over great numbers of important shows and galleries'.[21] He also showed the younger man some of the tricks of the dealer's trade. On one occasion when they were visiting an antique shop on Dublin's quays, Lane spotted a seventeenth-century Italian painting of some value. Rather than let the owner discover he knew its real worth, Lane persuaded Bodkin to act as though they only wanted a cheap canvas on which to practise cleaning techniques. By this means, he bought the work for a just few pounds. 'When the picture was cleaned and had turned out to be even finer than Lane had originally conjectured,' Bodkin remembered, 'he insisted on giving it to me as a present. This shrewdness and generosity warred perpetually in that strange character: but generosity was usually victorious.'[22] Writing in 1932 of his first encounter with Lane three decades earlier, Bodkin declared: 'I enrolled myself there and then as his humble follower and have not since wavered from that allegiance.'[23]

Charm in profusion was going to be needed if Lane hoped to persuade not just private individuals but also the relevant authorities to support his gallery cause. Dublin Corporation first signalled an interest in becoming associated with the project in February 1905 when its members unanimously agreed they should instruct the authority's Estates and Finance Committee to provide a sum of £500 per annum for the maintenance of a municipal gallery of modern art. After waiting almost a year, Lane decided to employ a number of complementary tactics to make certain this would be the case. By early 1906, 114 pictures and pieces of sculpture, many though by no means all from the Staats Forbes collection, had been either bought or promised to the prospective gallery. To this group, Lane now proposed adding a group of modern paintings that belonged to him and had a value in the region of £6,000. They would be given, however, 'conditional on the provision of a suitable gallery within the next two months'.[24]

The concept of a conditional gift had first been mentioned in the introduction to a catalogue produced in January 1905 for the National Museum show. Here Lane wrote that 'the small collection that I have formed myself', together with a number of third-party donations, would be presented to Dublin 'on the condition that certain steps are taken to place the "Gallery" on a sound basis'.[25] The unspecified contents of his 'small collection' would have been very different from what eventually became the conditional gift, as Lane had not yet bought many of the Impressionist works which were to be its most valuable element. Among the elected members of Dublin Corporation, therefore, his demand that a 'suitable gallery' be found initially met with little response. But the threat of his pictures being withdrawn had a galvanizing effect on Lane's friends and on 9th February 1906 they organized a public discussion in the main hall of the Royal Society of Antiquaries at 6 St Stephen's Green. The subject was the 'Proposed Gallery of Modern Art for Dublin', and the Earl of Mayo chaired a packed meeting at which the new Lord Lieutenant, Lord Aberdeen, who had only taken up his duties a few days earlier, was an unexpected guest. All the usual Lane adherents such as John B. Yeats, Horace Plunkett, Sarah Purser and Countess Markievicz were either present or else, like Colonel Hutcheson Pöe and the Earl of Drogheda, sent letters of support which were read out to the audience. Lord Aberdeen made a speech offering 'all good wishes for the success of the movement' and two resolutions were unanimously accepted: that a gallery of modern art was wanted in Ireland; and that definite steps be immediately taken to provide such a gallery.[26]

Those immediate steps only followed in June when Dublin Corporation once more chose to authorize its Estates and Finance Committee, this time with the task of finding, hiring and maintaining temporary premises 'in which art works could be preserved and exhibited' pending the erection of a permanent building in a suitable area of the city.[27] The annual costs involved were not to exceed the £500 already voted the previous year and the committee might act only after 'expert opinion' had been consulted over the quality of work being offered by Lane and his group to the new gallery. Sir Walter Armstrong and Nathaniel Hone were the experts in question and their opinions proved favourable, but a further twelve months would pass before a temporary site was taken.

It took two years, not two months, to find the 'suitable gallery' Lane had requested and he therefore had to revise the terms of his conditional gift. This delay does not appear to have troubled him very much, as he continued to add more paintings and sculpture to the existing collection. Some of those approached for help were understandably cautious; the Earl of Iveagh, for example, wrote that he would be prepared to donate two or three pictures of his choice, but only 'when a gallery has been set up'.[28] Art critics with whom Lane was familiar, such as Lady Colin Campbell, were asked to plead his case while he invited artists of his acquaintance to donate a work to the gallery.[29] Most were happy to do so because, at a time when few national institutions anywhere bought contemporary art, they could now be featured in a public collection. Walter Sickert, Roger Fry and William Rothenstein were among the English artists who agreed to donate a picture.[30] Other, more internationally famous practitioners expected payment, albeit at a reduced rate as Lane pleaded poverty. The Italian Giovanni Boldini, replying to a request for an example of his work, wrote that Dublin could have a portrait of Whistler for £2,000, even though, he said, a museum in Philadelphia had offered him $7,000 for the work.[31]

Lane was especially anxious for Auguste Rodin to be well represented in the new gallery. Through both John Tweed and George Wyndham (whose Rodin bust would be donated to Dublin), he therefore entered into negotiations with the sculptor, eventually agreeing in March 1906 to pay £200 for a bronze cast of *L'Age d'Arain*. Thanking Rodin for selling the work at cost, he wrote: 'Your genius will I feel sure inspire many young artists to do fine work ... I hope you will be able to let us possess it soon!'³² In fact, more than a year passed before *L'Age d'Arain* was sent to Ireland in late April 1907, but Lane used the intervening period to conduct further correspondence with Rodin in which he tried to negotiate for another piece of sculpture. 'I would not ask so much', he explained, 'if we were not a very poor people – especially the individuals who love art.'³³

The poverty of Ireland's art lovers had been made even clearer to him during the spring of 1906. At the beginning of the year, he had been invited by a group of Belfast citizens to organize an exhibition of modern art for their municipal art gallery. The Staats Forbes show in Dublin had excited a great deal of interest throughout the country and in January 1905 the *Northern Whig* suggested that Belfast ought to have its own gallery of modern art.³⁴ This proposal reflected the ideas expressed a month earlier in the same newspaper by a Belfast resident called Maurice Joy, who had argued that his native city needed both a good gallery of modern art and, to encourage this ambition, a loan exhibition featuring pictures 'of the first order' which Hugh Lane might be asked to arrange.³⁵ Although the request took some time, when eventually forthcoming it provided an irresistible opportunity for Lane to bring his ideas on developing a national school to another Irish city. He agreed to assemble a representative collection of work for show during April and May. As in the Dublin exhibition of 1904/5, he went to a number of different sources for help, including private owners, some of the Staats Forbes pictures now owned by Dublin, Durand-Ruel in Paris and his own private collection.

When the show opened in Belfast's Municipal Art Gallery on 20 April 1906 it contained 143 works described by Lane as being the most representative exhibition of modern painting yet seen in Ireland. It was certainly a curious mixture of schools and styles which now hardly seem to have much in common, as Corot and Constable were hung alongside Renoir and Rossetti. Some of the most important Impressionist paintings – Manet's portrait of Eva Gonzales and his *Concert aux Tuileries*, Monet's view of Vétheuil, the *Vue de Louveciennes* by Pissarro – had been, or were about to be, bought by Lane from Durand-Ruel but others were simply on loan. Irish artists included Orpen, Lavery, Osborne and Sarah Cecilia Harrison. In his catalogue preface, Lane made a point of

Hugh Percy Lane aged four years and ten months (© Hugh Lane Municipal Gallery of Modern Art)

In fancy dress, which he would always love, September 1885, aged nine (© Hugh Lane Municipal Gallery of Modern Art)

In 1889 (© Hugh Lane Municipal Gallery of Modern Art)

Adelaide Lane, née Persse, Hugh Lane's mother (courtesy David Thistlethwaite)

James Lane, Hugh Lane's father, standing in the grounds of the Rectory at Redruth, Cornwall (courtesy P.R. Bradley)

Two works by John B. Yeats: a drawing of Hugh Lane, dated August 1905, and a painting of Lane's sister Ruth Shine, the only one of his siblings to whom he was close (courtesy of the National Gallery of Ireland)

Lady Gregory, Lane's aunt and most fervent supporter, painted by Antonio Mancini, 1908 (© Hugh Lane Municipal Gallery of Modern Art)

On the steps of Moore Abbey, Monasterevin, Co. Kildare, home of the Droghedas, who were among his earliest Irish friends (David Thistlethwaite)

The first home of the Municipal Gallery, in Harcourt Street, Dublin (© Hugh Lane Municipal Gallery of Modern Art)

Two cartoons by Max Beerbohm: *Sir Hugh Lane Producing Masterpieces for Dublin*, 1909, and *Sir Hugh Lane Guarding a Manet*, 1911 (© Hugh Lane Municipal Gallery of Modern Art)

A photograph of Antonio Mancini, inscribed by Mancini to Lane (David Thistlethwaite)

Top: Titian's *Portrait of a Man in a Red Cap*, which Lane bought and sold twice, making spectacular profits both times (Copyright The Frick Collection, New York)

Left: Self-portrait by Sarah Cecilia Harrison, whose admiration for Lane bordered on the unhealthy, particularly after his death when she claimed improbably that they had been engaged (© Hugh Lane Municipal Gallery of Modern Art)

Outside Lindsey House, London, with his chauffeur (© Hugh Lane Municipal Gallery of Modern Art)

On horseback, *c.* 1914 (© Hugh Lane Municipal Gallery of Modern Art)

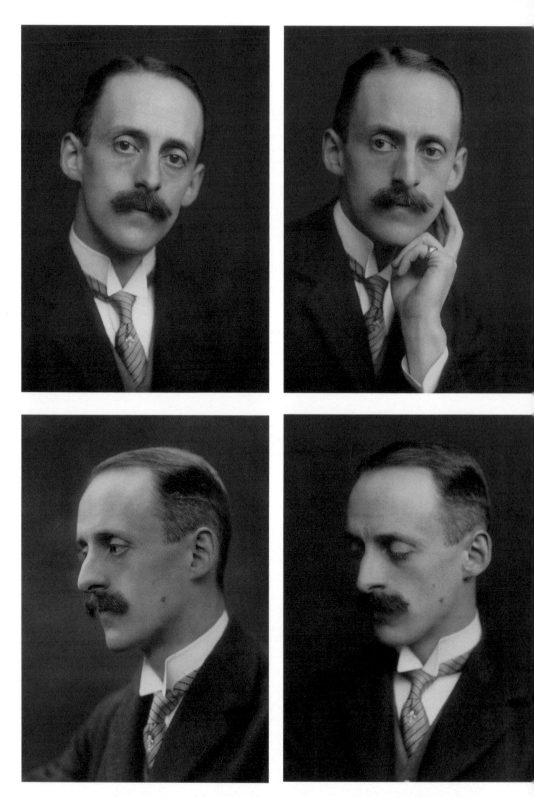

Series of studio portraits, *c.* 1912 (© Hugh Lane Municipal Gallery of Modern Art)

praising the 'enthusiasm of the artists and students whom I have met' during his time in Belfast, before going on to encourage them and their supporters to buy for their city the fifty-odd works in the show that were for sale, including another Monet canvas, together with pictures by Renoir, Sisley and Morisot. Were these paintings to be now purchased 'on advantageous terms', he argued, they would 'form a nucleus for the proposed modern gallery in Belfast'.[36] In the *Northern Whig* a week after the show opened, he had narrowed the list of pictures down to twenty which, he suggested 'would inspire the student and cultivate the public taste'.[37] The total cost of purchasing these twenty works Lane estimated to be £5,000. Among the artists in his abbreviated selection were Lavery and Orpen representing Ireland, Courbet, Vuillard, Corot, Morisot, Fantin Latour and Puvis de Chavannes for France, and the Englishmen Stott and Clausen. He then went on to say that if at least some of these pictures were bought by Belfast Corporation, he would donate a number of others from his own collection.

Despite this promise – and reminders from the *Northern Whig* to its readers that the purpose of the exhibition was to collect funds and pictures for a municipal collection – it quickly emerged that the burghers of Belfast were as reluctant as their equivalents in Dublin to invest in art. A year after the show closed, Ellen Duncan recalled in *The Athenaeum* 'the crowds of working-men who learnt to look upon Courbet and Manet as familiar friends',[38] but the city's wealthier inhabitants preferred to keep such friends at a distance. Perhaps their reluctance had nothing to do with aesthetics. By early May, C.H. Brett, a solicitor and member of the Belfast show's committee, was writing to Lane that 'You are, of course, right in theory in saying that art has no politics but alas in practice in this town politics do really get mixed up with everything'.[39] A fortnight later, Brett wrote again with the news that admission receipts had been steadily declining and his expectation was that no more than £200 would be collected for the picture fund. All hope of buying a single painting as fine as a Corot had therefore been abandoned, so could something less expensive be suggested?[40] The committee had set its heart on acquiring Lavery's *A Lady in Pink*, but at £600 this seemed impossibly expensive. In the end, Henri Le Sidaner's *Le Gouter au Jardin* and *Resting* by Orpen were bought for £210, while Lane donated a third picture, *The Goat Girl* by the English artist James Charles.

The effort to inspire enthusiasm for modern art in Belfast now petered out in disappointment and on 19 May the chairman of the local organizers, architect W.J. Gilliland, told Lane he had been incorrect to imagine that the northern city, despite possessing greater wealth, bore any comparison with its southern counterpart: 'Dublin as the metropolis contains a very large and cultured professional class which is practically non-existent in Belfast.'[41] But he and his companions intended to persist with annual shows in the hope that, eventually, their fellow citizens would come to recognize the necessity for a gallery of modern art. Lane was certainly willing to aid them in this aspiration. Three years after the first exhibition, he agreed to lend a number of pictures to the Ulster Arts Club's annual May exhibition even after one member reminded him 'that Belfast is a strange place in art matters'.[42] And in December 1910, after being once again asked for help in establishing a northern Irish art gallery, he prepared a document outlining his ideas on the subject. Insisting that only the purchase of truly excellent paintings from the finest contemporary masters would ensure local practitioners' standards improved, he observed that 'by buying good pictures the collection acquires a prestige that makes artists ready to give their work for considerably less than its market value'.[43] By then, this was a policy he had put to good effect in Dublin.

Many of Lane's friends believed his labours in Belfast had been not only unsuccessful but also insufficiently appreciated. However, they had anticipated this situation by arranging a public acknowledgement of his 'services in the cause of modern art in Ireland'.[44] In late January 1906, Lords Mayo and Drogheda, Colonel Hutcheson Pöe, George Russell and W.B. Yeats wrote to the country's newspapers that they planned to make a presentation to Lane and invited members of the public to offer whatever subscriptions they could afford.[45] The sums with which they opened the fund were relatively small – £10 from Pöe, £3 from Drogheda and Mayo, £1 from the two others – and nor did anyone else offer large contributions. The intention was to commission a portrait of Lane from one of the artists he most admired, John Singer Sargent; he had tried, without success, to borrow some work from him for the Belfast exhibition. Regrettably, when the subscription list eventually closed on 11 May, there was a considerable disparity between the amount of money needed (at least £200) and that actually received (in the region of £100), which must have been somewhat humiliating for the testimonial's intended recipient. Eventually, George Russell wrote to reassure Lane that Sargent 'has consented for love of you to paint you for whatever you will fetch as a testimonial'.[46] A head and shoulders portrait was eventually agreed. Wearing a loose coat and stock and holding a pair of gloves to his chest, the subject appears a dandified and romantic figure. There is little sense of Lane's nervous energy; he looks, on the contrary, languid and remote, as though the organization even of his own business had left him almost incapacitated. But this was a picture he dearly loved and, when he bought his own home in 1909, it was hung in a prominent place on the main stairs.

The portrait was formally presented to him on the afternoon of 11 January 1907 at a ceremony in Dublin's Hibernian Hotel. An accompanying framed testimonial contained watercolour illustrations by, among others, George Russell, Sarah Cecilia Harrison, Richard Caulfield Orpen and Nelly O'Brien, eldest sister of Lane's friend Dermod. The citation spoke of the recipient's 'strenuous labour for the public good, tireless energy, and splendid generosity; combined with brilliant organising capabilities and fine judgement'.[47] 'Never was a compliment better deserved', commented the *Freeman's Journal* afterwards,[48] although the *Irish Times* declared that 'the best compliment that could be paid to Mr Lane would be to complete the work which he designed and give the Dublin Gallery of Modern Art a local habitation as well as a name'.[49] Accepting the picture, Lane was so overcome with emotion that he burst into tears, although he recovered to thank his friends for their gift. He almost never spoke in public, but this was an exceptional occasion and he therefore forced himself to say a few words. He noted that opponents of the gallery project, unable to deny 'its unassailable soundness', had been reduced to attacking him. 'Therefore the personal abuse I have received I regard as the hallmark of the value of the scheme.'[50] It was a neat conceit, but while Lane and his admirers might clearly understand the worth of his intentions, not everyone else had been convinced.

8

THE GENTLEMAN PATRON

A fortnight after Lane was presented with his Sargent portrait, J.M.
Synge's *The Playboy of the Western World* made its première at the
Abbey Theatre. Although he does not appear to have attended the opening night on 26 January 1907, he was certainly in the audience for the
third night, when he helpfully pointed out troublemakers to the police
present. *The Abbey Row*, a satirical pamphlet published at the time,
included a cartoon called 'The Amateur Chucker-Out'; this showed a willowy Lane holding two burly figures apart. Orpen also made a drawing of
his friend holding a man over his slight and sinuous form. The riots
inspired by *The Playboy*, although ostensibly due to the author's language and his perceived slight on the morals of Irish womanhood, in reality had their origins in many of the same political and cultural disputes
that would also be stirred into existence by Lane's struggle to establish a
gallery of modern art in Dublin. In both instances, the impression had
been given that a self-appointed 'coterie' was attempting to deliver
instruction to the rest of the country; the latter, however, rarely chose to
listen except when an opportunity for disagreement arose. It was unfortunate that the main figures behind both the modern art gallery and the
Abbey Theatre should have come from the same privileged background –
or at least were believed to have done so. In *Vale* George Moore enter-
tainingly describes W.B. Yeats's attendance at a meeting in support of the
gallery project at which the poet denounced the Dublin bourgeoisie for

failing to support the project. This was Yeats as aspiring aristocrat and, Moore commented, 'we asked ourselves why our Willie Yeats should feel himself called upon to denounce his own class ... By virtue of our sub-scriptions we should cease to belong to the middle classes.'[1]

Yeats preferred to ally himself with the old order, although admittedly only those members who were anxious to work for the betterment of Ire-land. But did Ireland believe she was in need of betterment? The rioting in the Abbey Theatre's auditorium suggested not, or at least not in the way Yeats or Lane proposed. Much of the time, they and their circle tended to antagonize rather than encourage potential supporters. It was not just that Yeats, arrayed in a splendid fur coat, hectored audiences on the awfulness of the middle classes but that Lady Gregory declared: 'We would not allow any part of our audience to make itself final judge through preventing others from hearing and judging for themselves.'[2] She, like other members of the Irish literary and artistic revival, felt an almost missionary zeal for her work; the same devotion to a cause so many representatives of her class brought to converting other nations to Christianity or expanding the British empire by joining the army and civil service. But in this instance, the work was to be undertaken at home where most of the population proved resistant to ideologies proposed by an Anglo-Irish Protestant elite.

Typical of the latter's inability to appreciate the sensibilities of its audience were the arguments for self-improvement put forward by Horace Plunkett in his book *Ireland in the New Century*, published in 1904. Whatever beneficial proposals were included, these were over-looked because the author made the mistake of finding a connection between the country's lack of modernization and what he considered to be Irish Roman Catholic backwardness. Among this group of friends and allies, there was often, perhaps unconsciously, a quality of condescen-sion, a sense of speaking *de haut en bas*. In a document composed in November 1906 on the modern art gallery, Lane wrote: 'To ensure that the collection shall appeal to all classes in Dublin, I would suggest that one room should be set aside for loan pictures of a more popular order. The class that these will appeal to will rejoice in the constant change and variety.'[3] It is instructive to note how, because the pictures would be of a 'popular order', he only wanted them to be on loan and not part of the permanent collection.

Lane's difficulties in encouraging widespread support for his Irish projects were compounded by two additional problems. One of these was that, unlike Yeats, Lady Gregory *et al.*, he did not have the good fortune to find his efforts coinciding with a natural resurgence of talent in his field of endeavour. Whereas the literary movement's work was greatly aided by the emergence of many fine writers during the same period, nothing remotely similar occurred in Ireland's visual arts. Between the time of Lane's initial engagement with the country and his death fifteen years later, little altered in terms of indigenous painting and sculpture. Many local artists, especially those associated with the RHA, remained hostile towards him and he received far greater help from his aunt's literary friends.

While he could not be held responsible for this handicap, the other difficulty was entirely of his own making. Lane's residence outside Ireland undermined the considerable efforts he made to help the country, particularly at a time when nationalist feeling was on the increase. His occupation as a dealer in London tended to give credence to the idea that whatever work he did for Ireland was to his personal advantage. Just such a belief was insinuated in the *United Irishman*, the strongly nationalist weekly newspaper edited by Arthur Griffith who seriously quarreled with W.B. Yeats over this very point.[4] Someone of Lane's worldly sophistication would scarcely be to the taste of Griffith, who wrote: 'Cosmopolitanism never produced a great artist nor a good man yet, and never will.'[5] These views were by no means exclusive to him. The 1900s saw a sharp rise in public expressions of hostility to outside interference in Irish affairs, as articulated by demagogic journalists of the period, such as D.P. Moran, who in his 1905 book of essays *The Philosophy of Irish Ireland* made plain the intention of the local population to make their own choices and decisions. But nor could Lane, Yeats or Lady Gregory necessarily rely on support from their own class. The greater part of the Anglo-Irish ascendency came to regard them and members of their circle with extreme suspicion because of a series of incidents: Maud Gonne's public opposition to Britain's war against the Boers in South Africa; Edward Martyn's presidency of Sinn Féin (and his remark that any Irishman who joined the British armed forced 'deserves to be flogged');[6] the failure of the Abbey Theatre to close as a mark of respect after the death of King Edward VII in May 1910; Constance Markievicz's attempts to burn a Union Jack during a visit to Ireland the following year by his successor George V. None of these were the actions of people loyal to the crown. So Lane was doubly an outsider, an art dealer based in London who spoke with an English accent, would soon accept a knighthood from the crown, associated with the Castle set in Dublin and simultaneously consorted with nationalist sympathizers even if he never publicly advocated their views.

Here lies a possible explanation why, despite a great deal of canvassing, albeit of the most discreet kind, in 1907 he failed yet again to secure an official position. His old foe, Lieutenant Colonel Plunkett, who as Director of the Science and Art Institutions in Dublin had been responsible for the National Museum, was due to retire and Lane decided he would like the job, particularly as the museum was now being given independent status. Although friends lobbied hard, in late August it became clear the post had been awarded to another candidate, Count George Plunkett, whose son Joseph Mary would later be a participant in the 1916 Easter Rising. Lane's supporters rallied around him with reassurances that 'you are a young man yet and your chance may come'.[7] They decided that Plunkett, because he was a Roman Catholic, had been chosen by the government to placate nationalists. The disappointed candidate meanwhile told his sister the experience had been 'too aggravating for words' and said he believed his cause had been thwarted by T.P. Gill of the Department of Agriculture and Technical Instruction, with whom he had fallen out over the aborted St Louis exhibition more than three years earlier.[8]

A more likely reason is that the officials responsible for the appointment recognized that Lane was unlikely, whatever he might say, to give the museum his complete attention. He was, after all, still acting as a dealer in London and attracting as much publicity for this as for his work on behalf of art in Ireland. These were particularly busy times for Lane who, after scaling down his professional activities in the first years of the century, had now started once again to make considerable amounts of money from dealing in old masters. Among the most sensational – and widely reported – of his purchases during this period was the acquisition of a Titian portrait at Christie's on 12 May 1906 for 2,000 guineas. Then believed to represent Lorenzo de Medici but now more usually known as the *Portrait of a Man in a Red Cap*, it was to pass in and out of Lane's collection. The Titian was reproduced in publications throughout Europe and greatly admired; in early December 1906, for example, Bernard Berenson, who was visiting London from Italy, wrote to make an appointment with its owner to see the picture.[9] Attention of this kind could only enhance Lane's reputation as an important dealer. Another much-publicized addition to his stock came on 10 August 1907 when, also at Christie's, he bid against a number of other London dealers to gain possession of a small picture 'begrimed and generally in bad condition to the uninitiated' but attributed to Watteau;[10] this he eventually won for £2,625. Christie's was the auction house from which he most often bought, although he also used a number of others including the nearby Robinson & Fisher's and Foster's on Pall Mall. Some years earlier, he had written to Sir Algernon Coote that he found all his 'good bargains' at Christie's and Robinson & Fisher's; 'Last Sat. week I picked up a wonderful picture at the former place by the rare Ver Meer of Delft for £110 (I'd have got it for £5 but that one other man had spotted it) – I have since been offered by a dealer £1500 cash for it – and refused!'[11]

It was at Christie's that he met Alec Martin, another of the young men who were to become his protégés. Born in 1884, Martin had joined the auction house as a messenger at the age of twelve; he spent his entire career at Christie's where he eventually became managing director. Like Lane when young, he was eager to learn and during the long summer holidays while the London auctioneers closed down for several months, he would travel to Paris, take whatever work was available and study the Louvre's collection of pictures. He also learned a great deal about paintings from his older friend but in turn was able to be of service by bidding at Christie's on behalf of Lane, who did not like his professional rivals to see which lots he wanted. Alec Martin gave his friend the gift of a Pekinese puppy, named Tinko, to which Lane became devoted; 'His face would light up at the sound of its tiny bark or its bell', Lady Gregory remembered. If invited out to lunch, he would remark: 'There's Tinko – is there enough for him?'[12] That Lane made a lasting impact on the young Christie's employee is undoubtable. When Martin's wife gave birth to a son in April 1917, the child was christened Hugh Percy after his father's late friend; and seventeen years later, on hearing he had received a knighthood, Martin told Lane's sister Ruth: 'I have striven to follow the splendid example of Hugh to whom I owe an enormous lot. He befriended me, encouraged & helped me when I surely needed it.'[13] As late as 1961, a decade before his own death and more than forty-five years after that of his mentor, he could still write: 'Lane's friendship to me is a very precious thing.'[14]

Even while buying and selling old masters, Lane was adding to his own private collection of modern pictures. In November 1907 he sent his aunt a postcard from Paris informing her that he had just 'given myself a Renoir (value £1,600) as a birthday present!'[15] This was *Les Parapluies,* of which, Lane was told by Durand-Ruel shortly afterwards, Renoir had said: 'C'est une des toiles qui lui ont conte le plus de peine et de travail.'[16] Expensive birthday presents, coupled with his involvement in the creation of an Irish gallery of modern art, meant Lane was never held in the highest professional regard by some of his art-world colleagues. Nor, despite his considerable wealth, was he by any means the most successful dealer of the period; that position was determinedly held by Joseph Duveen. The two men knew each other but were never friends. Duveen regarded Lane as an 'amateur', overly preoccupied with his gentlemanly status, his social life and with non-commercial projects.[17] Lane, on the other hand, found his rival coarse and far too interested in making money. In March 1911, for example, the New York branch of Duveen's was successfully prosecuted for defrauding American customs by grossly undervaluing works of art shipped over from Europe. Joseph Duveen was a businessman who treated old masters strictly as commodities. This was not Lane's approach to his work. He repeatedly told friends how much he hated to sell the pictures he had bought. In an appreciation written for *The Burlington* after Lane's death, Henry Tonks declared: 'If he had ambitions, it would be very difficult to say what they were; at least they were not those of a dealer.'[18]

This meant that he could make mistakes or be tricked. In 1906, ten years after working with E.T. Turner, he met the older dealer again and agreed to exchange 92 relatively minor pictures he had in stock for a single painting by J. M. W. Turner estimated to be worth £3,200. Having 'no knowledge or interest' in the English artist, he failed to examine the work closely and only later discovered it was a fake. A long legal case followed as he attempted to regain the value of his lost pictures.[19] His loathing for the law and for lawyers, already well developed, was intensified during the same year by a case brought against him by the Carfax Gallery and its co-owner at the time, Robert Ross. Lane had given the gallery Gainsborough's portrait of his daughter Margaret (now in the National Gallery, London) to sell on his behalf. When this failed to find a buyer, he took the picture back and persuaded the South African collector Alfred Beit, whom he had met in July 1905, to purchase it. Ross and the Carfax then demanded £525 as a percentage of the profit made and, when Lane refused, took him to court for the money. In late May 1906, just as the Belfast exhibition was due to close, Lane's solicitors were advising him that Beit would have to appear as a witness because 'his evidence is very material to your case'.[20] Unfortunately, by this date Alfred Beit was in the German town of Wiesbaden with a terminal heart condition; he only returned to England to die at his country house on 16 July. The case therefore went ahead without Beit and Lane lost.

Lane's capacity for making errors of judgement extended to other areas, as evidenced by his championing of the Neapolitan painter Antonio Mancini. He had first met the artist, twenty-three years his senior, when visiting Rome in the autumn of 1904. Lane had been given an introduction to Mancini by Mary Hunter, the wife of a wealthy northern English industrialist and sister of the composer Ethel Smyth. Mrs Hunter aspired to be an art patron and numbered among her circle of favourites the novelist Edith Wharton, the composer Percy Grainger, John Singer Sargent and Auguste Rodin. She was a enthusiastic advocate not just of Mancini but also Annie Swynnerton, a now almost-forgotten English artist who lived in Rome and painted allegorical works in a loosely impressionistic style. Mary Hunter was a keen admirer of her work ('Sargent says she is too good to be popular'[21]) and Lane seems also to have become a fan during the 1904 visit to Rome, as Mrs Swynnerton subsequently wrote to him: 'You overwhelm me with your too flattering opinion of my poor work'.[22] However, he was even more taken with Mancini, from whom he commissioned a portrait. This substantial canvas, two and a quarter metres tall and more than a metre wide, was considered by Lane's friends to be his best likeness. It shows the young dealer, still not yet thirty, seated before a pale green curtain dressed in a blue suit and surrounded by a profusion of *objets d'art*. More than any other portrait, it suggests his highly-strung character, as he stares nervously ahead and gives the impression of being ready to take flight at the slightest provocation.

The picture must have greatly appealed to its subject, because he not only bought other examples of Mancini's work (four were to be included in his conditional gift to Dublin) but decided to bring the artist to Ireland. This became possible in September 1907 as the Italian artist was then staying with Mary Hunter at her English country house. Now in his fifties, for much of his life he had been very poor and was thrilled with the attention belatedly being paid to him. A small, rotund and voluble man, Mancini was usually unintelligible in speech and print, and not just because of his very slight knowledge of English. A letter sent to Lane from an Italian-speaking friend who had agreed to help the artist with his correspondence comments, 'I think now I have written all Mancini wants – if it is incoherent, don't blame me – believe me he is more so – standing over me dictating impossible phrases'. The writer concludes: 'Kindest messages from me – weird messages from Mancini'.[23] Mrs Hunter found him equally difficult to understand – on one occasion, she characterized him as 'quite honest but not sane or practical'[24] – but nonetheless invited him to England to paint her two children.

The portrait finished, she was so keen to offload him onto Lane that she paid a minder to escort the artist to Dublin, in case he managed to lose his way en route. Thanks to these precautions, he crossed the Irish Sea safely in late September and was installed in the United Services Club, where members were baffled by his incomprehensible effusions and habit of bowing low before everyone he met. He was taken to the Abbey Theatre for special performances of Synge's *Riders to the Sea* and Yeats's *Cathleen ni Houlihan*. There were also dinners at the United Arts Club attended by himself, Augustus John and the actress Mrs Pat Campbell. But Lane had not brought him over to enjoy a holiday. Mancini was expected to earn his time in Ireland – a period, incidentally, he little enjoyed because the country's climate did not suit him – by painting a series of portraits. The cost of these would be £200 for a large canvas and between £80 and £100 for smaller pictures, but Lane as usual was determined to negotiate lower fees, particularly as he was also expected to cover the costs of paper, canvas and paint. Eventually Mancini drew a number of people, including W.B. Yeats, in pastel and completed two oils, one of Lady Gregory which Synge, in an uncharacteristic (and inaccurate) effusion of praise declared 'the greatest portrait since Rembrandt'.[25]

The other oil portrait was of Lane's sister Ruth. In late April 1905 she had married a gentleman farmer called James Hickman Shine of Ballymacreese, Co. Limerick, but remained close to her brother who would try to persuade her to come to Dublin whenever he was in the city. In January 1908 he was once more arranging for Ruth to be presented at Dublin Castle, this time with her husband so that 'you can now brag to your neighbours that you are a Court favourite!'[26] He worried over her clothing ('I hope that your feathers and train are quite clean, as we may sit or dine with the Droghedas'[27]) and, because she had little money of her own, would regularly send to Limerick presents of a hat or jewellery as well as unsolicited advice about the decoration of her home. In return, in November 1907 she agreed to compile scrapbooks of all his press cuttings, filling at least seven volumes with this material over the next eight years. Lane had already commissioned her portrait from John B. Yeats and Orpen, but now wanted Mancini to undertake the same task. From mid-September onwards, even before the artist had arrived in Dublin, Ruth Shine was being advised by her brother as to what she should bring for her sittings; from an assortment of costumes, Mancini eventually decided to paint his subject in her white satin wedding dress. It was agreed the picture should give the impression of having been painted in a fruit grove, so she had to travel from Limerick with large branches of laurel; these were arranged behind her and then strung with oranges.

Mancini had a very distinctive way of composing his pictures. In front of the sitter, he would set up a large frame and across this would be stretched a sequence of fine threads. A matching web would then be crisscrossed over his own canvas and he would dart from frame to canvas, filling in each space on the latter. He was extravagant with paint and a rumour went around Dublin that Lane, who after all was paying for the materials, would drop into Mancini's studio each night and scrape some of the larger lumps off the canvas back onto the palette for reuse the following day. Eventually the weather drove Mancini to leave Dublin and return to Italy. His pictures, of which there are at least ten in the city's Municipal Gallery, are rarely exhibited today. Their reliance on impasto for effect now looks grotesquely bombastic and John B. Yeats's judgement of Mancini is unquestionably accurate. Writing to his son in October 1907, he dismissed the Italian as 'a wit rather than a serious artist'.[28] The following January, the *Pall Mall Gazette* was even harsher when its critic called Mancini 'not much more than a temporarily fashionable mannerist, whom it might have been as well to ignore'.[29] Not all the artists Lane chose to support have eventually proven to be worthy of his attention.

As John B. Yeats's remarks show, Mancini's limitations were apparent even at the time to at least some people in Lane's circle. Orpen, for example, was distinctly unenthusiastic about the Italian artist, ending one letter with a caricature entitled 'Portrait of Hugh P.L. by Charmini'.[30] On another occasion, he chided his friend for bringing 'this star' to Dublin because Mancini was 'not liked by the Orpen Planet'.[31] An element of professional jealousy was undoubtedly present here because Orpen felt Lane should support him and not other artists. By this time, he and Lane were sharing professional quarters in London, where in 1906 Orpen had taken a studio at 5 (later 8) South Bolton Gardens. The following year, for an annual rental of £60, Lane took some of this space from his friend, using it as a storage and display area for his stock of old masters as well as for furniture and china he had been accumulating. So extensive was this collection that it quickly spread through the building and Orpen was soon begging him to move some of it elsewhere, as negotiating a pathway around the rooms had become almost impossible. Lane responded that his taste in arrangement was considered rather good, but this information appeared of little interest to a painter trying to find enough space in which to work, particularly since one of his sitters in 1907 was his friend's father, the Reverend James Lane.[32] At the end of one letter, he included a drawing of the cluttered rooms with the message beside it: 'Puzzle, find the owner of the studio'.[33] He also suggested the house next door might be taken to provide additional space.

As Lane spent almost as much time in Dublin as London, Orpen frequently had to look after his voluminous correspondence and any clients who called by. Nor did he necessarily care for Lane entertaining on the premises when he was away. Understandably, therefore, his letters took on an aggrieved tone at this time and the warmth of friendship between the two men began to diminish. Not only did Orpen not care for Lane's patronage of other artists, but he seems to have been affronted that the dealer should be receiving so much public attention. When Lane was presented with his Sargent portrait, Orpen wrote that he was prepared to sit to the same artist, having done just as much, if not more, for Dublin except perhaps in the number of enemies made.[34] Over the next few years, especially after Lane bought his own house in 1909, they began to drift apart. Orpen no longer used nicknames in his letters but addressed his old friend more formally. By late 1912, they were quarrelling in a potentially damaging way over one of the contemporary Irish portraits Lane had commissioned many years before for £10 each. The subject was the Chief Secretary to Ireland, Augustine Birrell, and, having taken particular trouble over the work, Orpen was reluctant to part with it. Lane offered him a selection of porcelain and crystal ornaments in return for the picture, but those he sent around did not meet with the approval of Orpen who angrily returned them saying they were not what had first been offered to him.[35] Eventually Lane wrote what was, for him, an exceptionally aggressive letter, in which he announced that he would no longer humour Orpen and was now forwarding the £10 originally agreed.[36] The problem was resolved and the portrait added to the collection assembled by Lane, but this exchange indicates he was less tolerant of his friend's changeable ways than had once been the case. They kept in touch, albeit in a more desultory way, and Lane remained fond of Orpen's wife Grace (to whom he would bring presents of flowers) and her children. In August 1913 he agreed to be godfather to the Orpens' youngest daughter Diana, although he did not attend the christening but sent a silver cup.[37]

One reason for Lane's altered attitude towards the man who was once his closest friend may have been Orpen's harassment of him, almost from the outset, for money and assistance. On a jocular level, this could take the form of a dashed pen drawing showing the painter staring thirstily at an empty bottle beside an announcement that Lane's whisky was finished and he should send more.[38] But Orpen rarely missed an opportunity to make reference to his penury and the need for either cash or commissions. Lane was expected to supply both and, indeed, regularly did so. One of the most important jobs he found for Orpen was to paint the Vere Foster family whom Lane had first met when seeking pictures for the St Louis exhibition in 1904. Sir Vere Foster, a thirty-five-year-old baronet, lived with his pretty wife Charlotte Philippe, the daughter of a Norfolk rector, at Glyde Court in County Louth, a long, low Georgian house which had been Jacobeanized in the nineteenth century. They had little money and were attempting to modernize their home, but from the start Lane insisted they had to be painted by Orpen. Lady Foster pleaded poverty as well as her husband's personal distaste: 'Vere hates the idea of "sitting" and will only do so as a favour to me.'[39] Finally, in the summer of 1907 they gave in and Orpen was invited to stay at Glyde for the duration of the work. Because Lady Foster had a passion for donkeys, one of these had to be included in the picture, and as the elder of her two daughters, Biddie, liked to imagine she was really a boy called John, she was dressed for the occasion in a knickerbocker suit of brown velvet. Her mother and sister, on the other hand, were bedecked in feminine frills.

Whatever about their personal distaste, the Vere Fosters were probably unaware that Lane had only persuaded Orpen to paint them by paying him an advance of £100. Artist and sitters enjoyed each other's company immensely – Orpen would have pillow fights in the evening with the children – but the portrait was not a success. Sir Vere preferred to go shooting rather than stand around being painted, and Lady Foster, who was pregnant with her only son, spent large amounts of time in bed. Lane was obliged to negotiate between the two parties, especially after the picture had been finished and Lady Foster wrote telling him that in her opinion she and the other members of the family had been given the same facial expression as their donkey. 'If you knew of all the idiotic comments that tinkle through to us about the group,' she explained to him a year later, 'you would in a way understand my touchiness on the subject.'[40] Part of that touchiness may also have arisen because, in order to pay for the Orpen commission, the Vere Fosters had agreed to sell one of their finest pictures to Lane. This was a portrait of their ancestress Lady Elizabeth Foster, later Duchess of Devonshire, by Sir Thomas Lawrence. So that their friends need not know they had disposed of the work, Lane arranged for a copy to be made of it and this was hung in Glyde's drawing-room, a situation which soon caused Lady Foster equal agonies because 'I squirm and feel worse than in a dentist's chair when people admire the Lawrence! I always walk away at once.'[41]

The copying of pictures was a service Lane regularly offered to vendors who might not wish their need for ready money to be widely publicised. He was by no means the only dealer of the period to engage in this practice which had a long, if naturally secretive, history. Some owners of pictures, such as the fourth Earl of Bandon who had a weakness for gambling, were happy to replace their old masters with good-quality replicas. In a draft letter of November 1908, Lane wrote to the owner of a Gainsborough that 'If you thought of selling the picture I know of a wonderful copyist who could make you so perfect a copy of it which you could hang in the original frame now on your picture and which would be so like the original that no one except a few experts on close examination could tell the difference'.[42] In March 1914, Sir Algernon Coote (who the previous month had sold Lane a couple of pictures including Greuze's *The Capuchin Doll* – now in the National Gallery of Ireland – for £800) was enquiring how long it would take to make a good copy of a Hoppner portrait of his grandfather.[43] Sir Algernon was just one of a large number of Anglo-Irish aristocrats now taking advantage of Lane's interest in their pictures. Lord Castletown wrote offering a Ruysdael and two Guardis for £3,000,[44] Sir Arthur Vicars, former Ulster King of Arms, sent a list of Dutch, French and Italian paintings his elder half-brother Pierce O'Mahony wished to sell,[45] and artist Rose Barton hoped he would help her to raise cash by buying a Zoffany portrait.[46] Similarly, in June 1913, the ever-impoverished Lord Fermoy was keen to dispose of some of the few pictures still in his possession,[47] a pair of portraits originally thought to be by Gainsborough but more likely by Romney, for which he wanted £7,000. Other Irish landowners such as John Madden of Hilton Park in County

Monaghan, the Earl of Granard and Lord Monteagle for the moment merely asked his advice about the value of their artworks.[48] All of them were aware that political circumstances meant they might soon have to realize the worth of these assets. Not everyone was short of funds; Sir Algernon Coote still enjoyed a substantial income from his estates. But as he wrote to Lane in December 1913, 'A great deal depends on what happens in Ireland. In a year's time or even less, I may be forced to sell.'[49]

9
THE HARCOURT STREET GALLERY

In January 1906, Lane had promised to donate his personal collection of modern pictures to Dublin, provided a 'suitable gallery' was found to house them within two months. No such premises materialized and over the next eighteen months his promise came to be extended, as was the collection itself. Dublin City Council having empowered the Estates and Finance Committee to hire and maintain a temporary gallery for the sum of £500 already agreed, it was subsequently discovered that the Public Libraries Committee was actually the body legally empowered to deal with the matter. A further delay ensued when the latter authority decided to appoint its own sub-committee to take responsibility for the gallery. Meanwhile, more time passed. In January 1907 the *Irish Times* lamented that an opportunity had been missed to incorporate a municipal art gallery into the new college of science (now Government Buildings) on Upper Merrion Street, which was then being designed.[1] In fact, Lane would certainly not have been happy with such an arrangement, as he understandably thought the structure a monument to Edwardian excess and decried its florid style. In March, his brother Ambrose told him the Corporation had considered installing the gallery into an eighteenth-century octagonal exhibition room in the City Assembly House on South William Street, although he admitted the building was 'not much to look at outside and in a slum district'.[2]

Evidently this option did not meet with Lane's approval as he preferred to wait until early September when the Public Libraries sub-committee finally presented its report at a specially convened meeting of the city council. The chairman of the investigating group, Alderman Thomas Kelly, who was to be one of the gallery project's most loyal supporters on the local authority, recommended that the corporation hire a house at 17 Harcourt Street for £100 per annum. The urgency of the occasion was stressed because a few days earlier Lane had written to the Lord Mayor warning that if no conclusion were reached at the meeting, whatever about his own conditional gift, he did not think other prospective donors of pictures would wait any longer.[3] Nonetheless, there were objections from some councillors over the costs involved and further delays ensued. In late November, the city council received a letter from the Assistant Town Clerk on arrangements for the gallery and Alderman Kelly, along with his sub-committee, now proposed who should be given the post of director: 'Having regard for the energy and zeal displayed by Mr Hugh P. Lane in the forming of the collection, and to his special qualifications for the supervision of the hanging, cataloguing, etc. of the pictures, we consider no better selection could be made.'[4]

However, the directorship question was entirely academic until a site for the gallery could be confirmed and only on 2 December did the corporation finally agree to take the premises on Harcourt Street. A problem immediately arose when it emerged that the local authority did not have the legal right to take money from the Public Libraries Committee for the maintenance of a municipal gallery. A bill would have to be passed by Parliament in London to provide councillors with this power. The council therefore asked Lane once more to wait. This time he refused to do so. On hearing the news of a potential delay, Lady Gregory had immediately written to him urging that the gallery open, whether or not money was available for its upkeep, because the new institution would be 'exciting to the imagination and will awaken enthusiasms especially when articles are written about it'.[5] Two days after this letter, Lane in turn wrote to his sister in despair, saying 'I am in a hopeless fix with the Corporation who have done nothing in fact to make the Gallery legal – or to find the money to pay'.[6] But, legal or otherwise, the decision was taken to rent 17 Harcourt Street and open the Municipal Gallery of Modern Art there early the following year.

The large terraced property was known as Clonmell House. Completed in 1778, it had been begun by John Hatch, Seneschal of the Manor of St Sepulchre and Director of the Royal Canal. His former home on St Stephen's Green had been demolished when the newly laid-out Harcourt Street broke through into the square. Even before building work had been finished, the house was bought by John Scott, the Attorney General who was created first Earl of Clonmell in 1793. In 1830 the house had been divided into two sections, and it was the larger of these that the corporation now rented to serve as a temporary art gallery. Having been constructed as a domestic residence, the premises were never ideal for their new purpose. Although the principal rooms were well proportioned, their relative lack of light made hanging pictures to best advantage difficult. Lane also worried about security and particularly the risk of fire in an old property that had been neglected for some time.

Nevertheless, he agreed to the proposal and started to prepare for the gallery's official opening scheduled for late January 1908. He was placated, at least in part, by the Corporation's decision to follow his recommendation on how to avoid the potentially stultifying impact that becoming a municipal institution might have on the gallery. The local authority handed over responsibility for the project's management to a committee made up of two members each proposed by the National Gallery of Ireland and the Royal Hibernian Academy and four members taken from Lane's original Art Gallery Committee. As already agreed, he was appointed this body's honorary director. The role allowed him to remain in charge of the gallery even though officially it was now under the care of the Corporation and he was answerable to a supervisory board. The advantages of this arrangement were widely appreciated. In October 1910, almost three years after the Dublin gallery made its debut, the critic D.S. MacColl (by then keeper at the Tate Gallery) proposed that one-man collections were best 'because committees of art purchase lead to compromise'. In support of his argument, he pointed to Dublin 'where one man had been free to purchase and had been successful'.[7] Precisely the same point was made, and the same example cited, by Robert Ross in the *Daily Express* in May 1912.[8]

The directorship role satisfied outside observers as much as it irritated

Lane's foes. But the latter were much more incensed, according to Thomas Bodkin, by the remark with which he closed his preface in the catalogue published to mark the opening of the Harcourt Street premises. 'The opponents of the Gallery', he commented here, 'have been those who have not had the advantage of the study of these modern classics abroad, and who naturally cannot accept a standard so different from that which they have hitherto recognized.'[9] It was a triumphalist comment liable to increase rather than diminish antagonism towards him and his ambitions. But at the time he wrote those words, Lane was more concerned with ensuring all the work about to be placed on display would conform to his ideal for a gallery of modern art. Ever since the Staats Forbes exhibition four years earlier he had been accumulating pictures in anticipation of this event. In November 1907, for example, he negotiated to buy the late Irish painter Frank O'Meara's *Toward Night and Winter* for £50 from its English owner who insisted 'It is the best example of his work that I know of and a very important picture'.[10]

This would be just one of the very many paintings Lane would donate to the gallery; in all, approximately a third of its initial holdings were categorized as his gifts. In the 1908 catalogue preface, he wrote: 'I now hand over my collection of pictures and drawings of the British schools (70), and Rodin's masterpiece, "L'Age d'Airain." I also present the group of portraits of contemporary Irishmen and women (which will be added to as time goes on).'[11] In addition to this already generous contribution, he explained: 'I have also deposited here my collection of pictures by Continental artists, and intend to present the most of them, provided that the promised permanent building is erected on a suitable site within the next few years.' These pictures, Lane remarked, had been bought in order to make the gallery 'widely representative of the greatest painters of the nineteenth century'.[12] The work provisionally offered was an eclectic group. When in April 1917 Roger Fry reviewed the thirty-nine pictures formerly owned by Lane and by then the subject of an ownership dispute between London and Dublin, he wrote: 'They are a curiously mixed lot, reflecting no definite personal taste, but rather a sensitiveness to a number of diverse and conflicting artistic currents.'[13]

Indeed, the same remark could be made of the entire original Municipal

Gallery collection of some three hundred works assembled by Lane. It was displayed in eight rooms, the first of them given over to painters of Irish birth or descent. Here George Russell, or A.E. as he styled himself, was represented by eight pictures (seven of them part of the Lane gift) and Orpen by only one. There were five Nathaniel Hones, three Walter Osbornes and single examples of work by, among others, John B. Yeats, Sarah Cecilia Harrison (who wrote all the original catalogue entries), Constance Markievicz, Roderic O'Conor and John Lavery. Among the artists possessing rather tenuous Irish associations were Ambrose McEvoy and Mark Fisher. Room Two featured 'British Schools' running from Mrs Ambrose McEvoy (evidently, unlike her husband, she failed to be judged sufficiently Irish) to John Constable and taking in along the way Simeon Solomon, Philip Wilson Steer, Walter Sickert, James McNeill Whistler, George Clausen and Augustus John. On the staircase were hung the series of portraits of contemporary Irishmen and women commissioned by Lane and painted by John B. Yeats and Orpen, together with a handful of others from the brushes of Mancini, Count Markievicz and Sarah Purser.

In one room on the first floor, the French Impressionists 'and others' were displayed; the canvases by Monet (*Vétheuil: Sunshine and Snow*), Manet (the portrait of Eva Gonzales and *Le Concert aux Tuileries*), Renoir (*Les Parapluies*), Pissarro (*Printemps, Vue de Louveciennes*) and Vuillard (*The Mantelpiece*) among those which were to become part of Lane's contentious conditional gift. But there were also a number of outright donations to the gallery, such as Monet's view of Waterloo Bridge, London, given by Mrs Ella Fry, and Degas's *A Peasant Woman* for which funds had been raised by the artist Clara MacCarthy who had tragically died in childbirth eighteen months earlier. Lane's collection of Mancini's work also appeared here as did two paintings by the fashionable French portraitist Jacques Emile Blanche. Next to this room were shown examples of the French Barbizon school, the majority of them, including nine Corots and three Courbets, originally part of the Staats Forbes collection, and in certain instances given by supporters such as Lady Ardilaun, Colonel Hutcheson Pöe and the Earl of Mayo. But some of them – Fromentin's *The Slave*, *The Toilet* by Puvis de Chavannes, a Fantin-Latour still life – represented another portion of Lane's conditional gift.

Rooms Five and Six featured drawings and watercolours, a diverse assortment of almost ninety items which managed to take in Max Beerbohm caricatures (*Mr W.B. Yeats introducing Mr George Moore to the Queen of the Fairies*) as well as nude studies by Lord Leighton, a sketch of Lane's sister by Augustus John and a view of Lord Ardilaun's gardens at St Anne's in Clontarf executed by Rose Barton. Room Seven contained etchings and lithographs while a space on the staircase return was turned into a sculpture gallery holding no fewer than five works by Rodin (not least his *L'Age d'Airain*) plus three bronze figures of women by Maillol and a number of more academic pieces. To later generations, this really does look, in Fry's words, a 'curiously mixed lot'. But in the eyes of his contemporaries, what made Lane so exceptional was precisely that he had dared to assemble a reasonably representative selection of nineteenth-century art, something no public institution or individual had otherwise achieved. The seeming confusion in styles and schools accordingly becomes understandable. Interviewed in New York six years after Dublin's Municipal Gallery first opened, Lane observed: 'It is impossible to make a collection of living men's work with any certainty of its representing properly the art of the period.'[14] Perhaps, therefore, the pictures and sculpture put on show in Harcourt Street should be regarded as a hedged bet; a mélange of different styles and schools brought together so that whichever of them might eventually prove their worth, they would be represented in the gallery's collection. The implication that posterity could be the only reliable arbiter was made by Lane in his introduction to the 1908 catalogue, where he wrote that 'by ceding to the National Gallery those pictures which, having stood the test of time, are no longer modern', room would be made for representative examples 'of the movements of the day'.[15] He articulated the same views in an interview given to an American journalist in 1914, explaining that 'In choosing work for modern collections, you should give the artist the benefit of the doubt'. Therefore, a gallery such as that in Dublin 'should serve as a feeder and a sifter, a sort of artistic reduction furnace where a man's art work is held for the judgement of his fellows during his life, and if worthy passed after his death to that of coming generations'.[16] The gallery was to be a crucible in which the merits of every work of art on exhibition were put to the test and only those found worthy of preservation handed over to another institution, the National Gallery of Ireland. Of course, his wishes in this respect were not fulfilled; the Municipal Gallery was to retain all the work it had first acquired, declined to hand over pictures no longer considered modern to the National Gallery, and thereby fundamentally changed its character from that first imagined by Lane. The eclecticism of his collection can be seen as a gesture of humility. He may have been confident (sometimes erroneously) in the assessment of old masters but he recognized the impossibility of judging contemporary art objectively. Only time could manage that with any degree of success.

In early January 1908, around one thousand guests received invitations to the gallery's official opening; these were printed in both Irish and English. So too was the cover of the exhibition catalogue, a handsome publication containing a hundred illustrations along with full details of every work on display; it was on sale to visitors for one shilling. On the day itself, 20 January, the *Irish Times* hoped that now the gallery had come into being, Irish art would show improvement. Not only that, but 'this is a propitious moment for the public to shake off its apathy towards art, and give the artists a more genial and intelligent atmosphere to work in, as well as some more substantial encouragement'.[17]

The ceremony certainly suggested that Irish art could thenceforth expect ample encouragement. Held at 4 in the afternoon (and thereby permitting tea to be served, as Lane liked), it drew such a crowd that the rooms were packed, the old upper floors seemed under threat from the weight of people and the pictures could scarcely be seen. Formal speeches were made by Richard Caulfield Orpen and the Lord Mayor but, even though a vote of thanks to him was agreed among everyone present, Lane refused to say anything, preferring instead to hang back in one of the exhibition rooms. The following night his aunt gave a small supper party in his honour at which he was more relaxed. Guests here included the Markieviczes, Sarah Purser, W.B. Yeats, John Shawe-Taylor, Dermod O'Brien and Susan Mitchell 'who gave some of her clever parodies'. On this occasion, the actress Sara Allgood recited to Lane an edited version of lines from Yeats's *Cathleen ni Houlihan*:

He shall be remembered for ever,
He shall be alive for ever,
The people shall hear him for ever.[18]

There was praise in abundance for his work over the coming days. Within a fortnight, William Rothenstein wrote to him: 'I am perfectly willing to admit you to be a man of genius. That you have been able to make the most important collection of modern pictures, drawings and sculpture that has yet been brought together without great means other than your surprising energy and intuition ... is nothing short of a miracle.'[19] 'I hope you will come back to Dublin soon,' announced George Russell, because 'You are one of the few people alive in Ireland',[20] while William Orpen opted to send him a drawing showing Lane as a near-nude saint standing on the globe with a wreath hovering above his head. The public response was just as effusive. On 10 February, Dublin Corporation called a special meeting at which Lane was unanimously elected an Honorary Freeman of the City. Some years later, he bought an old silver container to hold the parchment presented to him by the local authority. (Ironically, this ornament was shaped like a ship and it had just been sent to him when he drowned aboard another vessel.) In 1908 he was also appointed a member of the Governing Body of University College Dublin. The councillors and academics were responding to the widespread approbation his efforts on behalf of Irish art had received. On 21 January, the *Irish Times* remarked 'Mr Lane has given the country its latest lesson in the enormous value of personality', the *Freeman's Journal* gratifyingly quoted D.S. MacColl's verdict that Dublin's new gallery was 'the first real attempt at a representative collection of modern art to be found in the British Isles',[23] and the *Irish Independent* repeated Lord Drogheda's remark that 'Budding Irish students can now study art without going abroad, except to study foreign effect', before going on to warn how the gallery would be 'mere waste of money if its advantages are not availed of'.[24] Prior to the opening, Lane had been chivvying the likes of W.B. Yeats and Lady Gregory to drum up as much publicity as possible for the project; the former wrote to him from London on 7 January that he was doing what he could among his own press contacts. But Lane need not have worried; Dublin's Municipal Gallery of Modern Art attracted a remarkable amount of international attention and was admired even by French art critics who, more than any others, would have had ample chance to see substantial collections of Impressionist painting. In late March, *Le Figaro* described Lane as an 'ingenious man' and spoke of how he had assembled the collection 'armed solely with a tenacious will and a passionate love of the beautiful'.[25] *Le Temps*'s critic was just as enchanted that he had experienced 'the most delightful surprise' in finding that Dublin now possessed such a 'wonderful collection of modern pictures'.[26] Lane's scrapbooks from this date include many cuttings on the same theme from publications as diverse as the New York *Evening Sun* and the *Statesman of Calcutta*.

At home, attendances immediately indicated that Dublin's latest attraction was proving popular; within two months of opening, the gallery had received more than 50,000 visitors and by early December, when the premises were briefly closed for cleaning and rehanging, that figure had risen to 168,753. Lane insisted the gallery be accessible to workers who might not have much free time, so opening hours were 10 a.m. to 6 p.m. and 8 p.m. to 10 p.m., Monday to Saturday and 2 to 6 p.m. on Sundays. Admission was free. Even if disadvantageous for attendance figures, perhaps a charge would have been advisable because before the gallery was much more than a week old, financial problems had arisen. The difficulty of Dublin Corporation being legally unable to oblige its own Libraries Committee to pay for a municipal gallery remained unresolved. But in any case, on 24 January, four days after the official opening, the Committee announced that it had already spent the year's budget and therefore had no further money to spend on anything until the end of March. The following morning, therefore, Dublin's public libraries closed because staff salaries could not be paid. The gallery would also have had to shut its newly opened doors except that Lane announced he and a group of the project's supporters would cover operational costs until the difficulty had been resolved satisfactorily. The same group also agreed to pay outstanding bills such as the £450 owed to the picture framers, Egan's on Ormond Quay.

Lane might not have been so sanguine over the matter had he realized how long that resolution would take. Three years later, the gallery was still effectively being run on private funds while a bill granting Dublin Corporation the legal power to support such a venture made its leisurely way through Parliament in London. In late April 1911, members of the gallery committee issued a public letter about this bill, appealing that it be given cross-party support even though, at the time, Unionist Party members had adopted a policy of blocking government measures in the House of Commons.[27] The appeal was successful; by mid-July the Public Libraries (Ireland) Bill had successfully passed through both houses of Parliament and into law, although it still took another year before Dublin Corporation finally raised money on local rates not just to support the gallery but to repay the outstanding debt of more than £2,200 which had been allowed to accrue since January 1908.

Lane, naturally, did not cease adding to the collection during this period. The Earl of Iveagh, who had said that he would make a donation once the gallery had been established, now kept his word and in late September 1908 donated three pictures he had bought that month: a view of Venice by James Holland, G.F. Watts's *Pretty Lucy Bond* and *Lilacs* by Millais. These might not have been altogether to Lane's taste. Writing to thank Lord Iveagh for the gift, he tactfully observed that the saccharine Millais 'will be very popular and is characteristic of his last period'.[28] More importantly, as he told his sister Ruth, 'This is most encouraging. The Dublin crowd will be tremendously impressed!'[29]

Meanwhile, he continued to promote Irish art outside the country, later that spring organizing a show of work at the Franco-British Exhibition in London; the pictures were displayed in an 'Irish village' called Ballymaclinton. Arranging such events meant he could meet young artists who were seeking outlets for their work. Any of them he considered sufficiently talented he would invite to give an example of their work to the Municipal Gallery. Not all were in a position to do so; one young painter, having explained his extreme impoverishment, declared that Lane's request for a free picture 'gives comic relief to an otherwise tragic position'.[30] Another responded to his letter with the blunt statement 'I am afraid that I don't feel very much in a giving away state just now'.[31] Sometimes Lane would commission an artist of his acquaintance to produce work for the gallery. In February 1909, Beatrice Elvery, who had been attempting for some time to meet just such a request, wrote to him: 'You see that is the worst of you; you said only the best was good enough & I'm so frightened because I know my stuff isn't the best.'[32] But most often, Lane simply bought or acquired work for the gallery as he, the Honorary Director, saw fit. Additions to the collection announced in August 1910 included pictures by Lavery, Frank Brangwyn, Arthur Studd, Gerald Kelly and Giovanni Boldini.[33] At the same time, he also gave a bust of Lady Gregory he had commissioned from Jacob Epstein and which had been executed during the preceding months. Almost two years later, in July 1912, he donated a further group of paintings by artists such as Hone, Boudin, Daubigny and Steer. On visits to Dublin during these years, he would periodically rehang one or several of the gallery's rooms to permit new work to be seen. Lane had been responsible for the first hanging, assisted by a few friends such as Bodkin, and the layout of each space therefore reflected his personal taste. A gallery caretaker later told Lady Gregory how 'He worked harder than any of us. He would be moving pictures and hanging and shifting them till far into the night.'[34]

To later eyes, the arrangement of pictures, placed close together and frequently hung two deep, looks excessively cramped. This impression is further enhanced by Lane's insistence on filling the rooms with items of furniture and vases of flowers. He always stressed the importance of the latter, encouraging visitors he knew to bring fresh foliage and blooms with them. Lady Gregory quoted the same caretaker saying: 'With flowers, too, he was wonderful. He would put them in so quick, and they would look just as if they were growing in the bowl.'[35] When Ellen Duncan took over responsibility for the Municipal Gallery in October 1914, his letter of congratulation to her included the plea: 'I hope that you will fill the vases with greens or flowers, it makes the Gallery look cared for.'[36] Lane was, as Thomas Bodkin later commented, 'amazingly fastidious'. His notepaper, for example, was chosen because its shade of azure blue harmonized well with the pink of the penny stamp.[37] According to Bodkin: 'Except in an emergency, he would never degrade it with two green halfpenny stamps.'[37]

At least where interior decoration was concerned, Lane's confidence in his own judgement was shared by many other people. Dermod O'Brien would remember: 'If he felt that your room required for its decorative completion, say an Aubusson carpet, as likely as not he would send one round on indefinite loan for the sheer joy of seeing the place perfected and satisfying to his eye when next he should happen to come.'[38] He was especially anxious about his sister Ruth's home in County Limerick, instructing her in September 1906 on the style of brass grate she should get for the drawing-room fireplace; 'If you will tell me the price of the one you want to buy I will hunt about here – & if I get what I like & it is beyond the price of it I will help you to buy it.'[39] 'Whenever he entered a room', Bodkin wrote of Lane, 'his swift eye would sum up its decorative possibilities.'[40] Many Irish country-house owners took advantage of his enthusiasm for interior decoration by having Lane advise them on their homes. In early January 1904, Lady Mayo wrote from Palmerstown thanking him 'for all the dirty and cold hard work you did here', and she would later ask him to perform similar duties for several of her friends. While Orpen was painting the Vere Fosters' portrait in 1907, Lane volunteered to help them reorganize the interior of Glyde Court, even though its châtelaine was reluctant to invest much money in this project. Pleading her impecunious state as usual, Lady Foster insisted: 'Honestly, at most I am sure £40 is the outside of what ought to be spent on our drawingroom.'[41]

Happily, Lane found much greater munificence at Killeen Castle, County Meath, where Daisy, Countess of Fingall was only too happy to fall in with his schemes for an overhaul of her home. Her husband, the premier Catholic peer in Ireland, had absolutely no interest in such matters and once said to her of Lane, 'He is a good fellow. It is a pity he is like that.'[43] Lady Fingall was delighted with his concern over the castle's appearance, as he helped her rearrange the principal rooms and reinstate many forgotten treasures. He persuaded her to paint the drawing-room walls the colour of pale stone and to have Dublin's best-known cabinet maker of the period, James Hicks, fill an alcove with delicate shelves on which a collection of *famille rose* and *famille vert* china was displayed. Lane told her 'Anything beautiful will go together – particularly anything Chinese'.[44] Hicks was also employed in an adjoining room transformed into a library, where he used old mahogany to make new bookcases to Lane's design; these cost Lady Fingall almost £1,000 but still she continued to ask for further assistance. 'I do not know how many weekends we worked,' she wrote in her memoirs when describing Lane. 'He was indefatigable. He would arrange a room a dozen times and rearrange it before he was satisfied ... I have a memory of Russell, the carpenter, sweating under his orders ... And Curtin the perfect butler helping to drag furniture about, although he had never been engaged for that.'[45]

Lady Fingall told how, in return for this assistance in getting her house in order, 'I had to give parties for his Gallery, and collect people and money to help him'. Lane, she said, was 'merciless when he wanted anything'.[46] He could be equally harsh in his disapproval of other people's taste. Dermod O'Brien said he sometimes gave offence by informing passing acquaintances 'that their pictures were not hung to their full advantage or that their chintzes were not in harmony'.[47] He told the proud owners of a portrait by Philip de Laszlo – an artist whose work he never liked – that 'the best place for it would be in the dark', and was so critical of the pictures he saw in a New York home that his host refused to speak to him throughout dinner.[48] Entering a room, he was known not merely to rearrange the ornaments, but even to take down the curtains if these failed to please him. He told one London hostess that her drawing-room was 'like a bazaar',[49] and in South Africa he informed a local collector that his paintings were worse than oleographs (pictures printed in oil colour) 'because they are bigger!'[50]

Lane was even critical of Lady Gregory's visual sense, writing of how in the Abbey Theatre she never seemed to mind how poor were the costumes or scenery of her plays.[51] Indeed, there was always something of a disparity between the richness of language and poverty of design in the company's productions. In May 1912, Lane undertook a scheme to redecorate the Abbey entirely, inside and out. He enlisted Lutyens to this cause and together they envisaged the building being given the appearance of an eighteenth-century theatre. He wanted the exterior to have a Georgian-style portico and balustrade while the interior design would include a wood-panelled balcony and a colour palette of black, white, gold and sienna yellow. By July, he was losing heart as both the decorators and the

Abbey's directors appeared equally indifferent to his plans which, for the building's interior, he expected to cost £500. According to Lane, everyone could be categorized as having taste or no taste or bad taste. He thought W.B. Yeats belonged to the last of these groups, telling Lady Gregory it would be as difficult to teach the poet taste as to teach him music.[52] Had he known of it, this opinion might have caused Yeats some disappointment, as four years earlier he had written from Paris that, thanks to Lane, he was now delighting in all kinds of pictures previously beyond his understanding.[53] Eventually the Abbey was redecorated but not to Lane's satisfaction. The job, he told his aunt, had been extremely badly done.[54] This was hardly an unusual outcome because not everyone demanded the same high standards. His own were so exacting that disappointment became customary.

10
LINDSEY HOUSE

On 8 February 1909, Eustace Lane in Dublin sent a telegram to his elder brother Hugh, saying simply 'Mother died one o'clock very quietly'.[1] If not quite a hypochondriac, Adelaide Lane had known ill-health for many years and death was as much a release for her children as for herself. The least directly affected was the oldest surviving, Harold, who remained in South Africa where he now became engaged to an English woman. Ruth, already married for the previous four years to James Hickman Shine, was no longer required to travel regularly from Limerick to Dublin. Ambrose Lane, now aged thirty-one, had trained and then practised for several years as a solicitor in Ireland; almost immediately after Adelaide Lane's death, he threw over this profession to follow his father's example and study divinity at Trinity College, Dublin. Ambrose had always been willing to assist his older brother Hugh's work for the modern art gallery but he soon moved to Canada where, following his ordination as an Anglican minister in 1914, he worked in a number of parishes in British Columbia. The youngest member of the family, Eustace Lane, who had remained living with his mother in Dublin, was now twenty-five. In early October 1909 he married a woman called Elizabeth Dawes, fifteen years his senior, at a registry office in Brentworth, Middlesex; none of his family appear to have been present at the ceremony. He later qualified as a solicitor but died in May 1914, after years of suffering from disseminated sclerosis.[2]

The Reverend James Lane did not remain a widower long, remarrying

barely six months after Adelaide's death. On this occasion, Hugh Lane
was a witness. Although the two men saw relatively little of one another
since they lived so far apart, they seem to have become increasingly fond
of one another. Lane commissioned Orpen to paint his father's portrait in
the summer of 1907 and also tried to help find a less remote parish than
Redruth for him. However, the Revd Lane remained in Cornwall until his
death in 1910, just a year after his second marriage. In a letter of condolence to Lane, Lady Gregory was unable to resist observing of his parents
that 'Two lives, and two natures, wère spoiled by this most unsuitable
marriage – but then where would the Dublin Gallery have been without
the union of those two temperaments?'[3]

At least James Lane lived to see his son Hugh, the result of that
'unsuitable' union, officially thanked for the work done in Dublin during
the preceding years. The king's birthday honours list in late June 1909
included a knighthood for Lane in recognition 'for his services to art'. He
was understandably delighted with the distinction, having, as Bodkin
succinctly explained, 'a frank taste for pomp and ceremony of all sorts'.[4]
As soon as the knighthood had been announced, Lady Gregory wrote to
congratulate her nephew. He replied: 'All my life has been stormy & my
work precarious. This establishes it a little and it will make a tremendous
difference to my future work in Ireland and here.' And he ended, 'I never
forget (with all my aggravating faults) how much I and all my family owe
to you for your patience & encouragement & to your fine example'.[5]
Becoming Sir Hugh while still only thirty-three was obviously a source of
considerable satisfaction to Lane. The knighthood not only appealed to
his snobbery and vanity but also confirmed that the government
approved of his gallery project in Ireland. And, just as important, the title
increased his status as a gentleman dealer. As Lady Gregory explained,
being a knight provided Lane with 'a sort of official rank without having
to explain what he had done, and this helped his work'.[6]

Given his new status, Lane felt he could no longer live in the series of
rented lodgings that had served as home ever since he settled in London
fourteen years earlier. He had first occupied rooms on the Harrow Road,
before moving to Duke Street and then to Jermyn Street. But these hardly
suited a dealer of his position. Nor was Orpen any longer willing to toler-

ate his friend storing large amounts of stock in South Bolton Gardens. So Lane began to search for a property to buy, and before the end of the summer he had found the ideal place. Overlooking the Thames in Chelsea, number 100 Cheyne Walk is called Lindsey House, although it is only the west wing of a building originally given that name. The site had belonged to Sir Theodore Mayerne in the early seventeenth century, but after his death it was bought during the reign of Charles II by the Earl of Lindsey, then Lord Chamberlain. He built the house now standing, which has the date 1674 cut into the porch. His successors later rented the property to a variety of tenants: Lady Plymouth and her son Lord Windsor at the time of Queen Anne; the Duchess of Rutland subsequently and then Lord Conway. In the mid-eighteenth century it was acquired by a Count Zinzendorf for the Moravian community and shortly afterwards divided into a number of separate dwellings.

In the portion he now bought, Lane undertook a lavish scheme of refurbishment in which the experience gained in friends' homes was put to good use. As Henry Tonks wrote in *The Burlington* after Lane's death, 'Balzac would have delighted in making the catalogue of his house'.[7] Jacobean oak panelling was installed in the main rooms, together with marble fireplaces from the same period. In the main hallway, he had a black and white chequered marble floor laid; on this stood a double rank of Ming stone figures. In his study, one prized item of furniture was a cabinet originally designed by William Kent for Burlington House and removed from there when the building had become home to the Royal Academy. The first-floor double drawing-room, panelled in oak, was fitted with carvings by Grinling Gibbons above the mantelpiece; the brass fireplace fittings had come from Windsor Castle. In the bay window stood an antique marble statue of Venus, her head turning to look out on the river below; together with her owner, this piece of sculpture can be seen in William Orpen's *Homage to Manet,* which was completed around the time Lane moved to Lindsey House. The dining-room, its panelled walls painted a pale green and white, had a floor that was covered with Louis XV Aubusson carpets on which stood an octagonal mahogany pedestal table and set of eight lattice-backed chairs; all of this furniture was believed to have been made by Chippendale for Queen Charlotte's house at Fort Belvedere.

Lane's love of oriental porcelain was attested by the enormous number of Japanese and Chinese vases and figurines in every room. He had no particular knowledge in this field, but simply trusted to instinct when buying, usually with success. Bodkin remembered a dinner in Lindsey House at which the curator of London's Whitechapel Gallery was so impressed with these ornaments that he asked to borrow some of them for an exhibition of oriental ceramics then being organized. Lane had to confess he had no idea which pieces were valuable and which not; he had simply bought each over the years as it caught his fancy.[8] He would sometimes give away items to guests who admired them; the actress Ellen Terry received a Chinese crystal figure as she left the house and the architect Herbert Baker was sent an ornament on which he had commented enthusiastically.[9] As at the Dublin gallery, he liked to have fresh flowers in the main rooms of his home. Lady Gregory suggested that for Lane 'flowers were a necessity, a part of the beauty of life; they must not only be fresh but of the right colour for the harmony of the room'.[10] She remembered his indignation once when he came into Lindsey House and found the drawing-room flowers had not been changed, even though there were visitors there.[11] After his sister Ruth came to live with him, whenever he went away Lane would write to remind her that fresh floral arrangements ought to be in place on his return.

Naturally, however, the most remarked-upon feature of the house was its collection of paintings. An easel in the drawing-room usually held the latest acquisition; Titian's portrait of Baldassare Castiglione, perhaps, or that by Ingres of the Duc d'Orleans. But old masters were hung all around the walls in every room. Lindsey House, after all, was not just Lane's home but also, in effect, his dealer's gallery. The pictures on display were for sale and periodically a rehang would be necessary to replace works that had found a buyer. Visitors never failed to be impressed by the wealth of art he owned. A feature on the house written for the *Connoisseur* just after Lane's death mentions many of the pictures now in the National Gallery of Ireland: the Titian; Sebastian del Piombo's portrait of Cardinal Ciocchi del Monte; a Chardin still life; two paintings then attributed to Uccello; a Greuze; a Claude Lorrain; three Gainsboroughs; two Romneys.[12] The house held less grandiose work too: family portraits;

paintings given to the owner (such as a Steer view of Lindsey House's garden inscribed 'To my friend Hugh Lane'); and Max Beerbohm caricatures.

If Lane's principal intention was to dazzle, he was rarely unsuccessful, as the enraptured letters of visitors to Lindsey House abundantly testify. After enjoying 'one of the most delightful weeks that I have ever spent' with Lane in London in August 1913, Bodkin wrote on his return to Dublin 'it is rather trying for eyes that have feasted for so many days on Titian, Rembrandt, Romney, Goya and El Greco to have to turn to my father's Shakespearian prints which now seem unusually shoddy'.[13] Guests were equally captivated by the garden laid out behind the house. It was designed for Lane by Edwin Lutyens, who would work with him on a number of other projects over the next few years. Lane soon became an admirer of Lutyens; in August 1910, the architect wrote to his wife: 'Lane came in – he is a walking advt. for me!!'[14] Working on Lindsey House's garden that same summer, Lutyens took advantage of an existing mulberry tree, said to be even older than the building itself, by creating a shallow lily pond lined in black marble beneath its branches. Long narrow paths led from a simple stone colonnade to the back wall where niches were created to shelter classical statues. While much of the garden was given over to grass and flagging, a flower border ran the length of the right-hand side. The result was described by *Country Life* in October 1912 as showing 'a refined classical flavour without being stiff'.[15] Lane paid the builders who carried out this work in part with pictures (his account books record a panel by the sixteenth-century Sienese mannerist Beccafumi being given to Messrs Cubitt for completing the job). He may have reached a similar arrangement with Lutyens, because the architect wrote to him in October 1910: 'Your portrait by Bonington looks ripping in my new dining room. I call her Mrs Langton – by Bonington out of Lane'.[16] On another occasion, he sent over a note to Lane asking 'Will you dine here & see your!! collection of pictures Saturday tomorrow evening 8 o'c?'[17]

Augustus John was also employed to work on Lindsey House, although with less happy results. The painter probably met Lane through William Orpen, with whom he had been a student at the Slade School and had subsequently established the Chelsea Art School in late 1903. Orpen introduced John to many members of his Irish circle and by December 1905 Lane was buying examples of the artist's work – two drawings from the Chenil Gallery in London for £8.8s each. In 1907 John visited Ireland, passing through Dublin where he simultaneously shocked and thrilled locals with his self-consciously bohemian manner before going to stay with Lady Gregory at Coole Park.

Although Lane happily accepted his donation of a picture for the Dublin gallery around this time, he always felt the artist's real métier was wall decoration. On buying Lindsey House, therefore, he commissioned John to paint a series of large panels for the hallway. Called *Lyric Fantasy* and showing a series of life-size figures moving through an imaginary landscape, the work was begun enthusiastically enough in October (especially once Lane had given John £100) but soon began to peter out. By early December 1909, the artist was complaining to Lady Ottoline Morrell not only that he would like years to do the job full justice but also that 'little Lane' was 'a silly creature and moreover an unmitigated snob'.[18] Within a fortnight of this letter he had fallen out completely with his patron, who was horrified to discover that John had been inviting gypsies he met on the road into Lindsey House. Lane, it seemed, 'proved too exasperating in his constant state of nervous agitation', so the incomplete panels, which had only been tacked onto the walls, were taken out of the house and moved to the artist's studio for completion.[19]

In February 1910 John sent Lane a postcard from Ravenna: 'I'm improving myself in Italy – aren't you glad? The decorations are getting on splendidly.'[20] But the much-promised work was never finished, even though Lane regularly advanced more money. As late as October 1913, he informed Dermod O'Brien that John was 'working at a splendid decoration for me',[21] and a month later he described the artist as 'the painter of most genius that England has produced for a hundred years'.[22] The following March John told his American patron John Quinn (who had similar problems extracting promised work from him) that he was 'actually getting Lane's big picture done at last'.[23] Despite the disappointment of this commission, the two men managed to remain on good terms and Lane continued to buy John's work; his final purchase before leaving for

New York in April 1915 was a portrait by the artist of the rebellious young poet Iris Tree. Typically, John had assured Quinn he could have first refusal of this work but then sold it to Lane for £150. Writing to thank him for buying the picture, the artist still offered reassurances that 'The big picture is getting on slowly – but I think well'.[24] However, with Lane's death, *Lyric Fantasy* was abandoned and the panels lost forever.

Because of John's undisciplined temperament, employing him was always going to be a risk, but one Lane had no qualms taking. His professional life, after all, was based on a series of gambles. It is, therefore, not surprising to discover that, despite his orderly character and fondness for small economies, Lane was a keen gambler. A letter from Richard Caulfield Orpen in May 1908 concludes with the sentiment 'I hope you'll back a winner tomorrow' beside a little sketch of a horse and jockey.[25] Lane would travel every spring to Monte Carlo, where he played nightly at the casino. He was quite prepared to throw away large sums of money on these occasions even while still dining in cheap restaurants. Bodkin believed he would annually 'lose several thousand pounds in a few weeks' play' and remembered that once he had become stranded in the South of France because there was no money left. Lane wired a request for more funds to his London banker J.J. Meagher who, trying to break this habit, was delighted to tell him later that telegrams had no legal validity; he therefore sent Lane nothing.[26] Lady Gregory records details of a notebook that her nephew kept in which he wrote down the results of his gambling: 'Won £540. Bought diamond and pearl necklet £280'; 'Lost in evening all capital, £400. Bought three pearl strings and olivine ring for £233.'[27] A friend once met Lane in Paris returning from Monte Carlo with no money, although his travelling bag was full of loose pearls. Lane collected gems throughout his career; the sale of Lindsey House's contents after his death contained twenty-four lots of jewellery including a rose diamond hair ornament said to have belonged to Marie Antoinette.[29] Some items he would give or lend to friends and members of his family, others were left to different women in his will. They were, presumably, another potential investment which, like all the paintings bought, he hoped would increase in value. Gambling may have been a means of relaxation over the next few years as Lane came under increasing pressure from a variety of sources. He also enjoyed playing cards, especially bridge. 'It is a delight-ful way of ending a hard day,' he told his sister Ruth when urging her to learn the game. 'I want so much to practise playing as everyone in London plays too well for me.'[30] He told Joseph Solomon: 'You must learn to play a chatty game of bridge. That will help you along.' However, the young South African architect wisely decided to disregard this advice, having seen that chat was not well-received during a game and that Lane 'talked more than people liked at bridge'.[31] His other method of relaxation in the evening was playing the piano. His aunt noticed when she stayed with him at Lindsey House how, should he come in looking 'white and jaded, dark rings under his tired eyes, the little frown of annoyance that I remember on his mother's face when she was crossed, he would sit down at the piano and play himself to a happier mood'.[32] But so engrained was his streak of frugality that when the friend who had lent him the instrument asked for its return, Lane would not buy a replacement.

Lady Gregory quickly became one of his most regular house guests as she had long since given up keeping a flat in London. For a few years, whenever visiting the city, she had stayed in hotels. Now, as she informed him in May 1912, instead of having to find lodgings, she had the delight of anticipating him acting as her host.[33] And he was insistent that she should treat Lindsey House as though it were her own home, telling her a bedroom was constantly at her disposal and setting aside another room so that she could receive her own guests. That same month, he told her another servant had been engaged 'in honour of your coming and will be able to give you dinner in the house'.[34] A couple called Turner were initially employed to manage Lindsey House but Lane discovered that they were pilfering from him and pocketing money he had left to pay bills. After their hurried departure, he hired another couple as butler and housekeeper, Frank and Cicely Loftus, who stayed with him for the rest of his life, though there were occasional upsets. In November 1913, Lady Gregory, then staying in the house while her nephew was away, wrote to tell him that Mrs Loftus, while dusting in the drawing-room, had accidentally upset Hogarth's portrait of the Western family (now in the National Gallery of Ireland) and a nail had gone through the canvas; the damage was minor and easily repaired.[35]

As a regular visitor, his aunt noticed that, although Lane had furnished the main part of the house luxuriously, he still preferred to live as simply as possible. His own bedroom was far less elaborately decorated than elsewhere; it had a plain white-painted bed and the walls were hung with old prints. If eating alone, he continued to go to inexpensive local restaurants for his meal. Some cousins who called to see him soon after he moved to Lindsey House remembered they had been offered a dinner of little more than bread and Bovril.[36] However, possession of a suitable room meant that he now began to give dinners, customarily for eight people since his table was octagonal and any additional guests had to be seated elsewhere. These occasions were usually for old friends and fellow members of the art world such as Henry Tonks, Philip Wilson Steer, Charles Aitken and D.S. MacColl. His favourite means of entertaining remained the afternoon tea party, and guests at such events were frequently more numerous and socially grander than those invited to dinner. Tea provided a relaxed opportunity on which to entertain new or potential clients. Lane told Bodkin that, much as he enjoyed his social life for its own sake, parties and dinners were 'good for trade'.[37]

After one such occasion, a visitor wrote to thank Lane for his hospitality and to ask if he could call again because 'When I came before, I was so much overwhelmed by the brilliant throng of ladies in furs that I saw nothing'.[38] That brilliant throng included some of the most prominent hostesses of Edwardian England including Maud, Lady Cunard; Lady Charles Beresford; Victoria, Lady Sackville; Sibyl Colefax; and Jennie Cornwallis-West (the former Lady Randolph Churchill). The last of these was responsible for organizing the Shakespeare Ball, best-known of the costume parties which were so much in vogue in London during the pre-war years. Held at the Royal Albert Hall on 20 June 1911, two days before King George V's coronation, it was an event to which Lane received a number of invitations. Ten days before the ball, Adele, Lady Meyer, an ardent socialite married to a rich banker, wrote snappily to him that while he could dine beforehand wherever suited him, 'I certainly expect you amongst my guests on Tuesday the 20th at 8.15 having asked you already three months ago'.[39] In fact, Lane – who adored fancy dress and owned several elaborate costumes including one outfit based on Spanish clothing from the reign of Philip II – took his own box at the Albert Hall. He brought with him his sister Ruth, dressed as Catharine of Aragon, and Lady Gregory who, having only been persuaded at the last minute to go, called herself Lady Woodville 'because she is mentioned only once in Shakespeare'.[40] As for the coronation, both Lady St Davids and Lady Cowdray invited him to watch the procession from their respective homes in Richmond Terrace and Carlton House Terrace.

Lane seems to have known few of the great political hostesses of the early twentieth century such as Lady Dorothy Nevill or Theresa, Lady Londonderry. Instead, his aristocratic social circle was based around women who, like himself, had strong artistic interests. The two with whom he developed the closest friendship in these years were the Duchess of Rutland and the Marchioness of Ripon. The exquisite Violet Rutland – Mrs Patrick Campbell called her 'the most beautiful thing I ever saw'[41] – married to an equally good-looking but notoriously dull man, was a highly talented sculptor; Rodin compared her work to that of Donatello. She also played the piano and sang well. To be part of her set was indisputably advantageous. But, as so often for a man in Lane's circumstances, the benefits were expected to be mutual. Invited to the ducal seat of Belvoir Castle, he had to look at the pictures it contained and give estimations of their worth. And then Lady Rutland began to enquire whether he would be interested in purchasing work, owned both by herself and by 'someone who has become very poor'. 'They might be of use to you,' she suggested, 'and anyhow, you could perhaps very kindly tell me if you thought them very good.'[42] Of course, the prices offered by Lane did not meet with her approbation – her husband, she informed him, 'hopes to get £25,000 for the Rubens alone – ah, do make people see how wonderful that particular Rubens is!'[43] When Lane was visiting Johannesburg in late 1910, she proposed in her usual exclamatory style: 'S. Africa! It sounds lovely to be going there – wouldn't a R.C. church in S. Africa want our 2 Murillos?'[44] Evidently they did not.

Violet Rutland shared a number of characteristics with Gladys Ripon, not least that they had both been lovers of the period's most notorious womanizer, Harry Cust. By the time she met Lane, however, Lady Ripon had put her amatory life in the past and was more interested in developing a reputation as a patron of the arts. In 1911, she welcomed her friend Diaghilev and the Ballets Russes to London. During their visit, she sent an invitation to Lane with the enticement that 'You will meet Pavlova & various other very interesting people – I think the dinner will amuse you – so please write & tell me you are coming to it'.[45]

By then she had moved an hour's drive out of the capital to a luxurious villa called Coombe Hill in Surrey. Here she entertained Lane, who was also invited for weekends to the Ripons' country house Studley Royal in Yorkshire. He gave her advice on how to decorate Coombe ('I am depressed at yr. having seen my bedroom before it was properly arranged', she wrote after one lunch)[46] and was soon offering the same help to her married daughter, Lady Juliet Duff, who lived in central London but still spent a great deal of time with Lady Ripon. Touchingly, the latter began to worry that Lane would 'grow so fashionable that you will have no more time for your quiet friend'.[47] Like many other women of his acquaintance, she also began to fuss over him, writing 'I hope you are better and resting'.[48] The maternal instincts felt towards him for so long by Lady Gregory now started to find many an echo. His women friends would become preoccupied with his health, offer him their homes in which to relax and insist that he needed to take better care of himself. He responded to this attention with alacrity. Bodkin's mother, for example, would insist when Lane came to her home in Dublin for dinner that he had to eat everything given to him 'like a good boy'.[49] Knowing his fondness for sweet food, she would always send him a large cake for his birthday and, shortly before he died, he gave her in return a drawing on the back of which was written 'To Arabella from Hugh who likes her good cakes and hates her bad bridge'.[50]

When discussing Lane's character, Bodkin argued that 'the society of women did not seem to give him any special pleasure'[51] but this scarcely seems to conform with the circumstances of his social life. Women greatly enjoyed Lane's company because he was polite, attentive and happy to spend time discussing their clothes and homes. Those to whom he grew closest were invariably women with whom he shared common interests. These included a prolific and popular American writer called Alice Williamson. An early subscriber to the Dublin modern art gallery (in

1904 she donated £25), lived for much of each year in the south of France where she wrote romantic novels with titles such as *The Princess Passes*, *The Love Pirate* and *The Lure of Monte Carlo*. Similarly, another long-standing female friend of Lane's was the composer Teresa del Riego, whose 250 works include familiar pieces like *Lead Kindly Light* and *Oh, Dry Those Tears* as well as less well-known tunes including *Thank God for a Garden* and *A Garden is a Lovesome Thing*. The two first met when they were both house guests of the musical Droghedas at Moore Abbey in 1902. Thereafter they remained close; Lane gave her a present of an amethyst necklace in 1905 (which she managed to lose the following year) and also a ring on the occasion of her marriage in 1908, when she effusively thanked him, saying 'You always choose such attractive designs in jewellery'.[52]

But the woman who came to know him especially well in these years was an Irish painter, Sarah Cecilia Harrison. Twelve years his senior and at six feet even taller than Lane, she had spent much of her youth in London, moving to Dublin in the late 1880s when she began to establish a reputation as a portraitist; in September 1908, Lane wrote to Bodkin's sister Judy suggesting she and her mother ought to be painted by Miss Harrison.[53] The artist executed at least two portraits of Lane, of whose gallery scheme she was one of the most ardent champions from the very start, writing to the *Irish Times* in December 1904 to announce her intention of subscribing £1 to the cause.[54] The following August, she wrote gushingly to thank him for the interest he had shown in her work and was soon undertaking any task he set her.[55] In late 1907, for example, she wrote all the entries for the Municipal Gallery catalogue. A month after the opening, she was ticking off her 'dearest friend', as she now addressed him, for not looking after himself properly and comparing him to a young boy; 'It seems ungrateful to a body like yours, which puts up with such shocking treatment without going on strike'.[56] A family interest in politics – her brother Henry had been a Nationalist M.P. and supporter of Parnell – led her to stand for election to Dublin Corporation in January 1912; she was the first woman to become a member of the authority, holding the seat for three years. While in office, she devoted much of her time to advancing the interests of Dublin's poor but also to arguing on behalf of

Lane during the period when his battle to secure a permanent home for the modern art gallery reached its climax. Her loyalty and devotion to him were without question but he did not always appreciate her support and nor, after he died, did the surviving members of his family. Many women claimed to have been close friends of Lane, but none was more determined to prove her case than Sarah Cecilia Harrison.

11
JOHANNESBURG

As any successful art dealer can testify, good social connections are beneficial for business. Among those enjoyed by Lane was his friendship with the Hon. Mrs Norman Grosvenor, a widow connected by marriage to the Duke of Westminster and by blood to many other English aristocratic families. Caroline Grosvenor, like so many women of Lane's acquaintance, had wide cultural interests; she not only painted (and exhibited) miniatures and watercolours, but also wrote three novels and several works of non-fiction and still found time to establish the Colonial Intelligence League (for Educated Women) as well as to become Chairwoman of the Women's Farm and Garden Association. Her daughter Susan was married to the author John Buchan, who in 1909 was writing a book called *Prester John*, based on his time in South Africa where in the early part of the century he had been private secretary to the High Commissioner. When the Buchans moved to a house in London's Portland Place, Lane as usual helped with the property's interior decoration; the drawing-room walls were covered in a blue French paper he had found for the couple.

Buchan dedicated *Prester John* to Lionel Phillips, an English-born entrepreneur who made his money as an employee and later partner of the South African mining company Wernher, Beit & Co. His implication in the Jameson Raid of 1895/6, one of the events which prefigured the Boer War almost four years later, meant that Phillips and his family had been obliged to return to London where they became close friends with one of their neighbours in Mayfair, Mrs Grosvenor. And although the Phillipses moved back to South Africa in 1906, they continued to maintain associations with England, not least because disposing of their country home, Tylney Hall in Hampshire, proved difficult. They had spent possibly as much as £800,000 on refurbishing the property but were now unable to find a buyer; they eventually sold Tylney, described by Lionel Phillips as 'that gigantic blunder',[1] in March 1916 for less than a tenth of what had been lavished on it.

Caroline Grosvenor was staying at the house in mid-April 1909 when she wrote to Lane suggesting he ought to call there and meet its châtelaine. Florence Phillips had once more travelled over from South Africa so that her daughter Edith could be a débutante during the current London season; her coming-out ball took place on 21 May at 26 Park Lane, former home of the late Alfred Beit. This event was still being arranged when Mrs Grosvenor sent her letter to Lane, informing him that he had been the subject of a conversation between the two women at the end of which Mrs Phillips had decided 'you were exactly the person she wanted to get hold of as she has got a huge scheme on foot for starting an exhibition in Johannesburg & also an industry for making furniture on the old Dutch models of which there are many in S. Africa'.[2]

Born Dorothea Sarah Florence Alexandra Ortlepp in South Africa in June 1863, Mrs Phillips (who became Lady Phillips after her husband was awarded what she called 'the beastly baronetcy' in January 1912[3]) had enormous energy despite lifelong ill-health; even when on one of her frequent health cures, she managed to maintain a voluminous correspondence. Much of her drive was channelled into assisting the development of Lionel Phillips's career, but she also found time to write *South African Recollections*, published just as the Boer War was declared, and *A Friendly Germany – Why Not?*, which appeared a year before the onset of the First World War. She was a woman of strong views stoutly expressed; her granddaughter later remembered seeing men reduced to tears after meeting Florence Phillips. However, inevitably for the period, much of her time was spent arranging the couple's different homes and their social life. Having settled in London at the end of the nineteenth century, the Phillipses were keen to make their mark, although these efforts were not always successful. In 1903, for example, they planned to give a concert at their London home where Nellie Melba would be among the performers. The date had first to be changed because it coincided with a State Ball and then, on the night itself, just as Mrs Phillips's guests arrived at her Grosvenor Square home, a fire broke out in the specially erected marquee and the entire event had to be cancelled.

By the time of her meeting with Lane, she had decided to turn her attention to the improvement of cultural life in Johannesburg, where she now spent the greater part of each year. Florence Phillips's own artistic judgement was by no means flawless; among her favourite expressions was the remark 'I know nothing whatever about pictures.'[4] This is borne out by the comments she wrote in an art book around the time Lane was introduced to her; of a Van Eyck Madonna in Bruges, she observed: 'The baby has a dear little face in this picture. Much more attractive than the usual ones.' Vermeer's *The Lacemaker* was summarily dismissed as 'Hideous', while she enthused of Frans Hals' *Servant and Child*: 'I love this. Idea for fancy dress for Jane.'[5] Following its donation to Lane's Municipal Gallery in 1910, her portrait painted by Giovanni Boldini six years earlier was described by the *Dublin Evening Telegraph Review* as 'incredibly vulgar'[6] and the collection she and her husband had assembled at Tylney Hall showed similarly erratic taste with a few good works hung alongside many others of dubious attribution. The fact that Lionel Phillips, although musical, had almost no interest in the visual arts and was colour-blind may help to explain why the pictures he bought were often so poor. Assembled over barely eighteen months in 1897/98, seventy-two paintings from the collection were sold at Christie's in April 1913 for a total of £40,750 with just four lots accounting for more than three quarters of this figure.

Like many other *nouveau riche* South Africans who came to England during this period having made large fortunes in gold and diamond mining, the Phillipses appear to have been primarily interested in art as a means to demonstrate their affluence. Lionel Phillips was certainly by no means the only Randlord during these years to acquire a London townhouse and a country estate – the traditional accoutrements of the British aristocrat – and then furnish both lavishly; Alfred and Otto Beit, Julius Wernher, Max Michaelis, Sigismund Neumann and Joseph Robinson were among those who did likewise. Although not all were English-born, the majority of them were Jewish and had started their careers with few material advantages. All of them depended, at least when first developing their collections, on auction houses and dealers for assistance. Lane had met Alfred Beit in 1905, the year before the latter's early death, and sold him a Gainsborough. Courtesy of the Phillipses, he later came to know Beit's younger brother Otto and encouraged him to follow his sibling's example in buying pictures such as *The Lute Player*, a work then attributed to Frans Hals. Otto Beit may also have bought Velazquez's *The Kitchen Maid* directly from Lane, since it was said to have been in the latter's possession in 1909. Lane had certainly acquired a work called *Woman Scouring Dishes* by Velazquez from Christie's in May 1902 for £115.10 but its dimensions were not the same as those of the Beit collection work, so *The Kitchen Maid* may have come from another source. In any case, the relationship between the two men was warmer than just that of dealer and client. 'Welcome back!' Beit wrote in January 1911, shortly after Lane had returned from South Africa. 'I was not certain about your return else would have caused a triumphal arch to be erected outside your house. But I am glad to know your [*sic*] back and I hope "well".'[7] Possibly at Lane's suggestion, he was later painted by William Orpen. Unfortunately, like the Vere Fosters before him, he judged the finished work only a limited success, informing Lane in April 1913 that 'while the room is beautifully done, I fear the likeness is not really satisfactory'.[8]

Otto Beit was a particularly courteous man, but some of his fellow Randlords proved far less mannerly, having had to struggle hard and endure privation while building their fortunes. They now arrived in England at a time when changing economic circumstances meant the traditional leaders of society had begun to lose their place; as Lady Dorothy Nevill put it in her 1906 *Reminiscences*, wealth 'usurped the place formerly held by wit and learning'.[9] And, gratifyingly for the likes of Lane, much of that wealth was spent on the accumulation of material possessions, especially those being disposed of by the old élite. Whereas the taste of their American equivalents initially inclined towards nineteenth-century academic painting and then, under the tutelage of Berenson and Duveen, tended to move on to early Italian work, the Randlords seem to have become particularly keen on seventeenth-century Dutch and Flemish art and British portraiture almost as soon as they could afford to buy such pictures. All were fields in which Lane was particularly proficient. Moving to England, the South African millionaires may have believed that possession of goods formerly owned by the aristocracy would bestow similar status on them. Among their favourite artists, for example, were Gainsborough, Reynolds, Hoppner, Romney and Lawrence. Lady Dorothy Nevill acidly observed that these arrivistes chose to surround themselves 'with the beautiful eighteenth-century portraits of the class they have conquered'.[10] In 1896, at a time when buying by South Africans was at its height, the twenty-eight most expensive pictures sold by London auction houses (all for sums greater than 1,400 guineas) were works by British painters.

The Phillipses owned several such works, including two Constables, two Romneys, a Reynolds and a Gainsborough. However, they were much less wealthy than other South African collectors, and Lionel Phillips's need to earn more money was one reason why he and his wife, after barely a decade in England, returned to Johannesburg. He had considered standing for election as a British MP but was informed by Sir Julius Wernher that, were he to do so, retirement from the company which provided him with an income would be necessary. Phillips was then effectively instructed by his superiors to move back to South Africa and supervise the company's business. By way of a consolation tribute to the Phillipses, Wernher helped to pay for the construction of their new home on the outskirts of Johannesburg, the Villa Arcadia designed by Herbert Baker. Removed from the cultural life of Europe to which she had become accustomed, Florence Phillips now decided to encourage its greater appreciation in an environment where artistic activity of any kind was barely known. Johannesburg had been founded in 1886; within three years, it had become the largest town in South Africa, and a decade after the arrival of the first settlers it had a population of around 100,000 people. The vast majority of them were men involved with mining. In 1908, when founding the Dorothea Club – a group established for women living in the area 'whose lives are for the most part very dreary, lonely and colourless' – Florence Phillips remarked that 'amidst such hideous surroundings even the most cheerful would become depressed'.[11]

To avoid this condition, she quickly immersed herself in local activity, becoming president of both the Ladies' Committee of the Witwatersrand Agricultural Society and the Ladies Branch of the Johannesburg Centre of the South African National Union, one object of which was to encourage 'the use of South African products and manufactures'. But these goods and businesses would have to be anglocentric in character; the Boer War had only ended in 1902 with the annexation as British colonies of the South African republics of the Transvaal and Orange Free State prior to their union with the Cape Colony and Natal into a single state in 1910. As former residents of Britain, the Phillipses were keen to promote a British cultural presence in South Africa and this aspiration underlay their encouragement of Johannesburg's civic development. Eventually Florence Phillips concluded that 'Johannesburg, of all places in the world, has need of an art gallery' because there was 'so much of the material side of life that we need something to lift us above that which is merely utilitarian, and to bring sweetness and light into the daily life of the city'.[12]

To launch this initiative, she planned an arts and crafts exhibition that was intended to contain at least some work on loan from British museums – particularly the Victoria and Albert in South Kensington – and would be shown in Johannesburg early in 1910. She wanted the gallery to have a distinctly educational tone, and her promotion of Britain as a source of cultural excellence in this project was unconcealed. Florence Phillips also appears to have been toying with an idea that the proposed city gallery might hold a collection of old master paintings. This was as far as her plans had developed when she was first introduced to Lane by their mutual friend Caroline Grosvenor in late April 1909. The meeting produced a *coup de foudre* of friendship as each responded to the other's temperament. Both Lane and Florence Phillips were strong-willed, impulsive and ambitious. They fast became close correspondents, and within a matter of months she was writing to him from another rest cure in Germany with the suggestion that he join her on a motoring tour of Italy. The trip began in late August 1909 and within days Edith Phillips was writing to her father, 'Sir Hugh is madly keen on everything and will not allow one to admire anything on one's own judgement. However, as he is fairly safe to follow, one is likely to be generally right!'[13] Since his new friend, by her own admission, knew 'nothing whatever' about pictures, Lane could happily play the part of cicerone through Italy's galleries, museums and churches. In Rome, he even managed to persuade Florence Phillips and her daughter to sit for portraits by the still loquacious and incomprehensible Mancini. On the return journey they spent time in Paris, where she was introduced to Rodin and the Russian-born sculptor Naoum Aronson, examples of whose work had already been acquired by Lane.

These contacts with contemporary artists arose because he had consistently told Florence Phillips from their first meeting that she should try to establish a gallery of modern art and not old masters in Johannesburg. Ignoring exclamations that 'she didn't like modern paintings',[14] Lane argued that the cost of good old pictures had already become prohibitive whereas an excellent collection of contemporary art could be assembled at once for relatively little money. When she attempted to plead that the time had not yet quite come to undertake this job and that she still needed to find money for a purchasing fund, Lane told her: 'Sell this fine house and its surroundings and use the money to make a great Gallery.'[15] Evidently he was even more persuasive than usual because the day after his first visit to Tylney Hall, Florence Phillips met him in London and bought three paintings by Philip Wilson Steer at an exhibition the artist was then holding in the Goupil Gallery. Even more impressively, in order to pay for the work, she seems to have sold a blue diamond ring only recently given to her by Lionel Phillips. The city's evening newspapers announced that Steer's *Corfe Castle*, *Limekiln* and *A Chelsea Window* had been bought for the projected Johannesburg Art Gallery.

Although a similar project had been conceived in Johannesburg back in 1904, want of local interest meant it never progressed very far. This time, however, the combined determination of the Phillipses and Lane ensured the gallery scheme would come to fruition. Florence Phillips assumed primary responsibility for fundraising. Recognizing the importance of stabilizing the hitherto transient population of Johannesburg, her husband informed Julius Wernher that 'it is absolutely necessary to cultivate the people's minds and teach them to regard this country as their home'.[16] Accordingly, he expected his fellow Randlords to donate either cash or pictures, or in some instances both. By the time Florence Phillips sailed back to South Africa in November 1909, more than £20,000 had been promised for the scheme and Lane had spent in the region of £6,000. When the initial collection went on display in Johannesburg, £33,000 had been collected. Among the most generous contributors were Otto Beit, who gave £10,000, Wernher (£5,000), Max Michaelis (£5,000), Sigismund Neumann (£4,500), Abe Bailey (£1,000) and Sammy Marks (£500).

Lane, meanwhile, was given sole responsibility for spending this money on art. As with Dublin, there was no personal financial gain to be had from his association with the project; he seems to have undertaken the work primarily because it gave him a second opportunity to establish a new gallery and, through this institution, to find a large audience with which to share his appreciation of modern art. As he had written in the preface to the 1904 Guildhall exhibition catalogue, a modern art gallery 'would create a standard of taste, and a feeling for the relative importance of painters. This would encourage the purchase of pictures, for people will not purchase where they do not know.'[17] South Africans may not have known much about modern art, but Lane was confident he did. Again as in Dublin, he was given the opportunity to assemble a collection almost without any outside interference, although in August 1910 Julius Wernher – who had built up his own impressive art collection during the preceding three decades – objected to the purchase of a work for Johannesburg by the French landscape artist Henri Joseph Harpignies because 'it is far too poetic for that material place'. Having authorized Lane three months earlier to buy a Millais, he now wondered 'whether for a beginning one shouldn't buy to a greater degree what I would call "direct pictures"'.[18]

In the final collection of 130 catalogued items Lane did manage to include two examples of Harpignies's work, one of them paid for by Otto Beit. Among the pictures, around 50 per cent of the works were landscape paintings and a further 30 per cent were genre/narrative scenes, with the balance made up of portraits and still lifes, together with some etchings, watercolours and drawings. In keeping with the anglocentric outlook of both the Phillipses and the English-resident Randlords who had paid for the collection, British painters predominated, accounting for more than 40 per cent of the total. They were a mixture of Victorian narrative artists such as Frith, Millais and Landseer (the last of these another of Wernher's choices) alongside some of Lane's favourite contemporaries including Augustus John (lent by Lane himself), William Orpen and Sargent. Among the non-British artists represented, there were three pictures apiece by Mancini and Boudin but only one each by Monet, Pissarro, Sisley, Puvis de Chavannes and Fantin-Latour, plus two Rodin sculptures. Other than a couple of pieces of sculpture, South African artists were entirely absent from the collection, an omission that did not trouble the gallery's donors.

The Johannesburg illustrated catalogue, which in design bears a strong resemblance to that produced for the Dublin gallery, contained an introduction by Lane who, in his remarks, indicated a belief that as yet there was no such thing as South African art. Such a view had already been articulated by Florence Phillips in July 1910 when, writing to a local newspaper, she had announced her 'hope that [a] South African School of Art will grow up', before going on to express the wish that a study of the masterpieces newly acquired for Johannesburg 'should be a help as well as an incentive to local artists'.[19] Likewise in his catalogue introduction, Lane argued that a student of art in Johannesburg could look at the pictures he had assembled 'with a mind free from pre-conceptions', remembering only the words of Sir Joshua Reynolds that 'The habit of contemplating and brooding over the ideas of great geniuses till you find yourself warmed by the contact is the sure method of an artist-like mind'.[20] Having further observed that the only works not deserving of encouragement 'are the products of mediocrity', Lane added: 'I should like to say here that I am not responsible for the choice of a few of the pictures in the Gallery, the choice of which I regret.'[21] This, presumably, was a retort to what he perceived as interference on the part of Wernher, who in July 1910 had commented to Lionel Phillips that Lane 'likes best pictures that do not reveal their beauty at a glance ... but of course every art man is a bit of a crank'.[22]

Most of the work destined for Johannesburg was shown at London's Whitechapel Gallery in two tranches during May/June and July 1910 to favourable reviews from the local press, which once again bemoaned the lack of any similar public collection closer to home. Roger Fry in *The Burlington*, for example, observed, 'It would be hardly too much to say that the new gallery which Johannesburg has just founded is already far more representative of the whole scope of modern British art than anything that we have in England.'[23] Similarly, the *Morning Post*'s critic was delighted to notice that 'Academic art is conspicuous by its absence'.[24] South African newspapers were, almost without exception, equally enthusiastic about the country's new acquisition.

In mid-September Lane sailed for Johannesburg so that he could hang the collection in what was intended to be a temporary home at the city's Transvaal University College. An exhibition of the pictures was formally opened here by the Duke and Duchess of Connaught (then on an official visit to South Africa) on 29 November 1910. Lane made a particular point of cultivating the Duke, one of Queen Victoria's younger sons, and his Prussian-born wife as well as their unmarried daughter Princess Patricia. Back in England the following spring, he engaged in now-customary methods of endearing himself: advising the Duchess on the decoration of her rooms and sending gifts of Chinese stands to Clarence House. Princess Patricia, meanwhile, received tips from him about her clothing; in June 1911 he told his sister he had been trying to persuade the princess 'to get a tussore silk dress trimmed with green like the one you tried on in Debenhams'.[25] The Connaughts (known as the "Cannots") responded to all this attention by inviting him for weekends to their country house, Bagshot Park in Surrey, from where he wrote to his sister Ruth Shine: 'I play bridge with the Duchess of evenings. She is as keen as I am and no better player.'[26] He then met the couple's elder daughter Margaret and her husband Crown Prince Gustavus Adolphus of Sweden when they came to England, and even Lady Gregory, who had long since forsaken London social life, was impressed when the entire family came to tea at Lindsey House.

For Lane, meeting the Connaughts was one of the happier results of his trip to South Africa, but the visit had its share of troubles, many of his own making. His views about the design of the Johannesburg gallery were as decisive as those he held about the building's contents. Even before leaving London, he had informed Lutyens that he was his choice for architect on the job.[27] But this appointment was hardly in the gift of Lane, particularly since the Johannesburg Municipal Council had already proven reluctant to pay for both the building's construction – the initial figure of £20,000 agreed in early 1910 eventually rose to £110,000 by the time work was due to start two years later – and then its maintenance. In many respects, the problems that now arose were forerunners of those Lane would face a few years later in Dublin, and in both cases their origins lay in his insensitivity or indifference to local opinion. Convinced of Lutyens's merits, he ignored the feelings of architects in South Africa, not least Herbert Baker, an Englishman who had moved to the Cape in 1892 where he soon ran the country's most successful practice.

At least the sensibilities of Baker were better understood by Lutyens, who was invited to join Lane in Johannesburg where he could produce suitable designs for the new gallery. Busy in Rome overseeing work on a British pavilion for the following year's international exhibition, the architect initially declined the job, then prevaricated for several weeks before the combined pleading of Lane and Florence Phillips persuaded him to sail for South Africa in mid-November. Disembarking at Cape Town, he was met by Baker, an old friend not seen for eighteen years, and taken on a tour of the city – during which the resident architect's work was paid particular attention – before the two of them departed by train for Johannesburg. Here they were met by Lane, and Lutyens was given rooms at the Phillips's Villa Arcadia so that he could work on designs for the gallery. His arrival caused a great deal of hostility in some quarters, with both the municipal government and the regional press enquiring why an architect from England had been brought over to work on a South African building.

A compromise was eventually reached whereby Lutyens would design the gallery but its construction would be supervised by a local. For the site in Johannesburg's Joubert Park, Lutyens imagined a large classical structure, the main gallery standing behind a portico based on that of the seventeenth-century St Paul's in Covent Garden, London. There would be a sculpture gallery behind and four linked pavilions containing respectively an art library, a temporary exhibition space, a furnished Dutch house (to reflect the history of South Africa's first white settlers) and the home of a curator who would also run an art school.

Work proceded slowly enough on the project, with a foundation stone being laid – in a shrubbery and during a thunderstorm – in October 1911, almost ten months after Lutyens and Lane had returned to England. And since its architect was now far away and involved in a wide variety of other projects, the gallery suffered a further delay due to lack of drawings from which the builders could work. The collection assembled by Lane was moved to its new home only in September 1915 when the central block and two pavilions were finished. By then he was dead and Florence Phillips had lost much of her enthusiasm for the gallery, refusing to attend an opening ceremony because the building as originally conceived was incomplete. But although acting as the new institution's honorary director when it first opened, Lane had quickly severed his ties with Johannesburg as established loyalties reasserted themselves. Even before leaving South Africa, on Christmas Day 1910 he wrote to Thomas Bodkin: 'I find that one cannot buy for two galleries (not the same sort of thing) as I want all the *bargains* for Dublin'.[28] Instead, he helped to ensure the appointment of his friend Robert Ross as a London-based director, sharing responsibility for further acquisitions with Henry Tonks, who was also living in England.

A sense of obligation to the Dublin project may not have been the only reason for his decision to distance himself from the Johannesburg gallery. Even while still in South Africa, relations with Florence Phillips had deteriorated. It is easy to see why these two equally strong-willed characters should, after an initial enthusiasm for each other's company, have begun to bicker. Their visions for the project undertaken together were quite different. Lane saw the gallery as a centre of contemporary artistic excellence in which only the finest examples of painting and sculpture would be shown. Florence Phillips's focus was far less narrow. Her better understanding of circumstances in Johannesburg led her to imagine the gallery as exercising a civilizing influence on the city through the widest variety of means possible. She wanted to incorporate a school of art and design in the scheme, a museum of industrial art and a library of art books. While in London during the spring of 1909 she had gathered together a large number of arts and crafts items placed on show in Johannesburg the following year. She specifically wished to include her collection of old lace and textiles displayed on that occasion in the 1910 exhibition arranged by Lane, but he opposed this desire and a quarrel ensued. Florence Phillips resolutely argued that the items be shown, and according to the gallery's temporary curator Albert Gyngell, 'All was done hurriedly, Sir Hugh objecting and Mrs Phillips insisting on the added interest to womenfolk by their inclusion'.[29]

Lane now seems to have become somewhat tactless in his remarks to other people about Florence Phillips, despite still enjoying her hospitality at the Villa Arcadia; she certainly heard back some unfavourable comments because she later told Robert Ross that 'Sir Hugh made some bad enemies in South Africa by talking against Mr Beit and myself and thus spoilt much of the really fine work that he did'.[30] At the time of Lane's departure from South Africa, she graciously wrote: 'If you think I have failed in my share, believe me it was due, certainly not to want of loyalty to you nor to the wish to shirk. I think on calmer reflection, you will realise that you have nothing to reproach me with except a personal antipathy, for which I am hardly to blame.'[31] In April 1911 Lutyens described to his wife the unhappy relations between the two former friends: 'He makes her cry and lose her temper – & he laughs & says it is good for her ... it is rude that is all!'[32] A year later, Lutyens told Herbert Baker of the dealer's increasing propensity to be critical of others, sticking his 'funny little Lane headed pins into everyone'.[33] Eventually, a truce was declared; in December 1912 Lane gave Florence Phillips a gift of two Chinese figurines, which, she excitedly informed Robert Ross, were evidently meant to be 'a gage of peace. I feel quite overpowered!'[34]

In itself, the disintegration of this friendship is of no great importance; as William Orpen had remarked back in 1907, Lane had a particular skill for making enemies. But Florence Phillips was representative of the people he had studiously cultivated until then for his professional advantage; they either possessed or had access to more money than aesthetic judgement, of which he had an abundance. In order to win their support for his schemes, he had to exercise discretion and avoid being too insistent on getting his own way. With the Johannesburg gallery, however, he wanted to have sole responsibility for every aspect of the project and behaved in a fashion which suggests increasing arrogance. Success would seem to have made Lane regard himself as an arbiter of excellence. When Dublin came to decide on a new location for its Municipal Gallery in 1913, he discovered that not everyone shared this opinion.

12

THE ONSET OF UNHAPPINESS

Because he was in South Africa at the time, Lane missed the infamous exhibition of Post-Impressionist painting organized by Roger Fry which opened at London's Grafton Galleries on 5 November 1910. The 'Art-Quake', as it was later dubbed by one participant, would probably not have been to his taste. The Duchess of Rutland, who had agreed to be a member of the honorary exhibition committee, subsequently wrote to the event's secretary Desmond McCarthy, 'I am so *horrified* at having my name associated with such an awful exhibition of horrors I am very much upset by it'.[1] Lane probably would have sympathized with these comments. Although a keen advocate of Impressionism, his taste does not seem to have advanced any further than this movement, which had, after all, been promoted by well-informed critics in Britain for many years before he took up the cause.

An indication of his taste can be gauged from the large oil *Homage to Manet* painted by William Orpen in South Bolton Gardens between 1906 and 1909, in which are portrayed many of the men whose ideas on modern art Lane shared. The work is dominated by one of his own pictures, Manet's portrait of Eva Gonzales, before which are assembled six admirers of the French master. The figures include Lane, naturally, but also George Moore placed well to the foreground, an open newspaper in his hands, holding forth in customary fashion to whomever would listen. Directly facing him is the artist Philip Wilson Steer. The other three men are D.S. MacColl, in his youth a painter but by then director of the Tate Gallery, the painter/teacher Henry Tonks and the artist Walter Sickert. All of them were considerably older than Lane – Moore by more than twenty years – and all had been involved in the struggle during the 1890s to introduce Impressionism and its ideas to a hostile British audience. Tonks, Sickert, Steer and MacColl had all been closely associated with the early years of the New English Arts Club, a group established in London in 1886 by French-inspired artists who felt out of sympathy with prevailing academic trends. Soon the common jibe became that the NEAC 'wasn't new, wasn't English, wasn't art and wasn't a club'. In the mid-1890s Tonks and Steer had begun teaching at the Slade School of Art, where they encouraged the next generation of artists including Orpen and Augustus John. Likewise, both Moore and MacColl had been advocates of Impressionism in the British press for close to two decades and their respective books *Modern Painting* (1893) and *Nineteenth Century Art* (1902) did much to promote the same cause.

But by the time Orpen came to paint the group, they were cultural revolutionaries grown middle-aged, belonging more to the artistic establishment than to any radical fringe and about to be superseded as critical pioneers by Roger Fry. Far from being open to new influences, they were becoming increasingly insular in their attitudes. In April 1911, for example, Tonks boasted to Lane: 'England is the only country that does not receive its education from Paris and has some kind of art which is its own. Notwithstanding the efforts of Fry and others, I believe it will continue to keep its independence.'[2] Those efforts were based around Fry's two Post-Impressionist exhibitions held in 1910 and 1912. The first of these contained at least eighteen works by Cézanne, eleven by Matisse, seven by Picasso, twenty-one by Van Gogh and forty-six by Gauguin. The second, which introduced Cubism to British audiences, again featured Picasso, Matisse and Cézanne, along with Braque, Derain and Vlaminck. Both shows incited considerable – although by no means universal – hostility among art critics, one of the most virulent of whom was Lane's friend Robert Ross. Writing in the *Morning Post* after the opening of the 1910 show, he declaimed: 'A date more favourable than the Fifth of November for revealing the existence of a wide-spread plot to destroy the whole fabric of European painting could hardly have been chosen.'[3] Cézanne was particularly reviled, along with Van Gogh (his pictures showed 'the twitch of the paralytic'[4] according to the *Athenaeum*) and Matisse. There was more than a touch of xenophobia about many of the show's more damning notices, summed up in Ross's insistence that work produced by members of the New English Art Club had 'far more life, far more art, far more originality' than anything emanating from the 'sensational Post-Impressionists'.[5]

Similar responses were forthcoming in Dublin when the United Arts Club hosted a selection of forty-seven pictures from the first London show in January 1911. The exhibition was arranged by Ellen Duncan, one of the club's founders and a supporter of Lane's gallery; she became the latter's first permanent curator in October 1914. Mrs Duncan, whose husband James was a civil servant in charge of teachers' pensions at Dublin Castle, played the piano and wrote critical essays on art. No youthful enthusiast of the modishly new, she had turned sixty when taking responsibility for bringing the Post-Impressionists to Ireland for the first time. Nevertheless, despite being married to a man who was indifferent to the idea of modern art, she showed greater awareness of and admiration for the new school's merits than did many more experienced Irish critics. George Russell, who had been a driving force behind the 1899 exhibition – intended to introduce local artists to current international trends – found he could say almost nothing favourable of Ellen Duncan's enterprise, writing in the *Irish Times* that 'A student of the diseases which affect old civilisations would find the Post-Impressionists an interesting pathological study'.[6] Only Gauguin, Denis and Signac were exempt from his criticism, while Thomas Bodkin in the *Freeman's Journal* added Van Gogh and Cézanne to this list. But Bodkin considered Picasso's portrait of Clovis Sagot 'a depressing failure to rival Van Gogh' and Matisse was dismissed as 'a mere artistic charlatan'.[7] Notwithstanding such hostility, Ellen Duncan arranged a second Post-Impressionist show incorporating examples of Cubism at the United Arts Club the following spring. This time, the *Irish Times's* anonymous art critic tried to be more sympathetic towards what was on show but eventually came to the conclusion that 'Judged by any ideas on the nature of pictorial art which I possess, the authors of some things I have seen at the Arts Club are either insane or impostors'.[8]

Publicly, Lane – until this point a leading advocate of modern art in Ireland – had nothing to say about the exhibitions in either London or Dublin, but he may very well have concurred with Dermod O'Brien, who wrote to him in February 1911, remarking that the Post-Impressionist pictures at the United Arts Club 'have been berated with a good deal of well deserved abuse. Don't get taken in by them. Whatever talent a few have as Impressionists, they have nothing of any interest to say as far as I could see.'[9] Privately, Lane did express reservations. When Thomas Bodkin enthused over Gauguin as early as 1906, his older friend warned him against showing too much sympathy for 'a barbaric and trivial type of art'.[10] Nine years later in New York, Lane argued the merits of modernism with the collector John Quinn, telling him Picasso's work was 'rubbish' and the latest experiments the result of weak and disordered imaginations. When Quinn insisted that critical judgement depended on what was defined as art, Lane's 'only answer was that painting was too beautiful a thing and too fine a medium to be distorted'.[11]

Of course, the most obvious way to assess his opinion of Post-Impressionist art is to see whether he gave the movement tangible support by buying it. This, after all, had always been Lane's way until now; he was more articulate with his wallet than with words. Although he was a good friend of Ellen Duncan, and a supporter of Roger Fry (Lane gave a loan to his experimental Omega workshops when these were set up in spring 1913), he does not seem to have shared the tastes of either. Nor did he respond on the couple of occasions when modern work was offered to him for sale: a Cézanne in May 1913 and a Renoir, a Cézanne and a Van Gogh the following February. 'Do these interest you?' enquired the critic and curator Frank Rutter, who was acting as intermediary for the vendor. 'If so, I will put you in communication with him.'[12] Presumably, since he made no effort to buy them, the pictures did not interest Lane, who, though still only in his mid-thirties, had begun to hold increasingly inflexible opinions. The curiosity and eagerness to learn which had been a mark of his temperament ten years earlier were now replaced by more inflexible attitudes.

Nor did this change of character apply only in relation to art. His disagreement with Florence Phillips indicated that Lane was no longer willing to be tolerant towards the perceived failings of his friends, and further proof of this was provided in 1911 when he quarrelled badly with Max Beerbohm. The diminutive caricaturist and writer had been an early admirer of William Orpen's wife Grace and later also became a friend of the painter, who in the spring of 1906 was writing to Lane that he and Beerbohm, then drama critic of the *Saturday Review*, had been to the theatre together.[13] Beerbohm also made several drawings of Lane, the best-known of which is *Sir Hugh Lane Producing Masterpieces for Dublin*, which shows the dealer standing in front of a crowd and extracting Corots and Manets from an old hat; the subject of this work bought the picture from the New English Art Club in mid-December 1909 for £12.12s. As was so often the case with Lane, a desire to play patron entered into his relationship with Beerbohm, particularly after the latter had resigned his position with the *Saturday Review* in 1910 and married an American actress called Florence Kahn. The couple moved to a villa outside Rapallo on the Italian Riviera but had relatively little money, so Lane tried to help Beerbohm organize an exhibition of his work at London's Leicester Galleries in April 1911. The artist was suitably appreciative of these efforts, calling his friend 'the onlie begetter'[14] of the event, but trouble arose after he had returned to Italy. Lane had decided to buy four pictures from the show and then concluded that their prices had been deliberately inflated after he indicated an interest. Having first accused the gallery's owners of attempting to wring extra money from him, he wrote an indignant letter to Beerbohm who replied in a conciliatory tone. Anxious that Lane might not harbour 'the utterly unjust and deplorable suspicion that you have been treated unfairly', he said there was absolutely no obligation to purchase three of the pictures and the fourth had always been intended as a present.[15] Eventually, in late June, one drawing was bought – with the gallery giving a 10 per cent discount – but the damage done to his friendship with Beerbohm was irreparable.

Lane's increasing irritability now became further aggravated by a combination of ill-health and personal unhappiness. That summer, he became very briefly engaged to 'a young girl, gentle, charming in whose presence he felt content and rest', as Lady Gregory discreetly described his fiancée.[16] Lady Clare Annesley was very young; at the time of her engagement to Lane, she had just turned eighteen and was therefore almost exactly half his age. Her father, the fifth Earl Annesley, was an Irish peer whose family seat was Castlewellan, a large, austere mid-nineteenth century castle in County Down. He had died three years earlier and she lived with her mother Priscilla, the earl's second wife. Originally from County Cavan, Lady Annesley was an exceptionally attractive woman described by Daisy Fingall, who first saw her when they were both débutantes at Dublin Castle, as having 'a profile like a Greek cameo ... The features are so perfect that they might be chiselled out of marble'.[17] A youthful and sociable widow, Priscilla Annesley was painted by John Lavery in spring 1911. By then she must already have met Lane, because in one letter written to him she exclaimed: 'It is too nice of you being interested in my being painted. I want to talk to you about it'.[18] The two certainly came to know each other better after Lane's return from South Africa, as in late February 1911 they went together to a fancy-dress ball, this time at the Chelsea Arts Club – she as Marie Antoinette, he as King Charles I. Lady Annesley had artistic aspirations for her daughter who, she hoped, might study at the Slade School. In fact, it was Clare Annesley's older half-sister Mabel who became an artist, noted particularly for her wood engravings and watercolours. The younger girl does seem to have been, as Lady Gregory noted, charming and gentle, but before the end of July Lane was writing to his aunt that the engagement – which had never been officially announced – was now off. 'Clare has decided that she is not in love with me & I think that she shows her good taste. For my part, I think that it may be as well for us both, as she is very young even for her years & she requires a patient husband & one who will spend his life in the country.'[19] He then admitted that, although they enjoyed similar interests, otherwise 'we had not much in common'.

Lane's willingness to conform to Clare Annesley's wishes suggests he had not been very emotionally involved on this occasion and that the engagement – like its cancellation – took place at her request. But he never forgot his erstwhile fiancée; in Lane's will, he left 'a piece of jewellery or a picture to Lady Clare Annesley'.[20] Although outliving him by

William Orpen, *Homage to Manet*. The figures pictured are George Moore (seated at left), Philip Wilson Steer (seated centre), D.S. MacColl (with moustache, standing), Walter Sickert (beside MacColl), Lane, and Henry Tonks (seated front). Manet's portrait of Eva Gonzales, recently purchased by Lane, hangs over the table. (© Manchester City Art Galleries)

Left: This painting was believed to be by Sir Thomas Lawrence when it was purchased by Lane in 1911; Lane removed overpainting to reveal George Romney's portrait of Mrs Edward Taylor.
Right: An actual Lawrence, his portrait of Lady Elizabeth Foster, bought by Lane from the Vere Foster family. (Courtesy of the National Gallery of Ireland)

Orpen's portrait of the Vere Foster family, as organized by Lane. Lady Foster later complained that Orpen had given the entire family the same facial expression as the donkey. (Courtesy of the National Gallery of Ireland)

Two paintings purchased for the Johannesburg Art Gallery: *A Chelsea Window* by Philip Wilson Steer, and *La Forêt* by Camille Pissarro (Collection: Johannesburg Art Gallery)

Left: El Greco, *St Francis Receiving the Stigmata*. Lane gave this painting to the National Gallery of Ireland shortly after being named its Director.

Right: *Portrait of a Woman Holding a Glove*, originally attributed to Rembrandt and intended for the gallery of Dutch and Flemish masters in Cape Town; now attributed to the Studio of Rembrandt (both images reproduced courtesy of the National Gallery of Ireland)

Peasants by a Lake, part of the Staats Forbes collection and believed to be a Corot until its resemblance to a Hungarian painting was noticed (Hugh Lane Municipal Gallery of Modern Art)

Another controversial painting: the attribution of Van Dyck's portrait of Count Oxenstierna, part of the Michaelis bequest to Cape Town, was questioned but eventually accepted (Michaelis Collection)

Two drawings of putative homes for the Municipal Gallery, made by William Walcott for Edwin Lutyens: a gallery in St Stephen's Green West (*top*) and a bridge over the river Liffey (Hugh Lane Municipal Gallery of Modern Art)

Renoir's *Les Parapluies*, purchased by Lane in 1907, became one of the jewels of the collection of thirty-nine 'conditional gift' paintings disputed between Dublin and London (National Gallery, London)

Hugh Lane, painted by Antonio Mancini (Hugh Lane Municipal Gallery of Modern Art)

half a century, she never remarried. He does not appear to have entertained the idea of matrimony again, although Lady Gregory recorded that he had often spoken to her on the subject. 'If I ever marry,' he told her, 'it will be that my wife's portrait may be painted by Sargent.'[21] And seemingly he discussed with Lutyens the prospect of designing a room with twelve panels, each of which would contain a picture of his spouse painted by a different artist.[22] Among those likely to have received these commissions were Sargent, Orpen, Mancini, Augustus John, Charles Shannon, Gerald Festus Kelly and Philip Wilson Steer. The last of these had started to work on a portrait of Clare Annesley during the summer of 1911 but he appears to have abandoned the canvas once she disengaged herself from Lane.

Might he have been happily married? Even his aunt had doubts, replying to the news of Clare Annesley's decision with the comment that 'it is wiser to break off at once if there is any doubt and indeed, I had not been very content about it at the end, for I am sure you ought to lie by for a while and let your strength build itself up'.[23] She tried to legitimize her unease by arguing that Lane's marriage 'might have been Ireland's loss',[24] but on another occasion, when asked whether her nephew and his prospective wife would be happy, Lady Gregory answered, 'Yes, if they lived in separate houses'.[25] Lane seems to have liked the idea of marriage mainly because he was fond of children. Thomas Bodkin remembered while staying in Lindsey House how Lane had called him over to the drawing-room window and pointed out 'with a note of sadness' his chauffeur who was wheeling a pram along the Embankment.[26] He was godfather to three children, the grandson of Lady Gregory and daughters of his cousin John Shawe-Taylor and William Orpen. The young Orpens he remained especially fond of, inviting them every summer to a party in Lindsey House's garden where they could eat mulberries from the old tree. Having promised one year that they might come to play with his Pekinese, Tinko, he became extremely anxious when the dog grew ill and then died a few days before the event. So he borrowed another Pekinese for the day even though the cost of insuring the animal was £100.[27] He always gave little presents such as china dishes or vases to his younger visitors.

That Lane entertained the possibility of marriage and children may seem surprising since the popular belief, at least in Ireland, has long been that he was not sexually attracted to women. It is easy to see why this notion should have arisen because Lane, in person and manner, had many of the characteristics commonly assigned to homosexuals. He was extremely concerned with his own appearance and with the appearance of his surroundings. He was attentive to members of the opposite sex but usually only in so far as the attention concerned their dress or jewellery. His voice and mannerisms were rather effeminate; an unsigned document written about Lane after his death describes him as giving the impression of 'a very feminine person, rather ineffective, but quite agreeable'.[28] But this in itself proves very little; effeminate men can be heterosexual, just as some homosexuals display extremely masculine traits.

Lane was certainly friendly with a number of well-known homosexuals; when he was just beginning his career as a dealer, he met Lord Ronald Sutherland Gower, a younger son of the second Duke of Sutherland. Thirty years older than Lane, the wealthy Lord Ronald was a part-time sculptor – he was responsible for the Shakespeare Memorial in Stratford-upon-Avon – and a full-time socialite; his many books included *My Reminiscences* and *Old Diaries, Records and Reminiscences*. The two men seem to have got to know each other during the spring of 1900, when Lane paid a visit to Gower's country home, Hammerfield in Kent; in May of that year, the latter wrote to thank his young friend for the present of a painting by Chardin (sadly not named), exclaiming: 'It's a delightful specimen of a rare master & I have always wished to possess a Chardin & now thanks to your great kindness I have one & a beauty.'[29] Together, the two men visited artists' studios in London and introduced each other to members of their respective circles; in July 1907, Lord Ronald informed Lane 'I shall much like to meet the "maestro" Sargent'.[30] Many years earlier, Gower had had an affair with the American journalist Morton Fullerton, who would later become Edith Wharton's lover, and had spent a great deal of time in the company of Oscar Wilde. However, when the latter was prosecuted for gross indecency in 1895, Lord Ronald expediently distanced himself by travelling around mainland Europe for a while – unlike another friend of Lane's, Robert Ross, who became

Wilde's literary executor. Ross's cultural interests were primarily visual: for many years he co-owned the Carfax Gallery in London; he was art editor of the *Morning Post*; and he bought pictures for the Johannesburg Gallery after Lane relinquished that role. Ross made little effort to hide his homosexuality and was, therefore, not acceptable in all circles. But he and Lane, despite their legal dispute of 1906, remained close friends even after Ross felt obliged to take Lord Alfred Douglas to court on widely publicized libel charges in November 1914. The following month, Lane was not only one of the three hundred signatories of a public testimonial in support for Ross but also invited him to a party at Lindsey House despite warnings from Alec Martin about the sensibilities of other guests. 'Then those people who don't like it may stay away,'[31] Lane replied. As a token of their friendship, in his final will Lane bequeathed Robert Ross £100.

Of course, neither Gower nor Ross was ever a social pariah; the former was connected with many of Britain's ducal families and among the latter's greatest supporters were the Liberal Prime Minister Herbert Asquith and his wife Margot. And association with either of them in no way necessarily implied common sexual inclinations; otherwise impossibly large sections of Edwardian society would have to be classified as homosexual. If this classification is to be applied to Lane, then it ought to be with the understanding that he may well not have been fully conscious of his own sexuality. He might have been homosexual but no material exists linking him except tangentially with known homosexuals such as Gower and Ross; the matter must therefore rest in the realm of conjecture. Alternatively, he may simply have been one of the many bachelors found in late nineteenth and early twentieth century Britain. The anonymous writer who described Lane as being 'a very feminine person' also declared, 'His interest in art was everything, it filled his life completely – human beings hardly counted.'[32]

Two letters written by William Orpen have been cited as indicative of Lane's homosexuality. One of these was sent to the painter's lover Evelyn St George in 1912. 'A terrible moment took place in my life last night,' Orpen informed her. 'Lane had dinner with me (notice the *me*) and I went back to his place with him about 11 and who should walk in but Tonks and Moore.'[33] What could this mean? Surely only that Orpen was discommoded by having to be civil late at night after an agreeable dinner with an old friend to two men, one a former teacher of his at the Slade School and the other an art critic, whose company he would rather not keep. The alternative inference that has been drawn from the letter is that Tonks and Moore might imagine Orpen and Lane were lovers, which is absurd. Orpen, after all, was married (and with a mistress to whom he was writing) while the two older men were both single. Orpen's other letter was sent to Lane himself in 1906: 'I went out yesterday afternoon with a friend of yours, I won't mention names – a male friend – critic of the drama – lives in Mayfair – do you know him – Because I'm anxious to find out a little more about him – My knowledge of him leads me to believe Etc Etc. I'll have my doubts of you soon.'[34] That friend, the letter subsequently indicates, was Max Beerbohm, a man who appears to have inspired jealousy in Orpen because of his long-standing friendship with the painter's wife Grace. There was never any suggestion that Beerbohm was homosexual; in fact, although a friend of Oscar Wilde, he had distanced himself somewhat from the writer after his disgrace in 1895. Again, therefore, this letter must be presumed to contain coded allusions to homosexuality only if the reader very much wishes to find them there. Otherwise, it represents nothing more than playful banter between two people who know one another well. Beerbohm, after all, eventually married, as did most of Lane's other close male friends, such as Alec Martin and Thomas Bodkin.

So too did a man who came to know him particularly well during this period and to whom he left £100 in his will, Joseph Solomon. Born near Cape Town in 1888, Solomon was working as a trainee architect in the offices of Herbert Baker when he met Lane during the latter's visit to South Africa. It was soon arranged that he should travel to Europe and spend some time with Lutyens; this he did between 1911 and 1913, and while working in London he stayed at Lindsey House on several occasions. On his return to Cape Town, he wrote to Lane: 'I can never adequately express my thanks to you for all you did for me. I owe you a debt of gratitude which it would be idle even to attempt to repay in any other way than an endeavour sincerely to repay your great kindness.' Lane's sympathy and advice, he insisted, would forever be 'influences which have helped to bring out whatever is good in me'.[35] Once more, there might be a temptation to imagine that relations between the two men went beyond friendship, especially when Solomon declared to Lane that 'no one will realise more than yourself how difficult it is to say the things one really feels'.[36] And yet, within a year of settling back in South Africa, he was writing news to London of finally meeting a woman he had previously admired from a distance in Lane's company ('you politely but firmly declined to discuss her & even went so far as to make a disparaging remark').[37] Before another three months had passed, he was engaged to be married to the woman, Jean Harkness, a touring actress. In reply, Lane dispensed with disparagement and sent congratulations instead, insisting that although the couple might have little money, 'If two people love each other, Providence will look after the well-matched pair.'[38] Thanking him for this encouraging letter, Solomon remarked 'There was so much sound wisdom and advice in it that I begin to believe that you have cheated some woman of great happiness!'[39]

Joseph Solomon was yet another young man dazzled by his older friend, of whom he wrote a brief memoir published in *Country Life in South Africa* in June 1915, barely a month after Lane's death. His text reveals a man who, in spite of everything he had achieved, was sometimes deeply unhappy and prone to self-doubt. Solomon described a 'pale, slender, dark-eyed knight with his trim, black beard, his slim hands and his poised, nervous, elusive manner' whose appearance was 'similar to the figures in the paintings of that strange seer, El Greco'.[40] He recalled an evening in London when, following dinner, guests including Moore, Tonks and Steer gathered in Lane's drawing-room and, while their host sat smoking in melancholy silence, remembered Synge who had died in 1909. After the others had left, Lane turned to Solomon and commented, 'How foolish to talk of Synge's small volume of work. Why generations after I, who have created nothing, am dead and forgotten, Ireland will be watching his plays.'[41] These words were echoed by Lane in November 1912 when, further depressed with lack of development regarding the Municipal Gallery, he told his aunt: 'Your wonderful combination of gifts has carried through what you have set out to do, while I with my one only talent of "taste" should never have attempted to work in Dublin.'[42]

While always superstitious, he now began to attach credence to omens and to what Solomon called 'days of ill-luck'.[43] He asked a number of fortune tellers to read his horoscope; a surviving fragment of one such document informed him that the particular combination of signs at his birth had produced 'a firm and powerful character, possessing magnetic power, keen judgement & great determination. Strong likes and dislikes probably, also an exacting & proud temper when vexed.'[44] W.B. Yeats was also requested to examine Lane's horoscope. The poet later told Lady Gregory that he had been able to tell when a long stream of good fortune had begun for his subject, but 'I told him also that he could not count upon his luck lasting more than a certain number of years longer'.[45] Perhaps because of this warning, Lane came to believe that he might die soon and had to finish as much work as possible in the time remaining. Except for his sister Ruth, none of his siblings enjoyed good health and were to die relatively young, which must have increased Lane's awareness of his own mortality. After his death, Lady Gregory was told by Yeats that her nephew 'was like a man who knew he had but a few years to live, and who raged against every obstacle to his purpose'.[46] She also heard from a member of Dublin Corporation, Thomas Kelly, that when he asked Lane why he was in such a hurry to achieve his ambitions, the reply had been 'Because I have not long to live'.[47] Similarly, the anonymous description of Lane in his extant papers includes an observation that he projected 'a sense of almost over-strained living – a silk thread stretched to the utmost which might snap at any moment'.[48]

The thread seems to have snapped in August 1911 when he retreated to a rest home in Bletchingley and abandoned contact with all but a handful of people. These included Lady Gregory and his sister Ruth, who communicated with one another their concerns over his welfare. 'Every day for months past has brought nearer this crisis', the older woman announced. 'I wonder he did not break down even more than he did.'[49] She was particularly worried because her other favourite nephew, John Shawe-Taylor, had recently died unexpectedly. To his aunt, Lane sent thanks for her many letters and confirmation that 'it is not all rest lying on one's back with one's thoughts only! It is the massage & regular hours that put on flesh & weight eventually.'[50] Since she was due to depart shortly to the United States, Lady Gregory took comfort in the news that Ruth Shine had travelled over from Ireland to spend time with her brother after he came out of the rest home. Suspicious of such places (Lady Gregory characterized one with which she was acquainted as 'most oppresive and deadly'),[51] they preferred to see him staying quietly at Lindsey House. But both women then became anxious again when he was forced to undergo a painful operation on his nose to correct breathing difficulties which interfered with sleep. As his aunt remembered, this problem meant that when she came to stay at Lindsey House, 'I would find him in the morning exhausted, white, taking his light breakfast in bed, lying late, irritable and nervous'.[52] Still she fretted when he and his doctor decided on surgery and only allowed herself to relax after learning from her niece that Lane was making a fast recovery.

In the meantime, the outside world was left to wonder what had become of him, since he opted to have all his correspondence handled by an old friend, the publisher and author Grant Richards. Three years older than Lane, Richards had set up his own firm in 1897 at the age of twenty-four; one of the first books to appear under his imprint was A.E. Housman's *A Shropshire Lad*, and despite two bankcruptcies he would go on to publish – after many vicissitudes – James Joyce's *Dubliners* in June 1914 as well as the novels of Ronald Firbank and Osbert Sitwell. In 1912, he produced his own first novel, a soufflé called *Caviare* which contains an instantly identifiable portrait of Lane, here given the name Sir Peter Bain. A Scottish – rather than Irish – art collector and dealer, Bain has arranged to donate £100,000 worth of pictures to the fictional city of Carburgh, on condition that the local authorities provide a gallery in which they may be displayed. He possesses an exceptional eye for art but has trouble articulating his opinions on the subject, explaining: 'I can't write about painting. I express myself by acquiring pictures. That's my way of criticism, my method of expression.' Among his most conspicuous traits are a deep sense of pessimism and a reluctance to spend money unnecessarily. He and *Caviare*'s hero, the Hon. Charles Caerleon, pass several days in one another's company in the south of France, during which time the reader learns that while Bain's 'purse and his time and his energy were at everyone's disposal, he continued out of mere perversity to assist the legend of his meanness'. His home in London is described as 'a residence out of the Thousand and One Nights', he cheerily loses money at Monte Carlo's casino and yet he instructs Caerleon 'if only he'd be sensible and eat at A.B.C. shops, he'd save so much money that he could have all the modern pictures he wanted'.[53] Richards's portrayal of his friend was affectionate and easily recognized, especially since the circumstances of Bain's upbringing and early career were exactly the same as those of Lane. Soon after the book's publication, Lane received a letter from Gerald Kelly addressed to 'Dear Sir Peter Bain' in which the artist commented of Grant Richards: 'He's done you very proud – & has only spoilt one of your stories – from excess of caution.'[54]

Richards was a long-standing devotee of Lane, who made the publisher an executor of his will (in which he was also left £200). In September 1906, after the failure of the Carfax Gallery court case, Richards told Lane: 'My real concern is with your state of health ... as I have no confidence in your ability to look after yourself.'[55] During the autumn of 1911 he put that concern to good use by assuming all responsibility for Lane's substantial correspondence, informing everyone: 'He is not allowed to write letters and is indeed discouraged from receiving them or from attending to any business.'[56] The queries Richards dealt with were varied, ranging from the Italian sculptor Antonio Sciortino's repeated appeal for a commission to requests for news of Lane's health. A number of friends made reference to a much-reported theft from the Louvre in Paris which had just taken place, and suggested there must be a connection between this event and Lane's sudden disappearance. 'Art could never afford to lose both him and the Mona Lisa,' Sarah Purser told Grant Richards. 'Both I trust will soon be restored to us in excellent preservation.'[57] Leonardo's painting was eventually returned undamaged but Lane, although once more back working at various schemes before the end of the autumn, never regained the vitality and enthusiasm that had until then been two of his most attractive characteristics. His youthful zeal and impetuosity were forever lost. From now on, he started to convey the impression of living on borrowed time.

13
MAX MICHAELIS AND CAPE TOWN

Among the many people Florence and Lionel Phillips had asked for assistance when fund-raising on behalf of the Johannesburg Art Gallery in 1909/10 was Max Michaelis, who agreed to donate £5,000 to the project. In 1875 at the age of twenty-three, the German-born Michaelis had emigrated to South Africa where he helped to found the Cape Diamond Company (subsequently taken over by De Beer's) and became manager of the Central Mining and Investment Corporation, which looked after the business of Wernher, Beit & Co. Like many other Randlords, he was an Anglophile who, after making his money, settled in England in 1891. There he bought both a house in London and a country estate, Tandridge Court in Surrey, as well as following the example of Wernher and Beit by acquiring his own art collection which included work by Reynolds and Lawrence, together with Jan Steen, Canaletto, Lucas Cranach and Rosa Bonheur.

By leaving the Cape, he further enhanced an already widely-held opinion that the men who had reaped the greatest financial rewards from South Africa were most indifferent to the country's welfare. In 1904, the South African statesman General Jan Smuts declared that the Randlords regarded his native land with contempt. As far as they were concerned, he said, it was 'a black man's country, good enough to make money or a name in; but not good enough to be born or to die in'.[1] Michaelis must have seemed a stereotypical 'Hoggenheimer', the derogatory name given in South Africa to wealthy, and often Jewish, capitalists who allegedly took but never gave anything in return. In fact, he would confound this image in 1919 by returning to live near Cape Town and, five years earlier, by donating a collection of seventeenth century Dutch and Flemish paintings to South Africa. This collection had been assembled by, and bought from, Hugh Lane.

Michaelis's reasons for making so substantial a gift will always remain somewhat unclear because he never commented publicly on the subject. He was an extremely reticent man who valued his privacy and only once gave a press interview in which, it seems, the journalist involved eventually became exasperated by his subject's unwillingness to divulge any information. However, the most obvious motivation for offering South Africa a ready-made collection was to advance its benefactor's wish for a British title. By 1912, when Lionel Phillips received a baronetcy, Michaelis remained one of the few Randlords not yet in receipt of such an honour. He had already generously given £5,000 to the Johannesburg gallery, followed by a further £1,000 to buy a collection of art books for the same institution. But this assistance brought him relatively little personal publicity and therefore a more overt act of philanthropy appeared essential to ensure that he came to official notice. Among the conditions attached to his offer of the picture collection to South Africa was that it should always be known as the Max Michaelis Gift.

In making this donation, he was certainly encouraged by Florence Phillips, a friend for almost twenty years, who appears to have assured him that she would press his case for a title with General Smuts. The latter may have been responsible for first suggesting the idea of a gallery in South Africa of Dutch and Flemish art. Joseph Solomon certainly told Lady Gregory this was the case and that, following conversations with Smuts, Lane started to assemble a representative selection of pictures. According to Solomon, 'together we conspired to get our South African magnates to start a National Art Collection Fund, which might purchase works over a period of years'.[2] Following the conclusion of the Boer War, Smuts had played a major role in the 1910 creation of the South African Union and now wanted to continue the process of nation-building. So he outlined to Lane his proposal for a collection which 'might recall to the

Dutch population of the Dominion the glories of their past civilisation in the days when they first colonised South Africa, and, by the representation of the art in which the Dutch and English peoples first met in spirit, symbolise a new Union'.³ This concept of the collection acting as a symbol of reconciliation was frequently disseminated, and the story of Dutchman Jan van Riebeeck's landing at the Cape in 1652 just as often evoked. In May 1913, shortly before the paintings were dispatched for South Africa, a writer in *The Studio* spoke of the Michaelis gift as a collection in which affinities between Dutch and English taste were displayed, 'for it was always the English who, outside of Holland, were the greatest patrons of Dutch art'.⁴ Another reason for the extensive attention both the collection and its donor were to receive was that hitherto there had been almost no old master paintings of any quality on public display in South Africa. Many newspapers accordingly made the suggestion that these works could now form the basis of a national gallery for the country. At the time, Cape Town possessed a South African Art Gallery but its contents, housed in two rooms of the South African Museum, comprised mostly copies of old masters, poor academic pictures and plaster-cast reproductions of classical statuary. The proposed gift would be indisputably superior to anything yet seen on the Cape.

Florence Phillips may have had an unhappy experience when working with Lane, but she still recommended that Michaelis buy the collection of Flemish and Dutch pictures the dealer had assembled over the past two years. She must have regretted doing so because just as she heard Lane had been indiscreet about her in conversation, so word eventually came back that he was equally tactless on the subject of Michaelis. In November 1912 she observed to her husband 'I only hope and trust Sir Hugh will not talk too much',⁵ and around the same time, in a letter marked '*This is very private*' she asked Robert Ross to use his influence with Lane because 'He does not realise that these things get back frightfully and that the very walls have ears! If Mr Michaelis does the right thing in purchasing his pictures, suggest to him to let him have the due credit and his *motives* have nothing to do with Sir Hugh! And the more he is credited with being big and disinterested, the more will he live up to his reputation and the more will he influence others for good!'⁶

Enhancing his personal reputation was an important element in Lane's decision to sell the collection to Michaelis. Around the same time Florence Phillips was indirectly attempting to discourage him from gossiping about the prospective purchaser's motives, he told Lady Gregory of the personal satisfaction he derived from having created a gallery of old masters 'for a continent that wants one so badly'.[7] A month later, he wrote to a colleague that the creation of such a gallery had been one of his ambitions.[8] Here lies the explanation for why he agreed to sell the collection to Michaelis for such a reasonable price. When the two men first entered into negotiations on the subject in early 1912, the Randlord offered £70,000, which Lane refused as being too low. Protracted haggling then followed, with Michaelis attempting to keep the price down by appealing to Lane's vanity. On 18 October, for example, he wrote from Tandridge Court that while he was no judge of the quality or value of the pictures, 'I may say that, as regards the composition of this collection, it does you great credit and will do so – if it can be kept together'.[9] In return, Lane pleaded ill-health and suggested he might make more money by breaking up the collection and disposing of individual works. 'As I am still very unwell & have lost most of my ambition this is tempting as it would save me so many months of trouble and work.'[10] When Michaelis appeared unmoved by this threat, Lane announced he had definitely decided to sell the paintings to dealers who, he claimed, had been asking to buy them. 'I will try & enter an arrangement', he added, 'by which they will let you have them at a moderate percentage of profit. This will relieve me from all the work & responsibility organising the bother & expense of getting the pictures into order.'[11]

The tactic worked; by the beginning of November it was settled that, subject to certain conditions, Michaelis would buy the forty-seven works for £76,000.[12] Whatever claims he may have made in the course of negotiating the sale, this price indicates that ambition to claim responsibility for another new gallery was still a primary motivation for Lane, as he had probably spent the same amount of money assembling the collection. The highest sums were paid for pictures by Rembrandt, Steen, Ruysdael, Van Dyck and Frans Hals. He had bought the Rembrandt *Portrait of a Woman holding a Glove*, together with Steen's *As the Singing Leads, so the Dancing Follows*, at Agnew's in mid-May 1911 for £27,000. Van Dyck's *Portrait of Count John Oxenstierna* also came from Agnew's, where Lane had paid around £3,675 for the canvas a few days after the earlier purchases, and *Hilly Landscape near Bentheim* by Ruysdael had been sold at Christie's in December 1910 for 2,250 guineas. The Frans Hals *Portrait of a Woman* had been acquired from Joseph Duveen; the price is unknown but it probably cost him at least £20,000. Advised by Otto Beit, Michaelis agreed to take the entire group of paintings, provided their attributions were confirmed by the Director-General of Berlin's Museums, Dr Wilhelm von Bode.

Born in 1845, Bode was among the most influential figures in the European art world, a position he had acquired by a combination of political skill and intellectual ability. Nicknamed the 'Kunstkorporal' (the corporal of art) by his nearest rival Giovanni Morelli, Bode had built up the German national collection in the latter part of the nineteenth century through negotiating important purchases from members of Italy's impoverished aristocracy. When the Italian government passed legislation to discourage the flow of artworks out of the country, Bode began to buy instead from British collections such as those belonging to the Earl of Dudley and the Duke of Marlborough. His acquisitiveness was matched by brilliant scholarship; during his lifetime he published around fifty books and ten times that number of articles in periodicals all over Europe. He advised collectors, including Julius Wernher and both Alfred and Otto Beit, and often produced catalogues of the works he helped them to buy. Lane had been in communication with him as far back as 1905 when Bode had encouraged Alfred Beit to buy Gainsborough's portrait of his daughter Margaret from the dealer. In July 1905, Lane sent a letter of thanks to Berlin: 'I am very much obliged to you for your kind letter and for having written to Mr Beit about the "Gainsborough" ... I had intended bequeathing it to the Dublin Gallery, but I am obliged to sell it now to pay for the "Forbes" pictures which have been purchased as a nucleus of a *Modern Art Gallery*.'[13] In December 1906, Lane was again in touch with Bode, this time asking for his opinion on a possible Giorgione.[14] The German scholar's reputation suffered a setback in 1909, however, when a bust of Flora, bought for Berlin's Altes Museum on his recommendation and attributed by him to Leonardo da Vinci or his circle, was discovered to have within its base a piece of nineteenth-century cloth.

But Bode survived this humiliation (it now appears probable that the fabric had been inserted during repairs to the sculpture) and retained his pre-eminence particularly in the field of seventeenth-century Dutch painting, the subject on which Michaelis now chose to ask for advice. In late November 1912, the Randlord went to Berlin with photographs of the pictures assembled by Lane. Bode had several meetings with Michaelis over the following two months and provided the necessary reassurances about the quality of the work being offered. Van Dyck's portrait of Count Oxenstierna was the painting over which there had been most concern, as no references could be found to it among standard works on the painter. On 23 November, Michaelis wrote to Lane saying he had seen Bode the previous day, when 'He spoke most admiringly of the Van Dyck. I mentioned your Metsu and he would much like to see the picture. Could you send it to him at the Kaiser-Friedrich Museum?'[15]

By early December Bode was in direct communication with Lane, again commenting favourably about the Van Dyck portrait and remarking on a still life then attributed to Barend van der Meer (and now believed to be by the German artist Georg Hainz) which, he observed, 'was interesting to me as it showed me an unknown master'. Bode's letter went on to remind Lane that a year later he had promised to present the Berlin gallery with a picture. 'Allow me to ask you whether you would be kind enough to do it at this occasion. If you are still willing to do so, please let me know what you would choose and send me kindly a photograph of it.'[16] For Bode, this was a common practice; in return for his assistance in confirming attributions, he would seek gifts of artwork from dealers and collectors. These were made, not to himself, but to the Berlin museums for which he was responsible. Wernher and the Beit brothers, who had benefited from his connoisseurship, all gave pictures to Bode and now Lane – dependent on the German scholar's opinion to close an important sale – was expected to do likewise. In a surviving draft of a letter sent to Berlin from Paris (where Lane was buying more pictures from a variety of dealers) Lane insists, 'I am not only willing but anxious to give you a picture for your museum ... The difficulty is to know what you would like amongst my remaining pictures. I have some good examples of the English school, Hogarth, Morland, R. Wilson and Zoffany.'[17] Bode chose none of these but, through his deputy Max Friedlander who visited London in late February 1913, opted for a portrait of a man by the French seventeenth-century artist Philippe de Champaigne. In March, Bode wrote a letter of thanks for the gift, commenting that Berlin until then had not possessed any paintings by de Champaigne, 'and this one is a sympathetic and good example of his art'.[18] Bought by Lane a year earlier at Christie's for £52, ten shillings, the portrait remained in Berlin until the end of the Second World War in 1945, when it disappeared.

Bode's support having been gained, Lane now arranged with the High Commissioner for South Africa Sir Richard Solomon that the collection of Dutch and Flemish pictures should be publicly exhibited in London prior to their dispatch for the Cape, as had been done with the Johannesburg Art Gallery's first group of acquisitions three years earlier. He had already been in contact with magazine editors such as Roger Fry at *The Burlington* to ensure the paintings were featured in their spring 1913 issues. Early notices certainly suggested Lane was right to look for attention. *The Burlington* proclaimed that the collection marked a new era for art history in the British Empire's more remote countries,[19] while the South African artist Edward Roworth, who had been given an opportunity to see the pictures in Lindsey House, told readers of the *Cape Times* that Lane's 'faultless taste and extraordinary judgement' had allowed him 'to acquire the greatest masters which are not exceeded by any gallery in the world, public or private'.[20] Joseph Solomon would later claim that through Lane's work, South Africa had come to own 'one of the choicest collections of its size and kind in the world'.[21]

This was an unhelpful exaggeration because, inevitably given the relatively small sum of money spent, the group of pictures had its flaws and omissions. In a 1933 interview with a South African newspaper, Florence Phillips insisted: 'The original collection was never considered by Sir Hugh Lane to be in the front rank. The price given for the whole collection was not as much as is given sometimes for one masterpiece.'[22] Within the group assembled by Lane, there were, for example, far more Dutch than Flemish paintings, and certain key artists of the seventeenth century, such as Rubens, were entirely absent. Even when an artist of the first rank was included, the picture might be a very poor example of his work. The condition of Gabriel Metsu's *Couple with a Child*, which had come from the Earl of Harrowby's collection, was especially bad. Lane's personal tastes were inevitably reflected in the choice of subject matter, with portraiture, still lifes and landscapes being in the majority. Michaelis obviously knew that the collection was not without its failings; he informed Bode at the end of May 1913 that 'It was hardly intended to include masterpieces *only*, but to offer a general collection comprising good as well as minor paintings of a school which would be of special interest for those to whom it was meant'.[23]

Ever self-effacing – and perhaps having a premonition of potential trouble – Michaelis was reluctant for any work to be shown publicly in England, insisting that 'the proper occasion' to mark his gift would arise 'when the collection is placed on exhibition in Cape Town'.[24] However, keen to attract publicity in England for his discerning taste, Lane insisted on pressing ahead with arrangements for the London show. Accompanied by an illustrated catalogue, the collection went on public display at the Grosvenor Gallery on 23 May 1913. Lane must have regretted not heeding Michaelis's recommendation because the show attracted little praise and a great deal of censure from English art critics. In particular, Sir Claude Phillips, former keeper of London's Wallace Collection, wrote a damning article in *The Daily Telegraph* on 27 May, arguing that the Michaelis Gift was 'of very unequal merit, and as a whole, by no means qualified to gladden the hearts of serious students of Netherlandish masters'.[25] While accepting that the Frans Hals portrait was a masterpiece and that there were a number of other fine pictures in the exhibition, he insisted others were of very poor quality. Phillips, who had been a friend of Lane and whose remarks were believed in some quarters to have been inspired by professional jealousy, proposed that rather than donate a pre-assembled collection of such variable merits, Michaelis ought to have given a handful of outstanding masterpieces to South Africa where they could provide a nucleus for a future national gallery. He was especially critical of the attributions of two key works: the Van Dyck and Rembrandt portraits. Whereas the former had always been somewhat suspect, no such doubts ever appear to have hung over the Rembrandt picture. For more than three decades, this had been regarded in many quarters as one of the Dutch master's finest paintings. In March 1880 it had been included in the sale of Prince Demidoff's collection in Florence, where the picture was reputed to have made the largest sum yet made by a Rembrandt work. In fact, this was not the case but the Demidoff Rembrandt, as it came to be known, thereafter enjoyed exceptional status in the art world. In an eight-volume *Complete Works of Rembrandt* co-authored between 1897 and 1906 by Bode, who held the artist in the highest esteem, the picture was classified as an important work, its head 'painted very delicately with no trace of timidity in the handling'.[26]

The Demidoff portrait's credentials had been unquestioned until they were examined by Phillips in May 1913 and found to be faulty. Refusing to be influenced by what he described as the 'sentimental aspects of the case', he argued that the picture was more likely to have been painted by another seventeenth-century Dutch painter, Ferdinand Bol, who would eventually be represented in the Michaelis collection by a portrait of a woman.[27] Phillips's attribution was supported by Dr Abraham Bredius, an expert in this field; he had been director of the Mauritshuis in The Hague for twenty years until 1909 and had written extensively on the subject of Flemish and Dutch art. An intense and very public debate over the picture's merits – and authorship – now followed, causing Lane immense discomfiture. Not only had he paid a large sum for the portrait on the understanding that it had been painted by Rembrandt (and then charged Michaelis the same amount on the same basis), but his very credibility as a dealer was now open to question. Once again, his lack of serious scholarship had left him vulnerable to attack from more cautious and better-informed members of the art world.

His immediate instinct was to engage in a degree of damage limitation. The day after Phillips's article appeared in *The Daily Telegraph*, Lane wrote to Michaelis offering to take back the Rembrandt as well as the Van Dyck.[28] Michaelis replied that he would 'like to think matters over & to consider what will be the best solution for all concerned'.[29] Lane sent another letter insisting he was prepared to exchange the two portraits, but could not resist mixing the personal with the professional when he continued: 'If I only thought of myself I would ask you to let me have the whole collection back as I can sell several of the pictures immediately at a considerable profit.' However, because he still wished to fulfil 'my ambition of forming a public gallery of old masters for South Africa, I suggest that I can "bear up" a little longer'.[30] Meanwhile, Michaelis was in contact with Bode, reminding the German scholar that he had confirmed the authenticity of the Rembrandt, and enthused about the Van Dyck, in a letter written at the end of October 1912.[31] Michaelis now planned to write to *The Daily Telegraph* saying that the pictures criticized by Sir Claude Phillips 'were acquired under the advice of Dr Bode and that both the Union Government (of South Africa) and myself are content to abide by his opinion'.[32] Bode, however, asked that this letter not be sent and also resisted requests that he write to the South African High Commissioner with reassurances about the Rembrandt and Van Dyck attributions. Pushed into giving judgement of some kind, he finally seems to have recommended that Michaelis keep the Van Dyck but not the Rembrandt.

Attempting to remain on good terms with both parties, Bode then wrote to Lane confirming once more his attribution of the latter portrait. Indeed, in a long letter he consistently enthused over the picture, declaring: 'I assert that it is incredible to me how Rembrandt could be doubted and Bol be named as the artist ... The "Lady with the Glove" is in conception a characteristic Rembrandt portrait, as painted by him from 1632 to 1636 and occasionally also from 1640 to 1642.'[33] A few weeks later, Alois Hauser, who had cleaned the Rembrandt for Lane in Berlin, also wrote testifying to both his own and Bode's conviction as to the painting's attribution.[34] Under considerable stress and suffering from spells of giddiness, Lane found reassurance in this support, which was further enhanced when Max Friedlander again travelled to London and confirmed the Rembrandt attribution once more. Nonetheless, Lane felt obliged to abide by the offer he had made to Michaelis when the Phillips article first appeared; while the Van Dyck remained in the collection, the Rembrandt was returned to Lindsey House and another twenty-two Dutch and Flemish paintings went to Cape Town instead.

But the matter did not rest there. In February 1914, the fact that Bode had recommended Michaelis not keep the Rembrandt was leaked to the British press. Lane, who knew nothing of the German's duplicity, immediately wrote to *The Times*, decrying 'inaccurate' statements which had appeared about the Demidoff Rembrandt and quoting the letters Bode and Hauser had sent him the previous summer in which they both praised the painting.[35] The following day, however, Michaelis in turn wrote to the same newspaper confirming as true the rumours that Bode had advised him to return the Rembrandt[36] and, before a week had passed, Bredius wrote from Holland to both Lane and *The Times* putting forward once more his reasons for believing that the portrait, while unquestionably wonderful, had been painted by Ferdinand Bol and not Rembrandt.[37] Lane then contacted Bode, disagreeing with Bredius's analysis and arguing that 'Bol was always a feeble painter, and one who would not have existed but for his slavish imitation of the Master'.[38] He wanted Bode to come to his aid publicly but the latter, clearly fearing a counter-attack might not be successful, once again refused to write to the British press. Instead, Bode complained that Lane should not have published their private correspondence about the picture. However, it was pointed out that the document he particularly felt should have been kept private had contained a postscript telling Lane 'You can make use of this letter if you wish'.[39]

And with that, the subject was closed – at least during Lane's lifetime. Michaelis, who never received his baronetcy and was knighted only in 1924 after he had endowed a Chair of Fine Art at the new University of Cape Town, felt he had been duped by Lane; in March 1917 Robert Ross told Florence Phillips that Michaelis 'thinks he was done but really quite wrongly. The *Hals* alone is worth now what he gave for the whole collection even allowing that the quality of *some* of the pictures was not a very high one.'[40] The contested Rembrandt remained in Lane's possession and, after his death, passed to the National Gallery of Ireland where it is now catalogued as being from the Dutch master's studio. Similarly the portrait of Count Oxenstierna, which did travel to South Africa, is regarded as being from the studio of Van Dyck.

In Cape Town, that picture hangs, along with the rest of the collection, in a mid-eighteenth century building known as the Old Town House. This site had been chosen only after another fractious debate about where the Michaelis gift should be shown. Edward Roworth, for example, having had a chance to view the pictures in London, wrote to Lane from Kimberley in May 1913 asking whether it were possible for the collection to go to that town rather than Cape Town.[41] A case for Pretoria being the Michaelis Gift's recipient was also argued, not least by Florence Phillips, even though she could claim credit with coming up with the idea of Cape Town's Old Town House being suitable for alteration into a gallery. In early May 1913 she wrote to Lane: 'I think I have at last found a place for the housing of the Michaelis pictures ... The whole thing was at a standstill here & it was very fortunate I had a brilliant inspiration.' According to Lady Phillips, 'The Old Town House has all the advantages of beauty, accessibility & smallness, so that the collection will not be swamped'.[42] At the time, the building was terribly neglected, shabby and threatened with possible demolition. Having been transferred from the city's care into that of the Union Government, it therefore had to be completely refurbished.

The responsibility for this job went to Lane's friend, Joseph Solomon, who would shortly leave Herbert Baker's office and set up his own practice. He had been following the controversy in London over the pictures and loyally sending reassurances to Lindsey House that Claude Phillips's hostile *Daily Telegraph* review had not made much impact in South Africa: 'the spite in the article is so obvious that no person of any common sense could fail to see it'.[43] Solomon's intention was to convert the Cape Town property so that its interiors should evoke those of seventeenth-century Dutch domestic buildings and of The Hague's Mauritshuis 'instead of giving it a cold formal experience of a gallery'.[44] By September 1913 he had become almost totally dependent on Lane's advice for what changes should be made to the Old Town House, writing: 'It would help me very considerably if you would be kind enough to send me a sample of the green wool damask which you suggest ... Do you wish to hang the pictures by chains in the way you have them at Lindsey House or do you wish to conceal the means of hanging?' This particular letter ends by announcing that Solomon wanted 'to please you in the matter so that I hope you will write freely as to your ideas'.[45] An accompanying floor plan of the building in Cape Town carried further notes, including Solomon's intention, provided sufficient funding were available, to panel one room in a style similar to that of Lindsey House's drawing-room. At the time, it seemed possible Lane would travel again to South Africa to hang the collection in its new home but the trip was repeatedly delayed and finally cancelled, to Solomon's great disappointment. 'How I wish Sir Hugh could have seen it,' he told Ruth Shine some months after her brother's death. 'It will be my eternal regret.'[46] In January 1916 he wrote again to inform her of his plans for a garden attached to the Old Town House: 'I am making the fountain pond a memorial to Sir Hugh & am planting a mulberry tree over it in remembrance of Lindsey House.'[47] That year, he paid another visit to London and once more saw the home of his late friend before returning to South Africa, where he was given the enormous job of designing the new University of Cape Town. The task, however, overwhelmed him and in August 1920, suffering from insomnia and stress, Solomon fatally shot himself in the head.

14
CONTROVERSY

'The Song of Dublin'

COMMITTEE	We're looking for money
	For Manet and Monet
SUBSCRIBERS	And if we get any
	Will that put an ending
	To Lane and his lending?[1]

In late July 1912, the English novelist and playwright W. Somerset Maugham wrote to the *Irish Times* observing that, on a recent visit to Dublin, he had experienced great difficulty in locating the city's Municipal Gallery. 'We are generally assured', he concluded, 'that those pleasures are most enjoyed which are attained with most difficulty, and I can think of no other reason why the fact that Dublin possesses a Municipal Art Gallery of unrivalled excellence should be kept from the public like a discreditable secret.'[2] Maugham, who knew Lane in London, may have been encouraged to send this letter because, four and a half years after it had first opened in Harcourt Street, the future of the gallery had once more become the subject of public debate. A week earlier, on 19 July, the British Prime Minister Herbert Asquith, in Dublin to encourage support for the Home Rule Bill then being advocated by his Liberal Party government, called into the gallery with his family. They were shown around by

Lane, who had been pressing Dublin Castle to make sure Harcourt Street was included in the Asquiths' crowded itinerary. As he wrote to his sister Ruth, 'I hope very much the P.M. will come; it will impress the mob greatly'.[3] The outcome was just as he hoped. The Asquith visit was widely reported in the press, as was the news that, while admiring the pictures, the Prime Minister had 'deplored the fact that they had not a better building in which to show such a magnificent collection'.[4]

The campaign for a better building would now come to preoccupy Lane and his supporters. In his preface to the gallery catalogue published in January 1908, he had stated: 'I have also deposited here my collection of pictures by Continental artists, and intend to present the most of them, provided that the promised permanent building is erected on a suitable site within the next few years.'[5] It was only in July 1912 that Dublin Corporation acquired legal authority to levy funds for the maintenance of the gallery, and Lane immediately began pressing for more permanent premises to be found. He told Ruth Shine early that month: 'People are pretending to be very anxious for a gallery but not taking any sensible steps to get it. However, I am making the Lord Mayor announce my determined intention to remove my conditional gift in Jan. next unless the building is forthcoming.'[6] On 13 July, the *Irish Times* reported: 'a very real danger remains. We understand that many of the more valuable pictures in the collection have been lent by Sir Hugh Lane on the condition that adequate and suitable accommodation shall be provided for them.'[7]

Where or what that accommodation might be was as yet unclear, but Lane had already begun to make his own plans for its decoration. In spring 1912, he had offered three prizes of £100 each for artists to produce designs for panels measuring eight feet square to be approved by him and to be installed in the proposed new Dublin gallery. Announced in June and exhibited in London, the winning works were by Walter Bayes for *Irish Linen*, Frederick Cayley Robinson for *The Coming of St Patrick* and James Mark Willcox for *Deirdre presenting Cuchulain to her Husband*. Although their themes were Irish, the artists were not. Nor were most of the pictures which Lane continued to add to the Municipal Gallery's collection. In late July 1912, he announced a further donation of nine works including Millais's *The Return of the Dove to the Ark*,

Daubigny's *Portrait of Daumier as an Old Man* and a Boudin beach scene.[8]

Around the same time, Lane settled, at least in his own mind, where the new gallery should be located. This was St Stephen's Green, which had been open to the general public since 1880 when the cost of landscaping its park had been borne by Arthur Guinness, Lord Ardilaun. Twelve years later, a bronze statue of the benefactor had been erected on the west side of the Green facing the Royal College of Surgeons, and it was close to here that Lane now proposed the Municipal Gallery of Modern Art should be built. As with the Johannesburg project, he quickly decided who ought to be given the design job; on 21 August 1912 he told Lady Gregory, 'Lutyens has promised me to architect the new Gallery (Dublin) and *garden* in exchange for an Old Master, so that now we only want the £25,000 and Stephen's Green'.[9] By mid-October Lutyens had sent him preliminary sketches of the building, a long, low classical pavilion approached via a flight of steps and fronted by a spacious portico. It needed to be seen, the architect suggested, through feathery 'Corot-like' ash trees amidst which would stand 'faun nymphs or leprechauns', while Lord Ardilaun's statue would be relocated in a front piazza.[10] Lane was so pleased with this design that he promised to add £10,000 to what he had already promised if the site were given.

Unfortunately, neither the septuagenarian Ardilaun nor his wife – who had donated two pictures to the Harcourt Street gallery – were much taken with this scheme, and since the peer had been given a power of veto over what happened in St Stephen's Green when paying for its redesign, Lane's ambitions for this site were frustrated. What would formerly have been only a minor setback now affected Lane much more seriously, and in early November he sent an ultimatum to Dublin's Town Clerk: 'I hereby hand over to the Corporation of Dublin the works of art named in the enclosed list (list 1) "Lane Gift", on the condition that they are always on view free to the public.' This list included Lane's Irish, British and American pictures together with a number of European works such as Rodin's *L'Age d'Airain*. However, he continued, 'The other pictures etc. (list 2) "Lane Collection" will be removed from Dublin at the end of January 1913 if the building of a new and suitable Gallery is not decided upon. But, if the provision of a Gallery is definitely arranged for, the pictures and sculptures will remain on loan until it is built, when they will also be given to the city.'[11] This second group comprised thirty-nine paintings, not least Lane's examples of Impressionism by Manet, Monet, Degas, Renoir, Sisley and Pissarro. He seems to have felt even the threat of the pictures' removal would make little difference, because eight days later he wrote to his aunt from Dublin: 'I have decided to sell my Manet etc. to S. Africa if I remove them at the end of January. I am too ill to do anything more for this horrible country where one can only collect advice. There is not a soul in Dublin with any organising ability.'[12]

In this last opinion, he was about to be proven wrong. On 16 November, the city's Lord Mayor Lorcan Sherlock called together a number of interested individuals, including the Earl of Mayo, Sir Walter Armstrong, Sarah Purser, Sarah Cecilia Harrison, Sir Frederick Shaw and Sir William Hutcheson Pöe, to discuss the site question with him at the Mansion House. Here they formed what was called the Committee for the Provision of a Permanent Municipal Art Gallery (later known more simply as the Mansion House Committee) and decided to hold a public meeting in the same location at the end of the month. Miss Harrison was appointed the organization's secretary and Hutcheson Pöe, Shaw and Sherlock made joint treasurers. In the meantime, members of the new body wrote to the Irish press stessing the urgency of the problem and pointing out that Lane's conditional gift was now worth at least £60,000, 'which is considerably more than the total cost of the pictures forming our National Gallery in Merrion Square'.[13] For the moment, all the country's newspapers were in agreement that the gallery cause was worthy of support, with the *Sunday Independent* declaring: 'It will be seen that speedy action is necessary if these beautiful pictures – the envy of the artistic world – are to be saved for the city.'[14]

The public meeting of 29 November attracted a substantial attendance as well as letters of support for the gallery scheme from, among others, the leader of the Nationalist Party, John Redmond, the Chief Secretary for Ireland Augustine Birrell, George Bernard Shaw – who remembered spending happy hours in the National Gallery of Ireland as a child and donated £100 – and W.B. Yeats. The last of these wrote that 'The men of wealth or the men in power must save this collection'.[15] As a man in power, the Lord Mayor explained that while the Corporation's powers and funds were limited, he felt it could afford to set aside £2,000 annually for the gallery; half of this money would cover maintenance costs and the other half would be used for repayments on a loan taken out to pay for the erection of a new building. However, given that a site would also have to be found and paid for, Yeats's 'men of wealth' still had their part to play. Unhappily, Ireland's leading man of wealth had already declined to help. Ever since Lord Iveagh had donated three pictures to the Municipal Gallery in the autumn of 1908, Lane had been hoping he might be persuaded to do more for the cause of modern art in Ireland. However, Iveagh – like his brother Lord Ardilaun – now proved himself unwilling to be persuaded. Approached for assistance by Lady Mayo, he tersely responded: 'I fear I cannot offer you any advice as to what steps you ought to take in the matter of Sir Hugh Lane's pictures'.[16] As the recipient of this 'haughty letter' observed, Lord Iveagh had effectively declared 'Go to the devil, I will have nothing to do with you'.[17] So, if the exceptionally wealthy would not help, less wealthy members of the public needed to donate between £17,000 and £20,000 over the next two months in order to ensure that the pictures remained in Ireland. A subscription fund was therefore opened, its first donation coming from a never-identified Canadian known only to Lane, who informed the Dublin committee that this mystery donor would give £2,500 provided the balance 'be subscribed by end of January, and that I approve of site and architect'.[18]

On 11 December, Lady Gregory reported to her nephew: 'As to the Dublin meeting I think you have come out all right anyhow, for whether the money is raised or not, your gist has been recognized and advertised, and no one can pretend not to know what you have done and suffered.'[19] She then left Ireland with the Abbey Theatre company for a North American tour which turned into a fund-raising exercise for the Dublin gallery. By the time Lady Gregory departed, just over £5,000 had been collected from local supporters for the scheme – only a quarter of the amount required. So while in Chicago in mid-January 1913, she gave interviews on the subject to the local press, the Abbey presented a matinee performance in aid of the gallery at which £200 was raised, and a group of businessmen then pledged a further £1,000. The same sum was also guaranteed by groups in Philadelphia and Montreal, while Lady Gregory managed to raise additional funds in Boston and New York. Among her other fund-raising initiatives was the production of a linen handkerchief designed by John B. Yeats and carrying images of the theatre company's leading players, as well as a scene from Shaw's *The Shewing-Up of Blanco Posnet*; this item was sold for $1 apiece in aid of the gallery building project. 'If the pictures are saved for Dublin,' Lane wrote to Lady Gregory, 'it is entirely owing to you and the generosity of your American friends.'[20]

But in Dublin new troubles had arisen, initiated perhaps unwittingly by W.B. Yeats who, on 11 January, had published in the *Irish Times* his poem 'The Gift', which was subtitled 'To a friend who promises a bigger subscription than his first to the Dublin Municipal Gallery if the amount collected proves that there is a considerable "popular demand" for the pictures'. The friend in question was Lord Ardilaun, who had incurred the wrath of Yeats by declining to permit St Stephen's Green be used as a site for the gallery and then made matters worse by commenting that there seemed little public support for the project. On the other hand, in mid-December he offered the not-inconsiderable sum of £500 to the building fund, an amount equalled in Ireland only by Hutcheson Pöe. Yeats's poem, contrasting the mean-minded pence and half-pennies of Paudeen and Biddy with the noble generosity of Italian Renaissance patrons, met with Lane's approval; he had told its author that he now 'hated Dublin'.[21] But the piece was hardly likely to encourage Ardilaun into offering additional aid, especially as it was followed by an article on the same page of the *Irish Times* headed 'Art and Aristocracy' in which 'our upper classes' were urged to act as their more beneficent predecessors had done and provide financial assistance for the country's cultural development.[22]

It was only at the end of March that Lord Ardilaun finally replied to critics of his behaviour over St Stephen's Green. Writing to the Irish press from the south of France, he pointed out that the site Lane had wanted was in 'the most beautiful bit of this landscape garden' and that, by the terms of agreement reached when he first offered to pay for its refurbishment, he was forbidden 'from erecting or allowing to be erected any building on the spot'.[23] In the meantime, the poem had caused consider-able indignation in Ireland. The *Irish Catholic*, which had previously decried the extravagance of spending large sums on a gallery 'at a time when the citizens cannot find money for rehousing their poor',[24] now denounced the 'snobbish aristocracy' it claimed was behind the scheme.[25] Similarly, one *Irish Times* reader wrote to the newspaper that Yeats 'can-not free his wings from the viscous stuff that hinders *la petite noblesse de campagne* from rightly estimating its place in a society which no longer rests on the minute pivot of aristocracy but firmly turns on the broader base of popular will and choice'.[26]

The concept of noble patronage espoused by the poet and, as he thought, embodied by Lane was out of step with the increasingly democ-ratic mood of the time, even though the gallery scheme's most formida-ble foe to emerge now had the temperament of an autocrat. Yeats's tone of lofty condescension had caught the attention of the entrepreneur William Martin Murphy, who decided to reply on behalf of the Paudeens of Ireland. Born in Bantry, Co. Cork, in 1844, Murphy was one of the country's wealthiest men, responsible for building railways in Ireland and overseas, and for creating Dublin's highly efficient tramway service. Tall and spare, there was something of the ascetic about him; although a keen supporter of Home Rule, he had strongly opposed Parnell and now brought the same energy to bear against the gallery project. In 1905, Mur-phy had founded his own mass-market daily newspaper, the *Irish Inde-pendent*, but cleverly he chose not to use its columns in which to attack Lane *et al.* A week after Yeats's poem was published, Murphy wrote to the *Daily Express* objecting to the Corporation's proposed expenditure of ratepayers' money on what he termed 'fads or luxuries' at a time when the city's priority ought to be the replacement of 'the foetid slums of Dublin by cheap and decent habitation for the people'. Insisting that he admired the public spirit of the subscribers to the gallery project, he asked only that they achieve their ambition through private benefactions and not the public purse. While he appreciated good pictures, 'I would rather see in the city of Dublin one block of sanitary houses at low rents replacing a reeking slum than all the pictures Corot and Degas ever painted'.[27] Two days later, he wrote to the *Irish Times* on the same subject, sneeringly referring to those who worshipped at 'the shrine of Saint Sir Hugh Lane' and suggesting they 'moderate their ecstasies' by looking at Dublin's deplorable housing conditions.[28]

As subsequent newspaper editorials and correspondents pointed out, Murphy had created a false dilemma: the Corporation had not set aside a certain sum of money to be spent on either a gallery or new homes for the poor, and failure to support one would not necessarily make any difference to the cause of the other. But he was a figure of considerable authority in the city and his opposition could – and would – threaten the gallery's future. Nevertheless, for the moment, the Corporation decided to ignore Murphy's arguments and on 20 January its members voted to provide £22,000 from local rates for the erection of a new building provided the Mansion House Committee presented a site free of all charge, along with a further £3,000 towards the construction costs. On hearing news of this decision in London, Lane, who had been on holiday in Monte Carlo until 1 February, agreed to waive the time limit he had imposed the previous year and allow the conditional gift pictures to remain in Dublin for the moment. In an interview with the *Irish Times* ten days later, he pronounced: 'I am satisfied with the progress that has been made, and I am ready, when the essential features of the scheme are satisfactorily settled, as I hope they will be before I return to London, to proceed with the formalities of handing over the pictures.'[29]

Provided the Mansion House Committee could continue to raise money successfully, the new gallery seemed set to be built. But another problem now became apparent, due to the difficulty of finding a suitable site and Lane's insistence that he have final say in this matter. After Lord Ardilaun had refused permission to build in St Stephen's Green, many other locations had been considered, among them Merrion Square, the old Turkish baths on Lincoln Place, a disused skating rink on Earlsfort Terrace, the former College of Science on the eastern side of St Stephen's Green (a building subsequently occupied by the Board of Works), a derelict site on Lord Edward Street and an old stableyard on the south side of the Mansion House. None of these met with Lane's approval. He objected to Merrion Square, for example, because it was too quiet a residential area and therefore unlikely to attract sufficient visitors, despite the presence there of the National Gallery of Ireland. 'I feel it to be essential that the house in which the collection is to be placed shall be the most perfect building possible, a work of art in itself,' he told the *Irish Times*, 'and that it shall have a situation favourable to its architectural beauty.'[30] To his aunt he explained: 'The Mansion House site does not give us any scope for a fine building which is even more necessary to Dublin than pictures. It is more than 100 years since a good piece of architecture has been raised in Ireland.'[31]

To his mind, that good piece of architecture would be a bridge gallery spanning the river Liffey. The idea had first been proposed the previous November when Sarah Harrison was contacted by a Dublin architect, Frank Craig, who subsequently sent a copy of his correspondence to the *Freeman's Journal* and the *Irish Times*. He suggested the gallery should be built over the river, but attached to the eastern side of O'Connell Bridge between Burgh and Eden Quays. While there might be certain technical difficulties, he argued this design 'should meet all Sir Hugh Lane's requirements as to a central situation, and from an architectural point of view would offer opportunities which a Continental town would eagerly grasp. In fact, it might almost be said that we have the example of Florence for such an arrangement.'[32] The bridge scheme immediately appealed to Lane and his supporters, not least because – like Yeats's 'The Gift' – it contained resonances of Renaissance Italy; but by late January (when 383 subscribers had promised £6,532 for the gallery) Grattan Bridge further up-river was being considered in preference to O'Connell Bridge. Early the following month, fresh urgency was given to the search for a site when a violent storm in Dublin blew off part of the roof of the Harcourt Street gallery, damaging work in the sculpture room. Attention shifted to another river crossing, the Ha'penny Bridge, pedestrian in both function and design. Then covered in advertising hoardings, this footbridge, although still standing today, had always been intended to have a relatively short lifespan. Lane imagined its replacement as a spacious sequence of rooms through which the city's population could continue to walk while simultaneously having the opportunity to admire works of contemporary art. 'Instead of the present eyesore,' he told the *Irish Times* on 11 February, 'a beautiful gallery would be seen from O'Connell Bridge.'[33]

As intense correspondence in Irish newspapers throughout spring 1913 testified, the audacity of his intentions could not be ignored. Among the many reasons for opposing his plan cited by letter writers was a concern that the Liffey's frequently noxious fumes might damage paintings and an anxiety that the river's western view would be blocked by a large structure rising at least forty feet high; on the latter point, a surprising number of citizens now declared themselves passionate admirers of the Liffey skyline at sunset. On 19 February, even the customarily supportive *Irish Times* was obliged to conclude that a river gallery was not popular; 'The objections to it are many and are almost universally felt'.[34] Despite this opposition, however, exactly a month later, the Corporation held a special meeting at which the adoption of a bridge site, subject to the approval of the Board of Trade, was agreed by a majority of councillors. The authority would give £22,000 as already promised, but the balance of the £45,000 that Lutyens expected his bridge gallery to cost had to come from private funds. The *Irish Times* exclaimed, 'Today art-lovers in Dublin and throughout Ireland will breathe a sigh of relief. Sir Hugh Lane's splendid gift has been saved to the city.'[35]

This was wishful thinking because the debate had not been concluded yet. In the same newspaper, a local architect called E.A. Aston now published his plans for a new 'central highway' running from north to south Dublin, which was intended to encourage the redevelopment of an area almost totally given over to dereliction and slums. Beginning at the junction of Mary and Henry Streets and concluding on Dame Street, this new route would cross the river at precisely the point where the metal bridge stood but would permit vehicular traffic and not just pedestrians.[36] Widely debated – and broadly supported by commercial business interests in the capital – this scheme, had it been implemented, would have precluded the gallery bridge on the same site.

But the greatest disquiet was engendered by Lane's choice of architect: once again he insisted that Lutyens be given the job. The architect considered this 'an idea so full of imagination and possibility that it is almost impossible to resist'.[37] He produced a plan showing broad stone-clad and top-lit pavilions on either side of the quays linked by a single-span porticoed bridge. The challenge remained to win popular support in

Dublin for this design. Back in early December 1912, a correspondent signing himself 'Corkman' had predicted that the key problem with the gallery project in the months ahead would be Lane's demand that he be given final approval of both site and architect. With regard to the latter, 'Corkman' pointed out, 'he suggests a foreigner who happens to have a large practice in England. We have plenty of good architects in Ireland quite capable of doing the work.' Lane, he concluded, was guilty of arrogance, insisting on the retention of certain 'rights' even though public money was to be spent on the gallery.[38]

Other dissenting voices also demanded to be heard. Both the Royal Institute of the Architects of Ireland and the Architectural Association of Ireland issued statements insisting that a public competition for the gallery scheme be held so that their own members could be considered for the task. Lane's placatory suggestion – that, as in Johannesburg, a local architect be given the opportunity to collaborate with Lutyens – understandably met with little support. He hoped that William Orpen's brother Richard, who had a successful practice in Dublin, might agree to be the project's Irish collaborator, but this proposal was rejected. As Richard Orpen's partner of the time observed, 'Had he consented, he would have been regarded by many people as a sort of local agent for Lutyens – an undignified position for a man of his status.'[39] Lane appears to have possessed no understanding of the depth of nationalist feeling that had arisen in Ireland during the previous decade, as evidenced by widespread support for the Home Rule Bill being promoted by the government in London. By early 1913, opposition to this bill among Ulster Unionists had in turn led to the creation of a Volunteer Force, and a political crisis, possibly even civil war, now seemed distinctly possible. Lane's determination to impose on Dublin an English architect – and Lutyens was universally seen as English, even though his mother Mary Gallwey had been Irish – was poorly timed and certain to cause offence.

His behaviour may be explained partly by ignorance of, even indifference to, politics and, more importantly, by his absence from Ireland for much of 1913. Discussing the gallery controversy with Lady Gregory, Alderman Thomas Kelly insisted: 'If Lane had stayed in this country, it would have been alright.'[40] But these were the very months when he was concluding arrangements for the Michaelis Gift and then attempting to resolve the difficulties that had arisen from the collection's show in London. His professional life was experiencing its own crisis at a time when poor health left him with little energy to engage in fresh disputes. Remaining in London, he left most of the gallery project's management to the Mansion House Committee; to his opponents, this behaviour only confirmed the impression that Lane was an Englishman determined to tell the Irish he knew what was best for them. As a correspondent to the *Irish Independent* on 20 August remarked, Lane's behaviour over the gallery was like that of his aunt, Lady Gregory, 'who says we must have the *Playboy of the West* [sic] with the help of England's police and England's police magistrates'.[41] In many respects, therefore, the gallery battle of 1913 can be read not as a dispute between those who cared about contemporary art and those who were indifferent to the subject but as a metaphor for the ongoing power struggle between the old Ascendency order and a new Ireland – nationalist, Catholic and middle-class – then taking definitive shape. For the latter group, acquiescing to Lane's demands would be a politically retrogressive act, ceding power back to a representative of the class from which they were still attempting to wrest it.

The impression of Lane as a cultural dictator was only confirmed when, at the end of April, he declared: 'I do not believe in listening to the "man in the street," as any new or original scheme is opposed by the "man in the street" because he does not understand it.'[42] Three months later, in a newspaper interview, he pronounced: 'All the Goths and Vandals, Huns and Visigoths, who don't know what is ugly or nice, or rather, who prefer the ugly to the beautiful, are in the opposition ... They are all people of bad taste, which is worse than no taste.'[43] The tone of his remarks was not helpful to the cause, as Lady Gregory observed when she wrote to Yeats that 'the ungraciousness of Hugh and the vulgarity of the opposition and the contempt shown towards art makes one ashamed as one so often is of Dublin'.[44]

Meanwhile, the gallery scheme's detractors grew more vociferous. Already at the end of March, a delegation of opponents to the scheme, including members of architectural and business groups, had met the

Lord Mayor and asked him to use his influence to have the Corporation's resolution in favour of the bridge site rescinded. They were unsuccessful but, conscious of the depth of public hostility to the gallery, the Corporation now began to engage in stalling tactics. Only in late June did it gather to examine a report from Lutyens on his design; and then, a motion that work be permitted to begin at once being rejected, more information was requested on such matters as 'the actual cost of the gallery' and the value and number of pictures in Lane's conditional gift. After these details were provided a week later, the Corporation asked if the gallery committee could amend its plans for the bridge site so that it might be used by vehicular as well as pedestrian traffic.

In early July, William Martin Murphy, now perceived by Lane and his supporters as their most dangerous opponent, announced his intention to set up a rival committee which would 'take every possible step to defeat the present proposals for building over the river'. His own newspaper had become a mouthpiece for Murphy's opinions on the gallery, and in the *Irish Independent* he commented: 'Outside of a very small number of people who see, or pretend to see, transcendent beauties in an eccentric school of French painting, the mass of people in Dublin don't care a thraneen whether Sir Hugh Lane's conditional pictures are left here or taken away.'[45] A few days later, one of that very small number, W.B. Yeats, speaking in London at an Abbey Theatre benefit performance in aid of the gallery, warned: 'If Hugh Lane is defeated, hundreds of young men and women all over the country will be discouraged ... Ireland will for many years become a little huckstering nation, groping for halfpence in a greasy till.'[46] In an introduction to his *Responsibilities* the following year, Yeats would declare that during the previous thirty years three public controversies had stirred his indignation: the downfall of Parnell; the dispute over Synge's *Playboy*; and the Corporation's failure to build a gallery for Lane's pictures.[47]

Even in late summer 1913 that failure did not yet seem inevitable, although support for Murphy's group was rapidly gaining ground after a public meeting in late July unanimously pledged opposition to the gallery. Lane's tactless response was to inform Dublin's Lord Mayor that a picture he had recently bought at Christie's for more than £4,500 and had intended to donate to the Municipal Gallery, he was now selling on to the National Gallery of Scotland. In a widely publicized letter announcing this intention, he declared the painting 'will serve as an historical monument to Dublin's want of public spirit and taste' before going on to insist that Lutyens's bridge design – 'one of the most beautiful and remarkable buildings of modern times' – would 'set a standard for Irish architects to work up to'.[48] He had, by now, lost patience even with his own supporters in Ireland, ungratefully telling Lady Gregory: 'I look on the Dublin crowd as hopeless. If I had a few Murphys on my side, all would have been well.'[49] She tried to placate him and, at the same time, gently suggested that while of course the bridge site 'ought to be pushed and held to as long as is possible' he might also like to reconsider the option of Merrion Square.[50] But by now Lane had become resolute: 'The site question has been gone into very thoroughly. Lutyens & myself & Sir W. Armstrong consider Merrion Square a very bad site.'[51] The matter was no longer open to discussion.

In the midst of so much disputation, there were occasional light moments. At the United Arts Club, a ditty on the bridge controversy was performed by Ellen Duncan's husband James and an architect called Frank Sparrow, who respectively played the parts of Lane and the Lord Mayor.

MAYOR: On the banks of the Liffey water,
                Where the main drain meets the sea;
                That's the very place we oughter
                Build our gallery.

LANE: On the site we have selected
                All the tramway men may see
                An ante-mortally erected
                Monument to me.

BOTH: Tho' in muddy waters fishing,
                All is fish that we shall get;
                All the fish for which we're wishing
                Will come to our net.[52]

The Corporation met again in late July, and again prevaricated, arranging for a sub-committee to meet with Lane who had come over to Dublin. On August 1st, he removed the conditional gift pictures from the Municipal Gallery. 'It is my last trump card,' he told Lady Gregory, adding that when the Corporation's delegates came to see him, 'I will show them the gaps and say that if they get me the river site I will return the lot'.[53] In fact, he went to see the sub-committee and came to an agreement whereby it would recommend to the Corporation that the bridge gallery be built in return for which Lane would promise to cover any costs above Lutyens's £45,000 estimate and permit the conditional gift pictures to be retained on display in the Mansion House for the next six weeks. 'You are applauded and I am more than ever proud of you,' wrote Lady Gregory when she heard his news. 'You have made a more generous offer than ever! I wonder what Murphy will say now.'[54] Murphy said nothing, but the Dublin Chamber of Commerce, of which he was president, passed a resolution protesting against the construction of anything other than a vehicular bridge over the Liffey. And two new groups opposed to the intended gallery now emerged, the Central Highways Committee and the River Liffey Protection Association, both of which sent deputations to the Corporation on 11 August. Ten days later, that body held yet another meeting to consider the gallery question but still could not reach a consensus. By this time, reasoned debate among the city's elected representatives had been almost abandoned in favour of such exchanges as:

> Mr Richardson: You are a liar.
> Mr Partridge: You are a corner boy.[55]

Lady Gregory would report the remarks of various Corporation members to Lane: how one had described Puvis de Chavannes's *Martyrdom of St John the Baptist* as 'a travesty of art' and another another had insisted that 'Irish artists could paint pictures like that if they liked'. As for Lutyens's design, a councillor announced this was 'an exact replica of a picture he had seen of a bridge' somewhere else.[56] Meanwhile, other business had now come to demand much of the Corporation's attention. At the start of September, the appalling condition of the city's housing was highlighted when two tenement buildings on Church Street collapsed, killing six people. To many Dubliners, the idea of spending £22,000 of the city's scarce funds on an art gallery seemed ever more preposterous. Just as seriously, in late August the labour leader James Larkin called a strike of the tramway unions, leading to a lockout of workers by the Dublin Employers Federation. Larkin had been an admirer of Lane's project, and his supporters in Dublin included William Orpen, George Russell and W.B. Yeats. Correspondingly, his greatest opponent was the owner of the Dublin United Tramways Company, William Martin Murphy. Thanks to the policies adopted by the Employers Federation, which Murphy had helped to establish two years earlier, before the end of September 1913 some 25,000 workers had been locked out of their jobs for refusing to sign a pledge that they would not join the Irish Transport and General Workers Union.

It was against this appalling backdrop that the Corporation met once more to attempt a resolution in the gallery dispute. And once more Lane seems not to have appreciated adequately the circumstances in Ireland, because he wrote to Lady Gregory: 'Quite a few apparently sane people have said to me sympathetically, "It is a pity that you chose this moment to ask for a gallery, what with the strike and the falling houses".'[57] For him, these disasters were inconveniences. For the Corporation, however, it was the gallery question that had become a tiresome matter about which far too much had been said and written without any result. Nor did Lane yet understand how much antagonism had been engendered by his advocacy of Lutyens. He told a journalist from the *Manchester Guardian* that patriotic arguments left him unimpressed, pointing out that 'the most beautiful and characteristic buildings in Dublin erected in the times of Irish Independence were almost without exception the work of English architects'.[58] In case this remark was insufficiently inflammatory, on 8 September, as the Corporation's members prepared to meet one more time, Yeats published his poem 'Romance in Ireland (On reading much of the correspondence against the Art Gallery)' in the *Irish Times*. Here he once again referred to fumbling in greasy tills as well as to shivering prayers, and contrasted the narrow meanness of contemporary Ireland with the dignity and romance of an earlier period, exemplified by three eighteenth-century Irish Protestants, Lord Edward Fitzgerald, Robert Emmet and Theobald Wolfe Tone. The Corporation members were unmoved by Yeats's words but still could not reach agreement on the gallery, so their decision was postponed for a further week. On this occasion, the number of representatives who turned up for the meeting was insufficient; some of those who were present alleged intimidation from opponents of the gallery scheme.

That group was in triumphalist mood. On 13 September, the *Dublin Saturday Herald* published a mock obituary: 'Yesterday in the Municipal Morgue an inquest was held on the remains of the Art Gallery project which was discovered in a very mutilated condition the previous day.'[59] Nonetheless, the Lord Mayor called one final special meeting on 19 September at which almost every elected representative was present. Sarah Harrison, Lane's most consistently loyal supporter and a member of the Corporation, moved a resolution approving the bridge site and all her friend's conditions. This had no possibility of winning sufficient support. An alternative motion was presented by one of her fellow councillors declaring the bridge site unsuitable and requiring Lane to leave the location and design of the gallery to the discretion of the Corporation. This was carried by thirty-two votes to twenty-five. That night, Lane announced he would be removing the conditional pictures from Dublin. He had lost the battle for the building of a new gallery.

15

TWO NATIONAL GALLERIES BECKON

Observed across the divide of more than eighty-five years, Lane's intractability appears to have been responsible for the failure of his art gallery plan in Dublin. Had he been prepared to compromise over the questions of site and architect, agreement with the Corporation might have been reached. But would the building have gone ahead? Within twelve months of the city authority's decision not to proceed with the project, the First World War had broken out and all such schemes were put on hold. Then came the Easter Rising and, once the war had ended in 1918, the struggle for Irish independence and the emergence of a new state. What likelihood was there of a gallery being constructed in the centre of Dublin during this volatile period? Lane himself, while obviously unaware of future events in Ireland, knew he would be wise to make alternative arrangements for his collection of pictures. As far back as January 1907, he had drafted a letter to Sir Charles Holroyd, Director of the National Gallery in London, offering that institution a two-year loan of his modern pictures, 'believing that the fact of their being shown in a famous London Gallery for a few years would make the Dublin authorities realise their merit & educational value. I am sorry to say that they think these pictures are not worth the price of the frames!'[1]

Nothing came of this approach, not least because shortly afterwards Dublin Corporation did bestir itself to lease the Harcourt Street gallery. But the possibility of London providing an alternative home for the works included in his conditional gift remained and in mid-January 1913, Lane wrote to Sarah Harrison telling her he expected to meet D.S. MacColl and Charles Aitken, respectively former and current Keeper of the Tate Gallery: 'They are making love to me – to try and get the Dublin pictures to found a new gallery in London'.[2] After this encounter, he told her that the two men, together with art connoisseur Robert Witt, had begged him 'to give the French pictures to London. They stated (semi-officially) that the Government would probably provide a Gallery and funds to make a Continental Gallery of Art, and that I would be asked to be director! I said that I would lend them the pictures for a time if I removed them from Dublin.'[3]

So in July 1913, as negotiations in Ireland dragged on, Lane contacted Sir Charles Holroyd and offered to lend the collection to the National Gallery. Soon Robert Ross was writing to Lane commiserating over the delays in Dublin but commenting of the pictures: 'I am wicked enough to hope that you would be so annoyed that you finally decide to give them to London. It will be one of the greatest coups of modern times.'[4] Holroyd seemed just as keen on this plan. Within a week of hearing from Lane, he replied that the offer of a loan was 'most welcome to me personally' and promised to raise the matter at the August meeting of the gallery board.[5] At the end of the month, Lane informed Lady Gregory that he had received a visit from Holroyd, accompanied by Lord Curzon, one of the National Gallery's trustees, and Charles Aitken. This delegation asked him to donate the pictures in question to London 'if they got a new building'. Still loyal to the concept of a new Irish gallery, he declined this offer for the paintings 'but offered to lend them to the N.G. This they are "considering".'[6] 'As I still hope that my work in Dublin will not prove a failure,' he explained to Curzon, 'I cannot think of giving them to any other gallery at present.'[7]

On 12 August, the National Gallery trustees duly informed Lane they would be happy to accept a loan of his conditional gift paintings 'on the understanding, however, that they will be unable to exhibit the pictures until the completion of a new room now under construction over the portico at Trafalgar Square'.[8] At the end of the month, Curzon in turn wrote to say: 'I am sorry for Dublin's sake that those stupid idiots there seem bent upon depriving themselves of your gallery ... However, it is our gain and I hope your arrangements for the loan exhibition in N.G. will go ahead alright.'⁹

And so, long before Dublin Corporation declared itself unable to accept Lane's terms, he had organized for the conditional gift to go to the National Gallery in London. After the vote of 18 September, a delay in the pictures' removal from Dublin arose because the city's dockers had joined Larkin's strike; almost nothing was permitted to leave the port. London was not the only beneficiary of a loan from Lane at this moment. At the end of August, the *Northern Whig* asked 'Is there a chance for Belfast?' and suggested 'If Sir Hugh made to the capital of the North the offer which Dublin has rejected, Belfast would be found more appreciative of the gift and more reasonable in meeting the wishes of the donor'.¹⁰ Three weeks later, the same newspaper reported that Lane had offered to lend Belfast's Free Library committee a selection of paintings by English artists.¹¹ His personal property, these had been removed from Dublin's Municipal Gallery at the same time as the conditional gift. Uncertain how best to respond to this proposal, the library's board chose to postpone making a decision for a fortnight. 'The result', chastised the *Northern Whig*, 'is that a handsome offer, the acceptance of which would have given pleasure to every true lover of art in Belfast, is shelved without even a word of thanks and recognition, and a slight is offered to Sir Hugh Lane which will probably produce a prompt withdrawal of the offer.'¹²

'Attach no importance to the course adopted yesterday by the Library and Technical Instruction Committee,' Belfast's Lord Mayor wrote to Lane, adding: 'If I had a conversation with you, as I shall hope to have, I assure you that you would merely smile at the actions of these gentlemen. Of course, the matter is serious as it seems to make Belfast ridiculous'.¹³ Hastily recognizing the error of its decision, the board now rescinded the earlier resolution and wrote a fulsome letter of thanks to Lane, who arrived in Belfast at the end of September to hang the pictures at the local art society's annual exhibition. Among the works he lent were a portrait of Lady Charles Beresford by Sargent, Burne-Jones's *Sleeping Princess*, views of Howth by Orpen and Hone, and two landscapes by Steer. One painting, Augustus John's monumental *Decorative Group*, caused controversy in some Belfast circles when it was observed that a woman carrying a child was not wearing a wedding ring.

Back in Dublin, the despondent members of the Mansion House Committee who had campaigned on behalf of the gallery now faced the task of returning to donors all their subscriptions, which now totalled close to £12,000. The following January, this group met for the last time and, having passed a resolution of appreciation for Lane's 'generous and public spirited effort in the cause of Art in Ireland', formally disbanded.[14] Lady Gregory was not so easily rid of her association with the campaign and its fund-raising efforts. Members of the Abbey Theatre company now began to argue that the money collected for the gallery at their benefit performances should be given to them. Lady Gregory wanted to retain the sum for what she hoped would be the next stage in Lane's battle for a new gallery; 'those play actors are the limit!' he sympathized when told of her troubles. 'Sooner than give them the money, do give it to Larkin to help him best Murphy!'[15] Eventually the players had to threaten Lady Gregory with legal proceedings before she would agree to arbitration. To her disappointment, the Irish Attorney-General gave an opinion in the performers' favour and eventually the money had to be released.

In any case, the likelihood of Lane engaging with the Corporation must have seemed remote. The fight of the previous year had left him exhausted and bitter. In late September, through the columns of the Irish press, he engaged in an undignified spat with one Dublin councillor, David Quaid, whom he accused of telling 'an impudent lie' about him – a lie, he then suggested, which 'can, perhaps, be excused on the grounds of stupidity'.[16] A few days later, writing to Lady Gregory from Belfast, he declared: 'I am always most anxious to get out of Ireland. My early romantic notion of it was got in my childhood [visits to] Galway & I am now so completely disillusioned that I don't want to be reminded of those early happy days.'[17] It was in this frame of mind that, back at Lindsey House in London the following month, he wrote a new will. This document bequeathed legacies to each member of his family and a wide circle of friends before going on to leave the bulk of his estate to the National Gallery of Ireland 'to be invested & the income to be spent on buying pictures of deceased painters of established merit'. His portrait by Sargent, the pictures currently on loan to Belfast and 'any modern pictures of merit (John drawings etc.)' were left to the Municipal Gallery but, significantly, Lane bequeathed the original conditional gift of paintings, then about to be lent to England's National Gallery, 'to found a collection of Modern Continental Art in London'. As his will went on to elaborate, he hoped the loss of the thirty-nine pictures 'will be remembered by the Dublin Municipality & others as an example of its want of public spirit in the year 1913 & for the folly of such bodies assuming to decide on questions of Art instead of relying on expert opinion'.[18] Telling Yeats of his actions a few weeks later, Lane explained that he had decided to wait for Home Rule in the hope that an Irish parliament would be more sympathetic than Dublin Corporation had been. In the meantime, according to Yeats, Lane would create 'a completely new collection' since he was 'tired of the old one and knows so much more now'.[19] When Lady Gregory then wrote to her nephew on the same subject, he responded in a franker fashion: 'You give me too much credit for my intentions towards Dublin. I hate the place & the people & the Gallery.'[20]

Persistent ill-health did little to improve his spirits. Two years earlier, he had been diagnosed as suffering from a nervous condition known as neurasthenia. First coined as a medical term in 1880, neurasthenia was a general term for a psychological illness with physical manifestations; in all cases, its causes were probably excessive stress and inner anxieties. Sufferers, who included Bernard Berenson during the same period, experienced constant weakness, irritability and a sense of overwhelming lassitude. Already in the autumn of 1911, Lane had told his aunt: 'The doctors say that I can never really be rid of neurasthenia – I have left it too long. But they say by living a quiet life without worry! that I shall get much better.'[21] For Lane, however, the following two years were plagued with worries and so his state only worsened. His hair now started to thin (he tried what the vendor promised him was 'the infallible cure for baldness'[22]) and he looked for means of recovering youthful vitality. By September 1913 he had opted to try a course of hypnosis. The costs were high, he informed Lady Gregory, twenty guineas for the first week and two guineas for each half hour thereafter, 'but it has done me no good so far'.[23] Perhaps this poor response was because he did not give the treatment his undivided attention. Thomas Bodkin travelled with him to one session and waited in Lane's car while the patient was supposed to be undergoing hypnosis. At the end of the session his friend emerged and told Bodkin the experience had been 'ineffectual so far as he could judge, and yet rather funny'. It transpired that after talking to Lane for a while, the specialist had left him alone with instructions to count to one thousand. But 'when he went out I just popped up and arranged his beastly mantelpiece for him, and when I heard him coming back, I lay on the couch and pretended to be asleep'.[24]

One of the sharpest portraits of Lane at this time was written by the American novelist Theodore Dreiser, who in early 1914 published a semi-fictional work called *A Traveller at Forty*. Based on time spent in Europe during the previous two years when he had taken several trips with Grant Richards, Dreiser's book features the former's friend Lane as Sir Scorp, 'an Irish knight and art critic, a gentleman who had some of the finest Manets in the world'. He is described as 'a pale, slender, dark-eyed man of thirty-five or thereabouts, with a keen, bird-like glance, a poised, nervous, sensitive manner, and that elusive subtlety of reference and speech which marks the notable intellectual wherever you find him'.[25] The name allotted to him, it soon becomes clear, derived from Lane's scorpion-like sarcasm and his inability to let any conversation pass without a sneer. Dreiser assigned several chapters of *A Traveller* to the holiday he took in the south of France with Richards (here called Barfleur) and Lane in early 1912. As in Richards's own novel, many of Lane's most distinctive character traits were noted here, not least an extravagance at the gaming tables of Monte Carlo contrasted with his resistance to the idea of spending money on food and drink. 'If Sir Scorp had been born with a religious, reforming spirit instead of a penchant for art,' wrote Dreiser, 'he would have been a St Francis of Assisi. As it was, without anything else to base it on, except Barfleur's gormandising propensities, he had already established moral censorship over our actions.'[26] In the mornings, Scorp is portrayed as unwilling to stir out of bed, where he could be found with 'his ascetic face crowned by his brownish black hair and set with those burning dark eyes – a figure of almost classic significance'.[27] When Dreiser departed alone for Italy, Scorp recommended a series of inexpensive restaurants and suggested he have his portrait painted by Mancini, 'which I could have done, he assured me, with a letter from him'.[28]

Unhappy as he was during much of this period, Lane at least found consolation in the company of his sister Ruth. Her husband James Hickman Shine had died in March 1912; as the couple had no children, legally she had no rights to his property, which passed to another relative. Left without a home, she came to live permanently with her brother at Lindsey House. It was an arrangement that suited them both, because of all his siblings Lane had always been closest to his sister, discussing all his work with her and insisting her taste had become 'a formidable rival to mine'.[29] Lady Gregory was equally pleased with this arrangement, since it meant someone would be almost permanently on hand to see to Lane's welfare. 'Do make him take you to a really good restaurant every evening and feed himself up,' she instructed her niece. 'He didn't eat half enough. Make him pay by the week for a meal at a tempting place and then he will feel it an economy using it, like a motor.'[30]

Ruth Shine's companionship was one boost at this time; another was the news that a wealthy American collector wished to buy one of the most valuable paintings then in his possession. Lane had bought Titian's portrait of Philip II of Spain from Agnew's in late 1912 for an undisclosed sum. On 10 November he told his sister that an intermediary called Mrs Newport had found someone willing to pay £60,000 for the picture; that person was a Mrs Emery of Cincinnati, who wished to present the Titian to her local museum, where it still remains.[31] When word of the sale became public, it caused a considerable stir in the English press. 'I've been on the track of this great painting for years,' Lane told one interviewer. 'I first saw it in Germany when I was a youth of nineteen and I was fascinated by the wonderful workmanship. No picture has affected me so strongly.'[32] 'I have been inundated with reporters today,' he informed Thomas Bodkin's mother when writing a letter of thanks for her usual birthday cake, 'about my "Titian" which I recently sold to an American collector who is giving it to a public gallery. The papers stated that I had sold it for £80,000. I wish I had! Still, it was a big sum for anyone to give who had only seen a photograph of it.'[33]

The Philip II portrait was Lane's first sale to the United States, which is extraordinary given the rapid growth in that market over the preceding decade as well as Lady Gregory's extensive trans-Atlantic contacts. She had been urging him for some time to travel to New York for business, conscious that from the late 1890s onwards the principal buyers of European old master paintings were American collectors such as J.P. Morgan, Benjamin Altman, Henry Clay Frick and the Bostonian Isabella Stewart Gardner. There is no obvious reason why Lane did not follow his aunt's advice – as well as the example of other dealers such as Joseph Duveen – and begin making commercial contacts with the United States. When he did eventually begin to consider negotiating with American millionaires, he operated through third parties such as Mrs Newport or Lady Gregory's great friend (and erstwhile lover) the Irish-American lawyer and advocate of modern art John Quinn. The two men had known each other for some years and Lane may have considered Quinn as a possible patron for the Dublin gallery; in late August 1909 Lady Gregory told her nephew he had made a great impression on the lawyer 'but I think he is more for buying pictures for himself than giving them away'.[34] By August 1912 Quinn, who gave as much support as Lane to both John B. Yeats and Augustus John, was offering to speak to Frick in New York about the Rembrandt portrait which would cause so much trouble with Max Michaelis the following spring. Lane was pessimistic about the chances of an American sale for the picture. 'If Frick does not write I will hardly be disappointed,' he wrote to Lady Gregory. 'Every picture buyer gets so many offers of this kind that nothing less than a good talk would awaken a real desire to see the picture.'[35]

As he had expected, Frick did not show interest in the Rembrandt, but following the Cincinnati sale Lane decided the United States was worth more attention than he had so far given it. In a draft letter to Mrs Newport, he declared: 'I think that America produces very remarkable women! You & Mrs Emery have no end of grit.'[36] Americans also appeared to have no end of money, unlike Lane who was then in need of funds. Within days of agreeing to sell the Titian, he wrote to Lady Gregory that a colleague, Charles Carstairs, who represented the American art dealers Knoedler & Co. in London, had invited him across the Atlantic. 'I rather dread the idea, but as I am hard up & it may lead to the selling of a picture (he wants me to lend him my Gainsboroughs for an exhibition he is arranging in New York) I think I must go.' Typically anxious not to spend more than was necessary on personal comfort, Lane added that he did not want to take Carstairs's advice on hotels, 'as he is most extravagant. Your kind of hotel will suit me better.'[37] Lane sent a trio of Gainsboroughs to New York but despite American collectors' widely acknowledged fondness for English portraits, none of these works found buyers; all three now belong to the National Gallery of Ireland. Nor did Lane personally fare well on his first visit to New York, where he arrived on 9 January 1914 and spent the next fortnight. He shared none of his aunt's enthusiasm for the city and its people, had little contact with John Quinn, was rebuffed by Mrs Gardner when he tried to meet her in Boston, and found the entire visit had served little purpose. 'I did not like the American collectors,' he announced on his return. 'They simply (most of them) buy pictures to outdo their neighbours & have no taste.'[38]

Back in London, he had to contend with the poor taste shown by another member of his circle. At the beginning of the year, George Moore published *Vale*, the third and final volume of his memoirs *Hail and Farewell*; wisely he had decided to leave Dublin and settle in London before the first volume, *Ave*, had come out in 1911. Extracts from the latest book had already appeared in the *English Review*, the January 1914 issue of this magazine carrying a chapter called 'Yeats, Lady Gregory and Synge'. The last of these was dead, but the other two did not care for the way in which they had been described by Moore. Specifically, Lady Gregory was outraged to read his claim that she had been an 'ardent soul-gatherer' when young and still living at Roxborough with her proselytising mother.[39] Given the tenor of the times in Ireland and her association with the Abbey Theatre, such accusations were especially damaging and Lady Gregory therefore demanded – and received – assurances from Moore's publisher that the text of *Vale* would be altered to remove any suggestion that she had ever attempted to convert Catholics to Protestantism. The author, meanwhile, wrote to reassure her that no harm had been intended by what he called his 'banter'.[40]

Presumably he expected readers to regard in a similar vein the portions of *Vale* in which Lane was discussed. In these pages, Moore cleverly ascribed many of his more crushing observations to Sir Thornley Stoker, a doctor and antiques collector who had been one of his neighbours in Dublin's Upper Ely Place. The brother of the novelist Bram Stoker, Sir Thornley had conveniently died in 1912 and was therefore not in a position to contest any remarks he was claimed to have made. In *Vale*, it is he who dismisses Lane as 'a London picture-dealer who had come to Ireland to see what he could pick up', while Moore is assigned the role of arguing the defence, insisting that Lane had 'got such pretty ways' and had wanted to 'revive the art of painting'.[41] But even his most supportive comments contained sly digs, such as the suggestion that when Lane called himself a collector rather than a dealer, he was engaging in a current fashion for euphemism: 'He is a collector who weeds out his collection. Let us call him a weeder; and let us never speak of the lavatory but of the cloak-room or the toilet-room'.[42]

Sly digs aside, Moore's exquisitely constructed and unquestionably entertaining prose contained two specific charges that caused Lane both offence and embarassment. One of these was evidence of a certain truth in Sir Thornley Stoker's denunciation of him as a dealer who had come to Ireland in search of pickings; Moore cited the instance of a Lancret painting lent by Sir Algernon Coote to the 1902 old masters exhibition at the RHA and subsequently bought by Lane, who then added a couple of other works before exchanging the lot with Durand-Ruel in Paris for Manet's *Eva Gonzales*. The publication of this transaction displeased both Coote and Lane, but the latter also had to read how, as a young man whose future profession had not yet been decided, he had been spotted examining Lady Gregory's dress one day at lunch. When his aunt went into her bedroom later that afternoon, she 'found her wardrobe open and Hugh trying on her skirts before the glass'.[43] Although Moore then makes clear that the possibility of a career in women's fashion lay behind this incident, an implication of transvestism was unmistakable. Back from New York, Lane informed his aunt: 'I think that I must injunct G. Moore also just as he is about to publish the book!'[44] However, the book's author now departed for Palestine and Lane, distracted by other matters, let *Vale* be published without any changes. On 9 March he asked Lady Gregory had she seen the work. 'It seems fairly nasty all round but I came off worst &

his perfectly untrue insinuations are of a damaging kind. I have asked the opinion of one or 2 friends, who say that an action would greatly advertise the book & they seem to think it had better be left alone.'[45] A month later, he wrote telling her Moore had returned to London and was claiming she had been the source for the dressing-up story. 'Later on he said, "now that I come to think of it to be *quite* accurate it was Yeats who told me which is the same thing".'[46] Moore later insisted he thought Lane would be pleased about the Coote story 'as it shows what a clever dealer you are'.[47] Although some changes were made to the relevant sections at Lane's insistence – to the author's great displeasure – the fundamental details were unaltered and continued to appear in subsequent editions of *Vale*. The idea that Lane liked to wear women's clothing therefore became widespread, although no one other than Moore ever made such a suggestion publicly. William Orpen's recollection of Lane as being keenly interested in supervising the appearance of women he knew is probably closer to the truth. 'Up to the time of his death,' wrote Orpen in *Stories of Old Ireland and Myself*, 'his great joy was to prepare his lady friends when they were going out to Court or balls. He had great art as a hairdresser, and he would deck their tresses with jewels and their ears with rings.'[48] Lane's preoccupation with clothing was like his concern with interior decoration; both reflected a desire to impose his standards of taste on the world around him.

Although irritated by Moore's behaviour, Lane was less upset than might have been expected because another issue now occupied his mind. After twenty-two years as Director of the National Gallery of Ireland, Sir Walter Armstrong was due to retire from the position at the end of March 1914. Lane keenly wanted the job and had begun campaigning for the appointment a year earlier. He had been a member of the board for the past decade, during which period he had advised on the purchase of a number of pictures, donated several to the gallery and lent others for exhibition, not least Titian's *Man in a Red Cap*. While diligent in his attendance at meetings during the first years after his appointment in 1903, he then began to send apologies for his absence with increasing regularity. Most notably, he did not attend a single board meeting between March 1910 and April 1913. But then, hearing news of Armstrong's departure the following year, Lane once more gave National Gallery business his attention and at the August meeting he presented the institution with a gift of five portraits. Earlier in the year, he discovered that his chief rival for Armstrong's post was his friend and ally Dermod O'Brien, the President of the RHA, to whom he had written in early April: 'If a "non-specialist" is to get the Dublin directorship, then I know of no one who deserves a "job" more than you do.' He continued, 'I have always contended that unless a director has a special "flair" – that he is an unnecessary appendage', before disingenuously explaining, 'The Dublin directorship used to be the great longing of my life & it is only serious ill-health & perhaps the realising of how little Dublin cares for work which may cost one one's life's blood that makes me dread a new task. Still, I *would* like to leave my mark at the N.G. and as old pictures are the one thing that I know anything about & really *enjoy* hanging, I feel that in 2 or 3 years – if I live, I may be able to do some lasting good.'⁴⁹ Meanwhile, he was evidently telling other friends of his determination to get the position; in mid-May Joseph Solomon was regretting that soon Lane would not be able to find time for a visit to Cape Town 'owing to your appointment as director of the National Gallery in Ireland'.⁵⁰ And at the end of July, Lane complained to Lady Gregory: 'I hear that Dermod O'Brien has been working at all the Governors of the National Gallery & that he will probably be appointed Director – very *deceitful* of him. But I won't compete.'⁵¹ Yet in late October he was insisting to O'Brien: 'I wish that I could feel any pleasure in the prospect of getting the job, but I feel very thoroughly discouraged with my native country & the gross misunderstanding of everything one tries to do for it.'⁵²

This refusal to confirm publicly his candidacy – due to earlier disappointment when applying for positions – caused some difficulty as the time for Armstrong's retirement drew closer. At the start of December, Lane confirmed to Sarah Purser that were he offered the directorship 'I would undertake to make it my first interest in life', but 'I do not want to *apply* for this post as I have nothing to gain by getting it and much to give'.⁵³ The outgoing director was among those who wanted Lane to be his successor, although he could take no active part in the selection process. However, as the year closed, Armstrong recommended that Lane write to the gallery's chairman J.P. Mahaffy declaring his interest in the position.[54] This advice was acted on the following day. 'I will not formally apply for the post as I do not wish to run the risk of a refusal,' Lane told Mahaffy. 'If you yourself feel that I am the best man for the job, I know that your influence with the board will carry more weight than any others.'[55] He also asked his aunt to intervene with Mahaffy. 'Tell him', he said, 'that if I am appointed to the National Gallery I will make it my adopted child.'[56] Lane then departed for the United States, leaving the matter for his fellow board members to decide. Lady Gregory worked away on his behalf and in January 1914 she felt confident enough to state that 'as far as I can ascertain a majority of the Trustees are safe for Hugh Lane'.[57]

By now, O'Brien had decided not to run for the job, and Lane's only rival was the gallery's registrar Walter Strickland, whose magisterial *Dictionary of Irish Artists* had been published in 1913. Although Strickland's academic qualifications were obviously superior to Lane's, he lacked the latter's social and political connections. Nor could he promise, as did Lane, to donate his salary to the gallery's picture-buying fund. Lane was, therefore, confident of securing the Directorship, particularly as Mahaffy had written to him early in the new year that he was 'in favour of offering you the appt'ment, though some pernickety people would have the thing advertised'.[58] The question of Armstrong's successor was discussed at a gallery meeting on 4 February 1914 when it was discovered that due to mid-nineteenth-century bye-law, a member of the board could not be eligible for the position of Director. Mahaffy therefore adjourned the meeting for three weeks to allow Lane to resign his membership, which he duly did. He was then further discreetly advised by Armstrong that he should inform the Chairman of his wish to be considered for the job. Lane did so very reluctantly on 20 February, and five days later when the board reconvened he was elected the National Gallery of Ireland's new Director 'by the majority of votes'.

Lane was staying with a house party in Buckinghamshire when he received the news and immediately wrote to Armstrong at the gallery expressing his delight: 'I can only say that I will do my utmost to deserve this important trust and to make it my principal interest in life.'[59] An abundance of congratulatory telegrams then arrived, among the first being Thomas Bodkin's 'Heartiest congratulations. We are at last in luck' and Sarah Harrison's 'Thank heaven. A thousand good wishes.' Lady Gregory confined herself simply to saying 'I congratulate Dublin and Ireland.'[60] To W.B. Yeats she was more effusive, writing: 'I awoke this morning more happy and satisfied than for a long time – almost radiant – because of Hugh's election to the Directorship yesterday. It seems as if that barren tide may have turned, and that the worst hour is over.'[61] The many letters sent to Lane by well-wishers included one from the Carlton Gallery's E.T. Turner, with whom he had had legal disputes in the past. 'I cannot help calling to mind at the present time', Turner wrote, 'how fully the intentions you mapped out to me for yourself some 15 or 16 years ago have matured and I know the directorship of one of our national galleries was always the height of your ambition.'[62] Lane's desire for an official position had at last been satisfied.

16
AN OFFICIAL POSITION

Three days after being appointed Director of the National Gallery of Ireland, Lane told Lady Gregory: 'I am feeling very depressed at my new
responsibilities, but I am sure that once I get started it will become
absorbing.'[1] After officially taking up the position on 1 April, he did
quickly become absorbed by the work, not least because the gallery
offered yet another opportunity to exercise his decorating talents. Parts of
the building had recently been refurbished, but Lane decided the work
was not to his liking and before the end of the month had started to leave
his own mark on the premises. The Treasury, which provided all funding
for the gallery and with which he was to be in constant dispute, refused to
give any money for this purpose and so, as he wrote to his aunt in late
April, 'I have begun rehanging and repainting (at my own expense) some
of the shabbier rooms & I have discovered a good picture by N Poussin at
the Castle which had been lent by the NG some years ago, so that I have
demanded its return!'[2] A month later, Lutyens wrote saying he was thinking of Lane 'having entirely redecorated the galleries out of your own
privy purse for the love of it'.[3] The new Director also discovered that he
was entitled to a court uniform. As none existed, he designed one for himself; when made up, it featured lavish quantities of gold embroidery
around the coat's collar and cuffs as well as an extravagantly plumed hat.

Among his more lasting achievements was the production of a new
catalogue for the gallery's collection. While much of the (unattributed)

contents were probably written by Walter Strickland, who continued to hold the position of Registrar, the frankness of opinions expressed certainly owed something to Lane. Daniel Maclise's *Merry Christmas in the Baron's Hall*, for example, is described as 'full of varied expression and complicated grouping; unhappily the colour is bad and the impasto leathery'.[4] Lane was especially conscious of gaps in the gallery's collection. He attempted to remedy any weaknesses by a mixture of purchases and personal donations. At his first board meeting on 22 April, he offered as an outright gift three pictures: a *Portrait of a Lady* by Veronese; a *Decorative Group* from Piazzetta and his studio; and El Greco's *St Francis Receiving the Stigmata*. Further paintings from his personal collection then followed. In June, he gave another four including a Gainsborough landscape, two still lifes by Francois Desportes and a portrait of a man then believed to be by Jacopo Bassano but now attributed to Annibale Carracci. The board was clearly taken aback by such generosity; Lane told his sister after he had presented this second tranche of pictures that the members who had attended the meeting 'said polite things, but I think inquire that they can't be genuine as I am giving them!'[5] Still that response did not prevent him from donating a further four works to the gallery in July. In total, Lane gave twenty-four paintings to the National Gallery of Ireland during his lifetime, and while Director he also lent a number of others – by Claude Lorrain, Poussin, Chardin and Tintoretto – which would later enter the institution's collection.

Such generosity was possible because even after taking up his new position Lane continued to live in London and to act as an art dealer. He therefore expected to make a substantial income from his professional activities. Lane had come to an agreement with the board that 'no conditions other than those provided in the National Gallery Act of 1854 (of which there are none) should apply to his hours of attendance',[6] thereby allowing him to become, in effect, a part-time Director – a role adopted by his successors for the next four decades. He had always intended that this should be the case; at the beginning of December 1913 he had told Sarah Purser (who joined the gallery board the following February), 'I would come to Dublin as often as it was necessary, but living there would make it impossible to pick up bargains or to get things given'.[7] To Mahaffy at the end of the same month, he was somewhat franker: 'I have felt the apathy and opposition of the Dublin public toward the modern gallery so greatly that I cannot live there.'[8] He therefore commuted almost monthly between London and Dublin, leaving Strickland to take care of the gallery for much of the time.

Lady Gregory had been trying for years to persuade her nephew he should live in Ireland. 'I wish you had a house here,' she wrote to him as far back as 1905. 'If George Moore would really go you could take his & give garden parties. But in spite of his farewells we expect to see him back again.'[9] Moore left Ireland for England in 1911 but Lane remained reluctant to move in the opposite direction. On one occasion, he did look at a number of Dublin houses with Oliver St John Gogarty and was especially taken by Delville, Mrs Delaney's former home in Glasnevin, which had been owned by an uncle of Daisy Fingall, Sir Patrick Keenan, in the latter part of the nineteenth century. However, Lane's disillusionment with the city remained so great that he would not consider living there even while entertaining the idea of a move from London.

When first diagnosed as suffering from neurasthenia, he had been advised by doctors that city life was not conducive to a full recovery. 'I have a motor car & have been taking trips to the country looking for a ruined palace to restore,' he told his aunt. 'It will be some time before I can hope to recover from this neurasthenia & as I am ordered quiet, fresh air & early hours, I must not live in London.'[10] In South Africa he had become an enthusiastic horseman and now started to hunt as often as he could every winter. Riding seems to have provided an antidote to stress and he showed the same recklessness in the saddle that he brought to the gaming tables of Monte Carlo. 'Did you ever realise his extraordinary courage?' Lady Gregory was asked by a mutual friend after Lane's death. 'With so nervous a physique it was remarkable. I noticed this concerning riding. He knew nothing of horses but didn't mind a mount of any kind.'[11] In November 1913 Lane told his sister of a drag hunt that had been 'as fast as a steeple chase & more devious. I fell off twice, once badly right onto my head & broke my hard riding hat to pieces & nearly my neck as well!'[12] That Christmas he wrote to her of his attending another hunt at which 'there were a good many spills owing to the bogs & big holes hidden by heather, but I brought my priceless horse back safely'.[13] Joseph Solomon commented to Lady Gregory, 'It seemed to me extraordinary, this recklessness and longing for rapidity on horseback in so frail a body. In motoring here it was just the same, he would have the chauffeur go at top speed, though all the time he sat up straight, and one could feel he was nervous.'[14]

By the summer of 1912, Lane was so committed to the concept of living in the country that he had begun letting potential purchasers view Lindsey House. Among the most interested parties was Daisy, Countess of Warwick, the former mistress of Edward VII (when Prince of Wales). Despite having converted to socialism some years earlier, Lady Warwick was still interested in buying the property and declared 'no house in all London could have any interest for me after seeing yours'.[15] Lane meanwhile took trips to the countryside and looked at a number of places, his plan being to acquire an Elizabethan or Jacobean house which he would furnish in period style. Eventually he narrowed down his choice to two buildings, a sixteenth-century moated manor in Sussex called Plumpton Place, and Kirby Hall in Northamptonshire, an enormous mansion contemporaneous with Longleat that had been allowed to fall into dereliction by the Earls of Winchilsea. Plumpton was eventually restored after the First World War by Lutyens for the owner of *Country Life*, Edward Hudson. Lane wanted the architect to take on Kirby Hall for him but was advised the job would cost at least £200,000, a sum neither he nor anyone else could afford to spend; the house remains a semi-ruin today. Although she enquired several times about the possibility of buying Lindsey House, Lady Warwick had announced after her first sight of his home: 'I shall not be at all surprised if you decline to sell at all because I cannot imagine your moving all your charming treasures to another place.'[16]

Nor did he do so; London remained his home because, as he pointed out to Mahaffy, it was 'the bargain centre of the world (in pictures)' and 'I can best serve the N.G. by living here'.[17] This explanation failed to impress the Treasury department in Dublin, which wrote to the gallery soon after he became Director to enquire 'whether by the terms of his appointment Sir Hugh Lane is required to devote his whole time to the public service'.[18] This official disquiet was certainly not dispelled by the information that Lane had promised to spend his annual salary of £500 plus £150 travel expenses on purchasing pictures, nor by the insistence of the gallery board that any limitations on his freedom would in their opinion 'militate against the interests of the Gallery, as the nature of the work devolving on him is such as can only be satisfactorily carried out by giving him considerable freedom of action in the performance of his official duties'.[19] A long correspondence then followed between the board and the Treasury in which the former sought salary increases for its staff and the latter attempted to understand the precise status of the new Director. The rise in Lane's salary (to £800 per annum) was refused and his position defined as being the same as that of any other civil servant except that he had no pension rights.[20]

Correspondence on this matter finally concluded in August 1914 – just as the British government declared war with Germany – but more letters began to pass back and forth between the gallery and the Treasury from early January of the following year. The Treasury announced that for the duration of the war, purchasing grants to all national institutions would be suspended because 'it would be absolutely wrong to ask Parliament to vote money for what might be considered a luxury, and could at best be described as culture, at a time when we are husbanding all our resources in a fight for existence'.[21] For weeks, Lane battled determinedly to have this decision reversed, arguing that the acquisition grant provided for Dublin was already significantly lower than sums given for the same purpose to the National Galleries in London and Edinburgh. 'During this year,' he explained, 'unexampled opportunities will present themselves for the purchase of important works at low prices, as many collections will be forced on the market owing to the effects of the war, and in the salerooms our grant of £1,000 will have a purchasing value which may never occur again.'[22] But the Treasury was unmoved; no funds were to be given to the gallery until the war ended.

Lane's observations on the depressed state of the art market and the low prices then being achieved at sales were based on personal experience: by the start of 1915 his own finances were in a parlous condition. In certain respects, the war had scarcely affected him, other than his chauffeur John Condon resigning in September 1914 in order to enlist, which meant the car could no longer be used for trips to the country. Neither Lane nor his friends seem to have given any consideration to the idea that he might sign up although, at thirty-eight he was younger than many other men who now did so; persistent ill-health and personal disinclination combined to make remote the prospect of his joining the British army.

But the war impinged in other ways, not least in the art market's precipitate collapse. As a dealer, Lane had always taken financial risks and these had been exacerbated by his lavish expenditure on behalf of the gallery of modern art in Ireland. In 1906, for example, he had borrowed £750 from Alfred Beit 'to pay for the pictures for the Dublin Gallery'.[23] This was money that could never be recouped, as he habitually gave away all the modern pictures in his collection. Ellen Duncan's husband James remembered Lane once telling him of a £30,000 debt which had to be paid before a certain date. When Duncan looked appalled at this idea, he was reassured: 'Don't worry, it will be alright. You've got it rather out of proportion. Think of a charwoman trying to raise thirty shillings and you'll get the idea.'[24] But while he sometimes realized substantial profits through sales of old masters, he could often spend just as much on acquiring new stock. El Greco's *St Francis*, which he donated to the National Gallery of Ireland in April 1914, was bought during one such spree. In December 1912, Lane went to Paris for the sale of the Rouart collection where his purchases included the *Woman in a Grey Shawl* then attributed to Goya (but now considered to have been painted by a follower of the artist). For this work, he was reported to have paid £5,680, although his own account book gives a figure of £6,248; whatever the sum, it was considered exceptionally high at the time and reported with astonishment in French newspapers. But on the same Paris trip, Lane also bought the El Greco from Durand-Ruel for £700, *Boy Standing on a Terrace* by Van Dyck for £8,000, Gainsborough's portrait of General Johnston for £3,000 and Sebastiano del Piombo's *Cardinal Antonio del Monte* for £9,500. A number of additional purchases brought his total expenditure in just over a week to almost £28,000.[25] However, none of the aforementioned paintings were sold during Lane's lifetime and so after his death they entered the collection of the National Gallery.

Obviously he had expected to dispose of this stock, and at a profit, relatively soon after its acquisition. But during 1913, problems with both the Michaelis Gift and the Dublin gallery meant Lane could pay little attention to his career as a dealer, and the following year other difficulties arose. The most immediately serious of these was the financial collapse of an important client, Arthur Grenfell. A gentleman broker in the City of London, Grenfell had experienced problems before but recovered from these thanks in part to the support of his father-in-law Lord Grey. He had bought a large number of pictures from Lane, not least Titian's *Portrait of a Man in a Red Cap*. In March 1911 he paid £30,000 for this painting, which Lane had bought at Christie's almost five years earlier for £2,205. Hearing this news, Caroline Grosvenor, who was a mutual friend, told him: 'I hardly know whether I am glad or sorry – I love them to have it but I should also have liked it always to have been yours'.[26] In the summer of 1914, Lane was given the opportunity to regain ownership of the Titian because, due to ill-advised speculation in Canadian companies, Arthur Grenfell had lost all his money and was obliged to sell whatever he could to realize funds. Among the first items to go were the collection of pictures he had built up with assistance from Lane, and the latter felt morally obliged to buy many of them back when they came up at Christie's in mid-June 1914. Lane paid relatively little for these repurchases – the Titian, for example, cost him £13,650 – but as other figures included £5,880 for the Lawrence portrait of Lady Elizabeth Foster (formerly owned by the Vere Fosters), £1,522 for two panels attributed to Ucello, £892 and ten shillings for Ferdinand Bol's *Portrait of a Lady* and £8,608 for Gainsborough's *Landscape with Cattle*, the total came to a rather daunting £31,000.[27]

This was not money Lane was likely to recoup quickly because, under the threat of war, the art market had entered recession as potential collectors lost their collective appetite. The situation only became worse once hostilities had been declared in August 1914. End-of-year reports from the principal auction houses revealed just how bad the situation had become. In 1914, the number of pictures in London selling for more than 1,000 guineas was forty-six; this compared to 124 the previous year. The season's best price had been the £13,650 paid by Lane for the Grenfell

Titian, the most important sale of 1914 since the major auction houses cancelled their programme of autumn sales. Not only were there fewer sales, but the prices achieved were a fraction of those made just a few years before. A Raeburn portrait that had fetched 800 guineas in 1911 was sold for just 300 guineas in 1914; similarly, Reynolds's *Portrait of Lady Hamilton as a Bacchante*, which sold for 1,500 guineas in 1911, went for a third of this figure three years later. It was, Lane told Thomas Bodkin, 'the worst season on record and the dealers against my things'.[28] He now found himself with a large amount of stock in his possession and very few opportunities for off-loading any of it. He already owed his bank, Williams Deacon of London, £30,000 and now needed to borrow the same amount again in order to pay for his purchases at the Grenfell sale; in the meantime, the pictures were in the care of Agnew's, which threatened to resell them if Lane failed to come up with the funds. However, given the depressed state of the market, the bank was understandably reluctant to extend its loan. Fearful of the consequences, not least to his reputation, Lane tried hard but without success to find buyers for some of the stock he held. A new friend, Raymond Wyer, who ran the Hackley Gallery of Fine Arts in Michigan, volunteered to see if any American purchasers could be found, but at the beginning of October confessed that all the collectors he had contacted 'seem disinclined to spend money at this time ... I believe your presence over here would help to bring about a sale or two.'[29]

As 1914 drew to a close, Lane was heavily in debt with no sign that the art market would improve in time to help him out of his predicament. He spent Christmas alone in London and wrote despondently to Lady Gregory shortly before the year ended: 'I suppose that it is always what one cares for most that gives us most trouble and anxiety. In my case it is the probable losing of all my pictures, which I must do unless I find a large sum by the 1st of April.'[30] But on the last day, the manager of Williams Deacon, J. Meagher, who was an admirer of Lane's work (and would be one of the executors of his will), managed to persuade his superiors to provide the additional £30,000. He went around to Lindsey House with the news, and found its owner sitting down to a solitary and typically frugal supper of two oranges and a piece of cake. Although Lane was now able to pay for the Grenfell pictures, he still had to find some means of paying back his £60,000 loan, and it was for this reason as much as the hope of finding new clients that he agreed to visit New York. Joseph Duveen had sent a number of paintings for sale across the Atlantic and while on board the SS *Mississippi* these had been damaged by a fire. Before agreeing a settlement Lloyds, the insurance company handling the matter, required an independent expert to look at the pictures and give an opinion on their value. Lane was offered this job and reluctantly agreed to do so.

Originally he was supposed to sail in February and at the beginning of the month, while in his office at the National Gallery of Ireland, he wrote a codicil to his will of October 1913 reversing the clause in the earlier document which left the 'conditional gift' group of pictures to the National Gallery in London. Instead, these works were to be given to the city of Dublin 'providing a suitable building is provided for them within five years of my death'. Similarly, the pictures on loan to Belfast were to be given to Dublin's Municipal Gallery, and so: 'If a building is provided within five years, the whole collection will be housed together. The sole Trustee in this question is to be my aunt, Lady Gregory.'[31] This codicil he signed or initialled in three places and then locked in his desk.

As Ruth Shine's diary noted, because Lane had 'a bad feverish cough which he won't take care of & Dr. will not insure him in consequence',[32] his departure for America was put off for two months and he had the opportunity to visit Dublin again in early April. Discovering that Lady Gregory was also in the city, he arranged to meet her at the National Gallery, where he was hanging a temporary exhibition of pictures belonging to the Provost of Trinity College. When she and Yeats called in during the afternoon, 'He took us through the rooms to show me all he had done and all he had given in those thirteen months'. Afterwards, over tea in his office, she told him: 'I am glad to see you in your right setting at last.' Five years later, she wrote: 'I like to remember him there, in authority, in love with his work, in harmony with all that was about him.'[33] As she left, he gave her a copy of the gallery's new catalogue signed 'To Aunt Augusta from the Director! April 8th 1915.'[34]

The following day, Lane returned to England. He was extremely nervous at the idea of travelling to America under wartime conditions. An English furniture dealer who met him just before his departure remembered 'he was so obviously ill at ease at the prospect of going away – his manner was disquieting & so unlike the intense and enthusiastic friend I had always welcomed. He spoke much of the journey and of the dangers of travel.'[35] In Dublin, the Land Commissioner William Bailey, who was a member of the National Gallery board, also could not forget how Lane 'seemed to have a prevision of the danger that he was running', having departed without 'the enthusiasm that usually characterised him'.[36] Arriving from Ireland at Euston Station in London, Lane met Alec Martin of Christie's, who had agreed to travel with him to Liverpool where he was due to board ship for New York. The two men took the train together, and the following morning 'we walked the streets and purchased a supply of cheap cigarettes which Hugh liked and could not get in America'.[37]

Just as he was due to depart, Lane received a telephone from Henriette Hind, the American-born wife of the English art critic and editor C. Lewis Hind. She had been acting as his intermediary with American collectors and now told him the Titian *Portrait of a Man in a Red Cap* repurchased at the Grenfell sale the previous year had been sold to Henry Frick for £50,000. A few days later, Frick also agreed to buy a second picture, Holbein's portrait of Thomas Cromwell, formerly owned by the Earl of Caledon and bought by Lane in Dublin exactly a year earlier for £38,000. Although the price he received for this work is not recorded, it must have been similar to, if not more than, what Frick paid for the Titian. Although he grumbled to his aunt that the two paintings had been sold 'at nearly cost price', Lane at least allowed that he was 'happy getting the Titian established in such a famous collection'.[38] Although his pressing financial problems had been resolved, it was now too late to change his plans and so he sailed for the United States on the evening of 11 April. To celebrate the unexpected reversal of fortune, he sent his sister a postcard asking her to order a new car, a Hupmobile, even though he still had no chauffeur.[39]

On 20 April, Lane arrived in New York where he was met by Knoedler's Charles Carstairs and his wife. The business of examining the damaged Duveen pictures seems to have taken up relatively little of his time and some of them were put up for auction while he was in the city.

During this visit he saw a great deal of John Quinn, who introduced him to people such as the contemporary-art dealer Harriet Bryant, and took him to dinner and the theatre and on a drive to the country for the weekend. Quinn wrote to tell Lady Gregory that although her nephew had been 'miserable' when he first arrived, after a few days he appeared 'to be enjoying it here very much'. 'I think he opened his heart to me more than perhaps to many people,' Quinn later remembered. 'There was nothing sentimental about him or maudlin, but at the same time at times he felt a sense of loneliness. He had told me all about his debts and his plans.'[40] Soon Lane was saying that had he not been expected back in Dublin for a meeting 'he would have liked to stay here two or three weeks longer'. As Quinn explained, 'It seemed a great relief to him after the grayness and darkness and gloom of London to come to this place where there were no wounded or sick people but dances in the hotels and the theatres going and so on.'[41] The two men bickered about contemporary art, with Lane insisting Quinn should not have followed Augustus John's recommendation to buy a series of Gauguin ceiling panels, although after a cocktail and champagne 'Lane who was in high spirits said "If I were to see John now I should probably agree with him that Gauguin's ceiling he advised you to buy was a great work of art and one of Gauguin's masterpieces".'[42] He then presented the American with a copy of the National Gallery of Ireland catalogue addressed 'To my rival, John Quinn'. Another New York acquaintance told Ruth Shine her brother had announced 'now that he had settled in and got to know some new people over here he would make frequent visits to America'.[43]

But Lane had not forgotten his commitments back in London. Before leaving Liverpool, he had promised to help Alec Martin with an art auction Christie's was holding to raise funds for the Red Cross. He donated a canvas by Sir Charles Eastlake, *The Sisters*, to this event, where it made £48.6s, but he also offered to see whether a sitter could be found in America for Sargent; the painter, who since 1907 had effectively refused to paint any more portraits, agreed to make an exception for the sake of the charity. When Lane was unable to find anyone in New York willing to take on this commitment, he sent a telegram to Christie's declaring he would pay £10,000 for the Sargent picture. On 27 April, Alec Martin told

Ruth Shine: 'The announcement was made today & was received with wild applause. It really is noble of Sir Hugh.'[44] The following day's newspapers were lavish in their praise of this gesture, the *Manchester Guardian* proclaiming: 'Sir Hugh Lane adds another to many instances of his extraordinary public spirits. He is not a rich man ... Formerly Sir Hugh had acquired a reputation for his rare skill in buying masterpieces more cheaply than anyone else but today he crowned it by buying more dearly than anyone else.'[45]

As Lane prepared to leave New York, he wrote to Lady Gregory, 'I feel better than I have done for years!'[46] She replied, 'I'm sure the sea voyage is doing you good in this nice weather – we have seen your sporting offer to Sargent in the papers.'[47] The night before his departure, he went to the theatre with Charles Carstairs and then on to see Henry Frick, thereby missing John Quinn who had called to his hotel to say goodbye, having failed to persuade Lane to stay on longer in New York. The latter was adamant he had to return at once to London, even after Quinn advised him against sailing during wartime on board the Cunard line's *Lusitania*, a British-registered vessel and therefore vulnerable to attacks from German submarines. On the morning of his departure, Saturday, 1 May, the German Imperial Embassy in Washington placed a notice in the principal American newspapers warning prospective passengers that persons sailing in the war zone on ships belonging to Great Britain or their allies 'do so at their own risk'. The notice was relatively small and the Cunard office subsequently reported the number of last-minute cancellations had been no greater than usual. Lane was not among those who chose to remain on shore. 'I am so sorry to have missed you,' he apologized to Quinn before going on to invite his new friend to come over to London during the summer 'and take pot luck at my house. You can do just as you like. I will I hope have a Hupmobile and we can run about looking at pictures and places ... I wish I had a few of your sort in Dublin and London to help to create a feeling of enthusiasm for the things I care for most.'[48] Quinn received this letter at his office on the day Lane left New York on board the *Lusitania*.

17
AFTERMATH

On the evening of Friday, 7 May 1915, Ruth Shine was at Lindsey House, where she had spent the previous week supervising a programme of spring-cleaning in anticipation of her brother's return the following day. Alec Martin arrived from Christie's to tell her that the *Lusitania* had been sunk off the coast of Cork and that he would go to the London offices of Cunard to see what other news was available. Later that night he sent her a note saying that the ship had gone down not far from land '& as the weather is good, there is good hope'.[1] For the moment, therefore, she remained in Chelsea. Lady Gregory, due to travel to London on Abbey Theatre business, was in Coole entertaining Augustus John and the Bernard Shaws when she received a telegram from John Quinn in New York saying he had heard of the *Lusitania*'s sinking and wondered whether Lane was safe. She sent the telegram to Yeats with a covering note declaring 'I am almost without hope, for I am sure he would have sent me a message if he had come to land – though it is possible he might be wounded or unconscious'.[2] Although Augustus John offered to accompany her, she then set out alone for London.

Reports of the *Lusitania* disaster were extensively carried by all the following day's papers. In the early afternoon, within sight of the coast of Cork and in completely calm seas, the liner had been struck by a single torpedo fired by a German submarine, the U-20 commanded by Walter Schwieger. By 3.30 p.m., less than twenty minutes after being hit, the

Lusitania had entirely disappeared beneath the water, with the loss of almost 1,200 lives. The speed of the tragedy, and the panic this induced among those on board, were offered as an explanation why quite so many passengers and crew drowned, but for some days afterwards there was a widespread belief that more than the official total of 764 survivors would be discovered.

On 9 May, therefore, Ruth Shine decided to travel to Cork 'hoping he may be found hurt & unknown'.[3] To assist the search for her brother, she arranged for notices to be printed and published in local newspapers; these carried a photograph of Lane and a description of his appearance including such personal details as his hair 'slightly turning grey, rather bald' and 'Wore cellular underclothing marked "H. Lane".'[4] Anyone with information about the missing man was asked to contact his cousin Charles Lane, a solicitor in Cork.

But nobody came forward, and soon Ruth Shine was writing to Alec Martin: 'There is no hope of finding him alive now ... It is not even certain his dear body can be found, as there are currents running off shore round this coast.'[5] 'I am like you hoping that his dear body may be found,' Mrs Loftus wrote to her from Lindsey House.[6] However, Lane's body was not among those eventually washed ashore. One survivor, Lady Allan, who was married to a Canadian railway magnate and had lost both her daughters on the *Lusitania*, later told Lady Gregory she saw Lane during the liner's last moments. He had not been wearing a lifebelt and announced that he was going in search of a wealthy American couple, the Pearsons, friends made during the voyage. Pale but calm, he remarked: 'This is a sad end for us all.' He was never seen again.[7]

Without a body to bury, Ruth Shine and Lady Gregory could only arrange a memorial service, held at Chelsea Old Church on the afternoon of 20 May; among those in attendance were Otto Beit, Robert Ross, Alec Martin, William Orpen, Grant Richards and Lord Curzon. A year later, a white marble plaque was erected on the south wall of the nave of St Luke's Church, Douglas, Co. Cork, within sight of where Lane had been born fewer than forty years before. 'To the dear memory of Hugh Lane Knt., Director of the National Gallery,' it reads. 'This tablet is placed here by his sorrowful sister Ruth Shine.'

Lane's death caused widespread shock and grief. 'I am afraid the poor boy is gone,' Quinn wrote to Lady Gregory four days after the *Lusitania* had been sunk. 'I don't know when anything outside a death in my own family has so distressed and depressed me.'⁸ 'All here in Dublin are stunned simply at the loss we all have had,' William Bailey told her. 'Two or three people have burst into tears when speaking of him to me in the street. People now know how much they loved him and what they have lost with him.'⁹ Half a century later, Thomas MacGreevy remembered meeting Sarah Purser in the National Gallery where she was overcome with grief: 'Oh, my poor Lane,' she cried, 'my poor Lane'.¹⁰ Many letters of condolence to Ruth Shine referred to the close bond between Lane and herself. 'I can find no words in which to tell you how deeply I feel for you & *how* much I sympathise with you in this terrible tragedy,' wrote Priscilla Annesley, who a few years earlier almost became Lane's mother-in-law. 'I know how devoted you & your brother were & it is just unthinkable to have to have to believe he is gone.'¹¹ Caroline Grosvenor's daughter Margaret commented: 'He was one of those people who always seemed to make everything round him brighter and happier – and the better one knew him, the more one admired & loved his wonderful kindness & generosity & above all his splendid enthusiasm.'¹²

More formal acknowledgements of his death were just as fulsome. 'The world has lost one of the most distinguished art connoisseurs and collectors,' announced the *Freeman's Journal*. 'His career was one of the romances of his time ... Out of nothing save his own knowledge and a charming manner, he brought together the most remarkable of all collections of modern art.'¹³ In the *Sunday Times*, art critic Frank Rutter called Lane's collection 'a lasting monument to his fine taste, his great generosity and his unflagging energy and enthusiasm',¹⁴ while C. Lewis Hind's appreciation in the *Daily Chronicle* opened by declaring 'Hugh Lane had genius' before going on to speak of 'his extraordinary faculty for discerning the greatness of a work of art, whatever condition of dirt, decay or repainting the picture might be in'.¹⁵ The *Irish Times*, which in the immediate aftermath of the tragedy had carried a notice simply recording 'There is no news of Sir Hugh Lane having been landed at Queenstown,'¹⁶ within days allowed itself to attest: 'We have not heard definitely the manner of his dying, but we can be sure from what we know of him, that he was unselfish and noble to the end'. Lane, the newspaper pronounced, 'was determined, so far as in him lay, to lift up the people of the country of his birth to an appreciation of that spirit of art that means so much more to a nation struggling for life than the quest after mere material well-being'.[17] Over the next year, the same publication offered further tributes to Lane, some of which were remarkable primarily for their unintentional bathos. A poem written by Martyn Howe of Trinity College, Dublin, and dedicated to the memory of Lane, concluded:

> And they, who left in life your praise unsaid
> May give you now, perchance, when you are dead
> The thanks that cannot reach you where you wait
> Among the shadows by the silent gate.[18]

Even more unforgettable were the lines composed by Percy French and published in the *Irish Times* in September 1916. The last verse ran:

> Some day, perchance, when from the skies
> He gazes with those kindly eyes,
> He'll see a sculptured shrine arise,
> A pillared fane;
> And know his gems are rightly set,
> And know that Dublin paid its debt,
> And know that we shall ne'er forget
> Hugh Lane.[19]

In the aftermath of his death there were more pressing difficulties to face than bad poetry. Lane, who had been at the centre of so many controversies during his lifetime, seemed to leave an almost equal number of problems to be resolved after his death. Among the most immediate was the question of a successor at the National Gallery of Ireland. The majority of board members had been his allies, especially recent appointees such as Bailey, Sarah Purser and Richard Orpen. They now considered between them who Lane would have wanted as the gallery's next Director;

among those stepping forward to offer himself for the job – perhaps a little too hastily given his close friendship with the deceased – was Thomas Bodkin, who in late May wrote to another board member, Dermod O'Brien, seeking the latter's support. According to Bodkin, Lane 'always encouraged and guided me' and 'I have some reason to know that as far back as 1913, he put on record his wish that I should be associated with his plans for a Municipal Gallery in the event of his death'.[20] But Bodkin also knew that the candidate with the most likely chance of securing the directorship was the Registrar, Walter Strickland, who had been Lane's rival on the previous occasion. Bodkin told O'Brien: 'Strickland's supporters will try to defer or put off the election, knowing that he is disqualified; for his retiring age was extended by the Treasury for the purpose of enabling him to continue for one year in the office of Registrar and not for the purpose of enabling him to compete for the Directorship.'[21]

At a special board meeting on 18 May called to place on record the board's regret at Lane's death, Strickland had, indeed, been asked to become acting Director, but Dr Mahaffy, who was both the Chairman and his leading supporter, now tried to have this appointment formalized, even though the Registrar reached the statutory retirement age of sixty-five in early June. A row now broke out within the board, with O'Brien protesting to Mahaffy how he had seen 'a day or two after the (last) meeting the announcement in the papers that the Registrar had been appointed as Director'[22] and the normally unruffled Lord Mayo announcing to Bailey: 'I was really thinking what action ought to be taken with regard to the extraordinary way in which Mr Strickland has been elected Director'.[23] Nonetheless, Strickland held on to the position for the following twelve months, although Mahaffy resigned his chairmanship after the July board meeting, following the appointment to the former Registrar's job of writer James Stephens, despite his not being on the shortlist of six (female) candidates.

The National Gallery's troubles did not end with the enforced retirement of Strickland in 1916, as his successor proved to be both opinionated and argumentative. Like Lane, Robert Langton Douglas was a successful, London-based art dealer who now saw the directorship of a national institution as providing an opportunity to enhance his reputation. A former Church of England clergyman, Langton was a far greater scholar than Lane had been, but a correspondingly less generous personal donor. His complicated personal life meant he had a considerable number of children to support on an annual salary now reduced to £300 for the duration of the war, which is one reason why he had to continue the practice of keeping the Directorship a part-time position. He saw a means of leaving a lasting legacy to the gallery in the terms of Lane's will; by the terms of this document, the bulk of his estate was to be invested, so that the resultant income could be spent on acquiring 'pictures of deceased painters of established merit'. Understandably, Douglas, who continued to receive no funding for new purchases from the Treasury, wished to assume responsibility for such acquisitions, but a majority of the board's members – led by Bodkin, who became one of their number in 1917 – argued that some of the pictures in Lane's possession at the time of his death should be retained by the gallery. Bodkin, who still had his own aspirations for the directorship, intensely disliked Douglas and the disagreement over Lane's will therefore became a struggle between two strong personalities.

In order to disregard the testator's intentions an application had to be made to the Courts, who were told by Grant Richards, one of the two executors appointed by Lane, that 'the Gallery could never buy such good pictures again with the money that they would have at their disposal'.[24] Douglas, on the contrary, argued: 'This statement is directly contrary to the facts & can be mathematically disproved by me by giving a list of the purchases that I have made in the last few years.'[25] He fought long and hard against the retention of any pictures, describing this plan to Dermod O'Brien as a 'gross interference with a plain testamentary disposition'. But despite his declaration that 'It is, it seems to me, a very serious thing to frustrate, to such an extent as is proposed, the clearly-expressed "purposes" of the testator,'[26] he was overruled by Bodkin *et al.* on the matter and, the National Gallery having gained the necessary legal approval, forty-two works were held back from the sale of Lane's property. The prices assigned to these works in 1917, when compared with the sums they had cost a few years earlier, show that the art market continued to be seriously depressed by ongoing war. The Sebastiano del Piombo *Por-*

trait of Cardinal Antonio del Monte, which had cost Lane £9,500 in December 1912, was now valued at £1,500; and Goya's *Woman in a Grey Shawl* had effectively halved its worth (to £3,000), as had Titian's *Portrait of Count Baldassare Castiglione* (bought for £11,000 in November 1913, estimated to be worth £5,500 four years later). It is no wonder that Douglas felt frustrated at the opportunities he was missing in the auction rooms when values had dropped so much over just a few seasons.

However, he was requested by the board to arrange an exhibition of the Lane Bequest pictures in the gallery; this was opened on 6 July 1918 by the Lord Lieutenant, Lord French. In the accompanying catalogue, Douglas took the opportunity to make his opinion of the works clear. As he pointed out, they were items which Lane 'happened to own when death suddenly overtook him. These forty-one pictures, then, were not selected for the Gallery by Sir Hugh Lane; nor did they form the carefully selected cabinet of a private collector who was also a great connoisseur; they are part of the stock that Lane as a dealer had in his possession at the time of his death. Nearly all of these pictures had been offered for sale by him and, had he lived, would have been offered for sale again.'[27] The Gallery's board and staff were in agreement that the commitment made by Lane less than a fortnight before his death to pay £10,000 for a portrait by Sargent should be honoured. The sitter had not been decided; John Quinn told Lady Gregory that Lane had been considering either Queen Mary or the Duke of Connaught's daughter Princess Patricia.[28] But the National Gallery board decided on the U.S. President Woodrow Wilson, who sat for Sargent in 1917; the finished work was widely exhibited in the United States before being brought to Dublin, where it entered the gallery's collection.

Meanwhile, the bulk of Lane's estate had gone to auction, beginning with his collection of jewellery; this made a total of £1,789 at Christie's on 27 June 1917 with the top price of £260 being paid for a diamond necklace. Early the following month, the balance of Lane's pictures were sold at Christie's over two days. Among the 123 lots were a number of paintings later generations of visitors to the National Gallery of Ireland must regret were let go: Pieter de Hooch's *A Musical Party* fetched £567, and Hogarth's *Street Scene* sold for £157.10s. Gainsborough's *Portrait of*

Admiral Vernon, bought by Lane for £735 at Christie's in June 1914, now went for £210; at Sotheby's in March 2000, the same painting made £172,000. Among the many portraits in Lane's collection were four works each by Lely and Van Dyck and three by Kneller, while other lots included paintings and drawings by Watteau, Cranach, Fra Bartolomeo, Reynolds, Steen, Wilson and Winterhalter.

Next his furniture was sold, the cabinet designed by William Kent for Burlington House making £136.10s and Chippendale's octagonal table designed for Queen Charlotte's house at Fort Belvedere £525. A pair of Chippendale carved and gilded mirrors was sold for £56.14s, and £90.6s was paid for a Kent part-gilded side table with marble top. The balance of household items were disposed of at Foster's auction rooms in late July when 326 lots as diverse as carpets and flower vases, picture frames and vegetable dishes were on offer. William Orpen paid £8.18.6 for a pair of old French carved models of eagles on carved and gilded columns with marble bases, and John Singer Sargent bought a *blanc de chine* vase for £10.10s. Now obliged to find somewhere else to live, Ruth Shine was permitted to buy a number of items from her brother's former home at probate prices; she paid £2 for his white painted bed and £3 for her own, £8 for a Queen Anne chest of drawers and £5 for some small pieces of jewellery. Finally, on 26 November, the art books assembled by Lane were auctioned by Christie's, where the catalogues of Alfred and Otto Beit, both volumes compiled by Wilhelm von Bode, went for £9.10s and £16.10s respectively. The freehold of Lindsey House itself had been sold two months earlier for £9,500. With this money, once all liabilities and government duties had been paid, the Gallery established a Lane fund worth between £1,000 and £3,000 annually; until the advent of the Shaw Fund in 1958, it was the institution's most valuable source of non-governmental income and has paid for over sixty pictures by artists such as Brueghel the Younger, Perugino, Hubert Robert and Delacroix.

Many of Lane's friends felt the desire to pay another kind of tribute to his memory, and within a month of the *Lusitania* disaster Lady Gregory was discussing who might be given the task of writing her nephew's biography. Although begun with the best of intentions, the project was to prove as vexatious as all those associated with Lane. To pay a fee to whomever was given the commission and to help cover publication costs during wartime, Alec Martin decided that friends of Lane should subscribe to a fund. Donations varied from £25 given by Florence Phillips to the more usual £5 offered by Caroline Grosvenor, the dowager Lady Drogheda and Joseph Solomon. By March 1916, almost £180 had been raised and the chosen author was getting to work. Initially Lady Gregory and Ruth Shine were unsure whether they wanted C. Lewis Hind or D.S. MacColl to undertake the task; in August 1915 they settled on the latter. MacColl, now Curator of the Wallace Collection, had, during his time as an art critic, been one of Lane's most articulate champions. Expectations of what he would produce were therefore high, even though he warned that his book would not be long, running to perhaps no more than 100 pages. 'Of course 100 pages w'd be very short,' Lady Gregory agreed with her niece in March 1916, 'but I think when MacColl sees the material & gets interested he is sure to do more. Anyhow too little is better than padding.'[29]

Blaming other obligations, MacColl was slow to start the task and had only begun to gather material in late June when he told Lady Gregory, 'I rely on you to whip up people in Ireland whom I do not know & who are in a position to furnish memories of Lane'.[30] In the same letter, he also insisted on his rights to authorial autonomy, at the time not a matter of dispute. Problems arose some months later, however, due to the argument between Dublin and London over possession of Lane's thirty-nine 'conditional gift' pictures. Left to the latter city in his 1913 will, they were then given to Ireland by the terms of his 1915 codicil. As this document had not been witnessed, it had moral but not legal validity; MacColl now stated in print his personal belief that the collection should remain in London and argued that this had really been Lane's intention. It was a belief strongly held but based on little more than McColl's conviction that the pictures ought not to be returned to Dublin after the way that city's authorities had behaved towards a putative benefactor. In support of his position, MacColl quoted from letters written by Lane in the autumn of 1913. He only remembered the dead man's anger and disappointment at that time and did not seem to have allowed for the possibility that over the next eighteen months Lane's attitude towards Dublin might have changed.

Lady Gregory was understandably angry with MacColl. Had she been aware of his views, she would never have invited him to become her nephew's biographer. She and Lane's other Irish supporters now chose to respond to MacColl on Christmas Eve 1916 in the letters page of the *Observer*, where W.B. Yeats, while praising the commissioned biographer's literary abilities, insisted that MacColl 'was never, however, among Sir Hugh Lane's more intimate friends and has had to go to others for all his material. Why does he claim special knowledge and why, above all, does he suggest that he is more impartial than other men?'[31] MacColl responded to these remarks privately by informing Lady Gregory that he released her 'from any obligation to me in the matter of Hugh Lane's life'[32] and publicly by writing to the *Observer* to say that while he felt some scruples about quoting from documents he had been given for the biography, 'they abundantly prove his deep disillusionment about Ireland, his detestation of place, people and gallery'.[33] He then returned his author's fee.

More than a year had been lost, and another writer had to be found as soon as possible. The task was now given to the art critic Martin Wood, who had known Lane even less well than MacColl but seemed keen; at the beginning of May 1917 Alec Martin wrote to Ruth Shine from Christie's, where he was preparing the sale of Lane's pictures and furnitures, to report that 'If Wood's anxiety to start is any index to his intention to get on with the work, we ought to see the book in some definite form before long'.[34] His optimism was misplaced, because in late August he told her: 'I shall have a quarrel with Martin Wood very soon if he does not make progress.'[35] The author proceeded at a leisurely pace because, he confessed to Lady Gregory, he had a weak heart and his specialist had ordered him not to undertake 'any prolonged piece of writing on account of the state of my health'.[36] It was not until May 1919, four years after Lane's death, that Wood finally handed over a manuscript to Alec Martin, who immediately condemned the work, as did Grant Richards, who had intended to be the publisher. The text, Martin declared, failed adequately to represent 'either in detail or in the spirit, our wishes for the biography'.[37] Hoping for a better response elsewhere, in mid-August the author sent a copy of his work to Lady Gregory. She was even more outraged than Alec Martin. 'I think it is on the whole hopelessly bad and unworthy, both as to that it leaves out – the fire & nobility – & what it puts in, belittling trifles that would be caught at by gossiping critics – I saw no merit whatever in it, outside the useful arrangement of events and collecting of dates.'[38] She especially objected to Martin Wood's preoccupation with trivia, such as an account of Lane's 'trying on a court suit after his knighthood and wearing "as his own stocking had holes" a pair of silk stockings lent by a "titled lady"'.[39]

There was, however, little time to reproach the biographer because in the autumn he had a stroke and died. Lady Gregory was now left with a useless manuscript and an irate sibling, as Martin Wood's brother now took up his cause and threatened to publish the book himself. Legal proceedings threatened, not least because the Wood family held on to the Lane papers which the deceased had been consulting. They would only give these back in return for Martin Wood's manuscript; after meeting his brother, Lady Gregory commented to Ruth Shine, 'if ever I had seen a rogue here was one, with a fixed smile and little hard eyes.'[40] It took more than three years of placatory intervention on the part of Alec Martin before the matter was settled and relevant documents exchanged between the two parties. All the money assiduously collected to pay for the book had to be spent on solicitors' fees and related costs.

In the meantime, Lady Gregory, understandably grown tired of waiting for someone else to write Lane's biography, had decided to take on the job herself. 'If I can further serve him by writing an account of his life less unworthy than this, ought I not to do it?' she asked Martin. The work she envisaged would be called *A Passionate Pilgrimage* and would evoke 'the fiery moments when he tried to realise his dream from childhood of making – here or there on the way, but above all in Ireland – the "palace of art" he had seen in his dreams'.[41] Published in late 1920, her book carried the more prosaic title *Hugh Lane's Life and Achievement, with some account of the Dublin galleries* and, due to the absence of the papers still in the possession of Martin Wood's family, depended heavily on her own memories and those of his friends she interviewed. Grant Richards failed to be among this number; he had now taken umbrage because Lady Gregory gave the book not to him but to her usual publisher, John Murray.

Richards had already caused offence by insisting he was entitled to a percentage of the profits should he publish the book and by instructing Lady Gregory that in her book on Lane 'you must give all his romantic side and all his little meannesses'. 'I resented this,' she declared. 'They were not meannesses; they were economies upon himself that he might give to others and make that gallery'.[42]

Grant Richards now threatened to consult his solicitors 'in view of the fact that I have announced the memoir of Sir Hugh Lane over & over again in the last three years'. He also claimed that, as an executor of Lane's will, he could prevent any papers or letters being used by Lady Gregory in her work.[43] No wonder that she told Ruth Shine, 'I found him dishonest on the business side and offensive on the personal side'.[44] It was the end of another long-standing friendship with a member of her nephew's circle. But she persisted in her intentions and Murray's did publish the biography, dedicated to Alec Martin, 'Hugh's friend and mine'. The book could hardly be described as objective about its subject, but Lady Gregory did not shy away from mentioning her nephew's faults: his snobbishness and stinginess where food was concerned; the damage he did to his own cause by refusing to compromise over the Dublin gallery site; and the unresolved difficulties he had left after his death by failing to have the 1915 codicil witnessed. However, as its name implies, *Hugh Lane's Life and Achievement* is celebratory in character and essentially uncritical in spirit. It was a book written from love and pride, and also grief because by the time she came to the task, Lady Gregory had lost not only her surrogate son but her real one also; a pilot in the Royal Flying Corps, Robert Gregory died in January 1918 when his plane was shot down over northern Italy. She was now almost seventy and her biography of Lane is imbued with poignancy as she looked back at ideals and hopes which were far too often unrealized; 'now it is for the dead I am living,'[45] she told Alec Martin. Preserving Lane's memory and fulfilling what she believed were his wishes became her most sacred duties for the rest of her life.

In keeping with the character of its author, Lady Gregory's book is meticulous in appreciative acknowledgement of anyone who had offered support to her nephew. It is, therefore, somewhat surprising to find only one passing reference to Sarah Cecilia Harrison, certainly one of his most devoted and powerful allies in the gallery struggle after she had been elected a member of Dublin Corporation in January 1912. Her loyalty to the cause was not necessarily reciprocated; other members of the pro-gallery group snidely referred to her as 'Saint Cecilia' and even Lane found she could be a liability. In late July 1913, in the midst of the bridge site debate, he wrote from Dublin to Lady Gregory: 'Miss Harrison is extraordinarily unpopular here. Everyone admitting her unselfish devotion to the cause, but she is very tactless – has many "bees in her bonnet"!'[46] Many of those bees related to improving the plight of Dublin's poor, but her first concern always remained Lane and the realization of his gallery. Even after the Corporation decisively rejected Lutyens's bridge design, she continued to hope the battle had not been completely lost; 'Miss Harrison writes rather often again!' Lane ironically observed to his sister in November 1913.[47] Whenever in London, she would call to Lindsey House and go shopping or to concerts with Ruth Shine.

After the *Lusitania* was sunk, the two women continued to see each other for some weeks. But then Sarah Harrison announced that her relationship with Lane had been closer than just that of a loyal friend; they were secretly engaged, she declared, and had intended to marry after he returned from the United States. A response of total disbelief from all quarters suggests this was a fantasy. There were many reasons not to give this story of an engagement any credence, not least the fact that Sarah Harrison was twelve years older than her supposed fiancé; his brief engagement in 1911 had been to a woman considerably younger, not older, than he. Lane had the companionship of his sister, to whom he was probably closer than anyone else, and had never shown any special interest in Sarah Harrison. Her letters to him, on the other hand, do suggest a rather hopeless devotion; while primarily concerned with Municipal Gallery business, they are invariably addressed to her 'Dearest friend' and, after expressions of concern for his well-being, conclude 'Ever yours, SCH'.[48]

Sarah Harrison now insisted only she knew the truth about the nature of her relationship with Lane and went further by denying the validity of both his 1913 will and its 1915 codicil; these were faked documents, she argued, and a real will still existed – or had been destroyed by members of Lane's family – which would reveal his real intentions towards her. He had left her £100 and a piece of jewellery but she refused to accept these because by doing so she would validate the will. In the years immediately after his death, during which time she stopped exhibiting any of her pictures, the dispute over Lane's will remained a private matter between herself and the members of his family. They naturally found her position deeply embarassing. While in Dublin in December 1918, Ruth Shine met a former editor of the *Freeman's Journal* who knew Sarah Harrison well and confirmed that 'she was quite mad on the subject of Hugh though quite sane on other things ... Dermod O'Brien told me she had been to see Steer with her story & floods of tears!'[49] Five years later, she decided to publicize her grievances in a formal statement and wrote to tell Lady Gregory of this intention, suggesting that they should first meet to discuss the issue. Lady Gregory's response was succinct; after thanking Sarah Harrison for her letter, she added 'I cannot think my going to Dublin to hear the statement you mention would serve any useful purpose'.[50] She asked Henry Harrison to speak to his sister but he replied saying that 'he has not seen her for months and that whenever he has any discussion with her he "wants to bash her head".'[51]

Sarah Harrison's statement denying the validity of Lane's will and codicil was first presented to Dublin Corporation in May 1924.[52] After this failed to achieve any satisfactory results, she began to badger the Irish press. When the *Freeman's Journal* received a letter from her on the subject, the newspaper's editor sent it to W.B. Yeats for his opinion; according to Lady Gregory, 'he was half inclined to let it be published to show how mad she is, but it was better not, our enemies might have made use of phrases. And Yeats says how the Dublin people are saying Miss Harrison drinks – and tho it may not be true it is as well they feel she is not a witness to be trusted.'[53] Unable to let the matter drop, in 1927 she published a pamphlet called *Inquiry concerning the Continental Pictures of Sir Hugh Lane, The Next Step*, the primary purpose of which was to argue that only she knew of Lane's real intentions regarding the disputed works and that the will and codicil should be disregarded. In case the arguments presented in support of this case were insufficiently powerful, she also claimed that a valuable collection of documents dealing with the subject had been stolen from a locked desk in her home. Ruth Shine was presented as an opportunist who had destroyed the real documents for the sake of financial gain, even though it was obvious that the principal beneficiaries from the 1913 will and subsequent codicil were not members of Lane's family but the National Galleries of Ireland and England. Although they took no legal action against her over the pamphlet's libellous remarks, Lane's family and friends now cut all contact with Sarah Harrison and so there was justifiable irritation when they learned in 1932 that Dublin Corporation had appointed her a member of the official Lane Bequest Claim Committee. 'I thought it peculiarly disgraceful', Thomas Bodkin told Lady Gregory, 'in view of her various crazy pronouncements on the subject of the will.'[54] The same year, Lane's old banker commented to Ruth Shine: 'Miss Harrison seems to be on the warpath again. I can't be bothered with her. Then I don't think anyone else can either.'[55]

Isolated by her own preoccupation with Lane, she had already decided to commemorate him alone, asking Lutyens in 1919 to design a memorial tablet. A decade later, she requested permission to erect this in St Anne's Church on Dawson Street, Dublin. Now placed on the wall of the building's north gallery, the plaque is dedicated 'To the beloved memory of Hugh Percy Lane, Knight' and records how 'Endowed with a passionate love of the beautiful, he dedicated his gifts to the service of Art and his Fortune to spreading a knowledge of it in his own country. The memory of his self-forgetful life, inspired by a devout and humble faith, is the precious possession of his friends.' While she continued to paint for some time more, until her death in July 1941 Sarah Harrison devoted much of her considerable energy to helping alleviate poverty in Dublin. Her other great devotion – to Hugh Lane – was not mentioned in the obituaries but in her studio were found two portraits she had painted of him; appropriately, one each of these is now owned by the National Gallery of Ireland and the Hugh Lane Municipal Gallery of Modern Art.

18
THE CONTESTED GIFT

Of all the many complications arising in the wake of Lane's demise, the most difficult and least easily resolved concerned the fate of his pictures. There were, for example, disputes between the National Gallery of Ireland and the Municipal Gallery of Modern Art over ownership of certain works, the rights of each institution being argued by Robert Langton Douglas and Ellen Duncan respectively. In his codicil, Lane had left to Dublin's Municipal Gallery the group of contemporary British paintings temporarily lent to Belfast and, while there were problems relating to the legality of the 1915 document, everyone in Ireland agreed about the collection's eventual destination. But Ellen Duncan understandably wanted to acquire as much as possible and asked that some of the modern pictures in Lane's ownership at the time of his death should now be offered to the Municipal Gallery. Douglas retaliated by quoting from the 1908 Harcourt Street catalogue in which Lane stated his hope 'that this Gallery will always fulfil the object for which it is intended, and – by ceding to the National Gallery those pictures which, having stood the test of time, are no longer modern – make room for good examples of the movements of the day'.[1] Precisely what steps, he asked Ellen Duncan, did the members of her own board propose 'to take to carry out the object for which Sir Hugh Lane founded their Gallery?'[2] Nonetheless, he and the National Gallery board were magnanimous and recognized that some works formerly in Lindsey House, while they ought to be seen in Dublin, were of too recent origin to find a home in the National Gallery, which only showed old masters. Harcourt Street therefore received a collection of more than sixty-five pictures by such artists as Orpen, Steer, Augustus John, Boudin, Corot and Mancini. Sargent's portrait of Lane also went to the Municipal Gallery.

In any case, both parties were united in a battle to regain possession for Ireland of the thirty-nine 'conditional gift' paintings which Lane had removed from Ireland in late September 1913 when his plans for a bridge gallery had been turned down by Dublin Corporation. At that time, he had imagined that these pictures would go on display at London's National Gallery in Trafalgar Square before the end of the year, but troubles had soon arisen. Lane had been prepared for problems, having told Lord Curzon in early August of that year that 'I confess to being quite out of sympathy with the English National Gallery, who seem only able to buy the dearest pictures on the market, and seem to be satisfied with a hopelessly old-fashioned method'.[3] But Curzon insisted 'I don't think we are as bad as we are painted,'[4] and when the gallery's Keeper and Secretary Hawes Turner wrote to confirm Lane's loan of his pictures all seemed well. The collection was accordingly brought to London, sent to the National Gallery and held in storage there while the building's new rooms, where it was to be shown, were completed. In late December, Lane together with the gallery's Director Sir Charles Holroyd supervised the hanging of the pictures and arranged that they would officially go on public view on 20 January 1914.

But before that date, the board began to indicate a change of mind about the paintings and their value. In mid-January they instructed Turner to write to Lane, informing him that they were 'disposed to think that, while some of these pictures are well worthy of temporary exhibition in the National Collection, there are others which hardly attain to the standard which would justify their inclusion'.[5] Sixteen of the thirty-nine works were deemed 'worthy of temporary exhibition' including the two by Manet, three by Corot, the Degas, an Ingres, a Mancini and Puvis de Chavannes's *The Toilet*. The same artist's *Martyrdom of St John the Baptist* was spurned, together with Monet's *Vétheuil: Sunshine and Snow*, Pissarro's *Printemps, Vue de Louveciennes* and Renoir's *Les Parapluies*.

These the board offered to store at Lane's convenience before going on to observe that the gallery had a rule that it only exhibited pictures 'in cases where there is a reasonable chance of their being acquired by the Board at a later date, either by purchase or gift or bequest'. Since funds were too limited to make purchase a viable option, Lane was requested 'before the Trustees proceed to the contemplated exhibition, to be good enough to inform them what are your views or intentions with regard to the future disposition of the pictures in question'.[6]

This offensive letter, which Lane contented himself with describing as 'singularly ungracious',[7] was sent to him while he was in the United States. He was justifiably incensed to read its contents on his return, and despite personal pleas for restraint from both Turner and Holroyd, he sent his response – drafted for him by D.S. MacColl – to the board in mid-February. Having noted that the gallery, and specifically Lord Curzon, had initially approached him about lending the collection to London, he went on to comment icily that he 'should never have dreamed of submitting my pictures for selection to members of the Board who, however distinguished in other respects, have no competence as experts in modern painting', and further added that any questions about his eventual intentions should have been asked before the offer of a loan had been accepted.[8] Although he made light of the matter in his correspondence to friends, Lane was seriously concerned. His intention in offering the pictures to London had been to win favourable publicity for the collection and thereby bring Dublin's authorities to their senses. Now he found himself attempting to negotiate with another organization which, after being initially amenable to his ideas, was proving increasingly intractable. 'I hope you won't give that London gallery anything – they are an absurd flock,' declared Lady Gregory, still hoping the pictures would return to Ireland in the near future.[9]

A standoff then followed in which Lane and the National Gallery expressed indignation at the behaviour of the other. In an attempt to resolve the disagreement, the board asked MacColl and Sargent to look at the collection and write a report on its merits. Not surprisingly given his friendship with the two authors, this document was entirely favourable to Lane's point of view and, as he told Lady Gregory, put the gallery's trustees 'in a rather awkward hole!'[10] But at the end of February Turner wrote again, a diplomatic letter in which he noted that 'some misunderstanding has arisen as to the circumstances in which the hospitality of the Gallery was offered to your collection', as a result of which the members of the board now felt 'they have no choice but to abandon the idea of exhibiting the collection, of which you will no doubt wish to resume possession'.[11] Embarrassed by this turn of events, preoccupied with his new appointment to the Dublin National Gallery and having nowhere to store the thirty-nine pictures, Lane was in no hurry to resume possession and so the collection remained in the basement of Trafalgar Square. Finally, in mid-October a new Keeper and Secretary C.H. Collins Baker sent Lane a note reminding him 'that we still have a large number of your pictures here', and that in view of the gallery's vulnerability to attack from German planes, the board would not be able to take responsibility should the collection suffer any damage.[12] Lane sent his response the following day, saying the paintings could remain in their present location as he was hoping to arrange for their exhibition in the Tate Gallery – 'It was this suggestion that induced me to refrain from publishing the particulars of this annoying affair' – and that 'I cannot even return the pictures to Dublin without removing the slur that has been cast on them'.[13]

The collection was not shown at the Tate and this continued affront to his taste and generosity, as much as a softening of attitude towards Ireland, was what caused Lane in February 1915 to write the codicil to his will according to which he left the thirty-nine pictures to Dublin. The existence of this codicil was not known in the immediate aftermath of Lane's death in May, when the only document found was the 1913 will leaving the collection to London. However, because he had told so many people of his change of heart, a search immediately began for a later will. The executors wrote in confidence to Lane's friends in Ireland such as Thomas Bodkin 'asking me to make enquiries as to any remarks he may have lately made about his will',[14] and, when this approach failed to yield results, advertised in the press on the same subject. John Quinn was consulted in case the deceased had drawn up the document while in New York, but he could give no help. It was Lady Gregory who decided to examine the locked drawers of her nephew's desk at the National Gallery of Ireland, and there in a sealed envelope the codicil was found. Her triumph at this discovery was short-lived because the paper had no legal validity; unlike the earlier will, it had never been witnessed. Under Scottish law witnesses would not have been necessary, and nor were they deemed so for wills left by men who died fighting for Britain during the war. But Lane's signature and initials on the codicil were judged to be insufficient and so the thirty-nine pictures belonged to London.

In this simple failure on Lane's part to follow correct legal procedure lay the origins of a dispute over ownership that was to cause much rancour between Britain and Ireland for the next thirty-five years and which has not been satisfactorily resolved to this day. A collection of thirty-nine paintings, in which neither country had shown great interest during Lane's lifetime, came to be the source of intense disagreement after his death. Both London and Dublin laid claim to outright possession of the works and refused to consider the possibility of compromise on the matter. At least part of the blame for the adoption of these intractable positions must lie with Lane's aunt. In early January 1917, when D.S. MacColl confirmed he would not be writing the biography of Lane, he proposed to Lady Gregory that the pictures be divided between the two countries: 'I am convinced that a scheme of alternate exhibition is the right solution, & I would use any influence I have to bring it about.'[15] But Lady Gregory, named as 'the sole Trustee in this question' in Lane's codicil, felt she had a duty not to yield any ground and for her the only option was that all the pictures be returned to, and exhibited in, Dublin. Had she been more amenable to compromise, the fight over the collection might have been resolved sooner. However, establishing Ireland's rightful ownership of the collection became a crusade for her and, especially after the death of Robert Gregory, no less than a reason for living; she was determined to see the pictures back in Dublin before her own death and used every means at her disposal to achieve this ambition. During negotiations with the British government in January 1922 over the implementation of the Anglo-Irish Treaty, for example, she had the matter of the Lane pictures raised by Michael Collins, who reported back to her that 'the attitude towards the return was not unsympathetic ... I most sincerely hope that we shall be successful in securing their return.'[16]

Such strenuous efforts make Lady Gregory's eventual failure all the more poignant. As she remarked in her biography of Lane, 'Personal sorrow and the advance of years and the grittiness of official discourtesy have done away with any joy of battle'.[17] Lennox Robinson later wrote, 'There is something heroic and pathetic in this old, importunate widow begging at this doorstep and that'.[18] She begged out of a sense of obligation to Lane and, at least in the years immediately after his death, with a certainty that she would see this mendicancy rewarded. To begin with, as the codicil's sole trustee she made a formal request for the return of the pictures and supported her claim with testimonials from Irish universities and institutions, as well as letters from as many as 150 individual artists in both Britain and Ireland. There was broad support for her application across all Irish political parties, with the Unionist leader Edward Carson being particularly helpful. In late October 1916, Robert Ross wrote to say he had just been staying for the weekend with the Prime Minister, Asquith, 'and I don't think I am indiscreet in telling you that he was extremely sympathetic to your views'.[19] Two months later, Ruth Shine wrote to *The Times* in defence of Lady Gregory's case: 'My brother had no business habits in the ordinary sense of the word and was ignorant of legal technicalities ... So little am I surprised at there being no witnesses to the codicil that my surprise is altogether that he should have written it so carefully.'[20] Around the same time, the board of the National Gallery in London responded to Lady Gregory's request for the pictures with expressions of regret that it could not overrule the terms of Lane's will but might in future consider lending some of the pictures to Dublin.[21] At the time, while there were obviously legal difficulties, these did not appear to be insuperable.

An intense correspondence, both public and private, followed over the next few months and in March 1917 the matter was raised in the House of Commons. Here a key difficulty in the resolution of the dispute was explained; the government argued that, except on the grounds that the pictures were forgeries and therefore worthless, an Act of Parliament would be necessary in order for London's National Gallery to repudiate Lane's bequest. The gallery's board now realized that its own cause was not helped by leaving the collection languishing in the basements of

Trafalgar Square and therefore arranged for it to go on exhibition. Many British art critics, while accepting that the group of pictures was uneven in quality, nonetheless found the show a revelation. Roger Fry was especially delighted by the Renoir, MacColl and Claude Phillips by the large Puvis de Chavannes. By arranging this exhibition, however belatedly, the National Gallery immensely strengthened its position because the potential loss to London was now much more widely appreciated. Public approbation meant the institution's board better understood the value of the bequest and was proportionately more reluctant to let it go elsewhere. In London, therefore, the legal status of Lane's will became more important than any consideration of his final intentions.

That Lane wished the pictures to return to Ireland was widely attested. Among those who made public statements on the matter was the deceased's cousin A.W. West, who reported that shortly before leaving Dublin for the final time, Lane had said 'definitely and unequivocably that he had decided, after all, to let Dublin have the pictures that he had sent to London'.[22] George Russell also confirmed that around the same date Lane had announced: 'Oh, Dublin will get the pictures all right. I made threats to frighten people here to get them to move.'[23] In Ireland, London's refusal to surrender the pictures looked like another instance of English perfidy and was treated as such. Obviously the small group that had always been supporters of Lane and his plan for a modern art gallery in Dublin campaigned for the collection's return on the basis of its aesthetic worth and the wishes of their late friend. But their number had not greatly increased and the inherent merits of the collection were probably no more appreciated than had ever been the case. However, by now in Dublin the pictures had become a metaphor for Irish rights being overruled by British self-interest and this, more than anything else, was what motivated the campaign for their return.

A large public meeting chaired by the Lord Mayor was held at the Mansion House in late January 1918 at which further appeals were made for Ireland's right to the pictures. Signatures were collected for petitions and prestigious names drafted to the cause. Later that year, Lady Gregory went to the National Gallery of Ireland where the old masters retained from her nephew's personal collection had gone on show, together with his portrait by Sargent. Looking at this picture, she wrote in her journal, 'The eyes seemed to follow me, seemed to reproach me for not having carried out what he had trusted me to do, the bringing back of the French pictures to Dublin.'[24]

But what more could she do other than continue her ceaseless round of appeals and meetings? The situation was further complicated once the First World War ended, as Ireland's struggle for independence from Britain and civil war made the latter's authorities even less interested in surrendering the Lane collection. The opinions expressed by the unionist author St John Ervine in early 1923 were widespread among English art lovers at the time; he argued that the paintings should not go back to Ireland because of 'the likelihood that on arrival in Dublin they would immediately be blown to pieces or burned by noble-minded Irregulars'.[25] Another view frequently articulated in London was that Lane, had he lived, would not have wanted the pictures to remain in an Ireland independent from Britain, although there was no evidence to show that his attitude towards the country would have differed from that of family and friends such as Lady Gregory, W.B. Yeats and Lord Mayo. In a 1948 lecture, Thomas Bodkin pointed out that when Lane first became interested in the development of Irish art, he had commissioned portraits from John B. Yeats and William Orpen of nationalists such as Michael Davitt and William O'Brien. 'He was an Irishman first and last,' Bodkin insisted, 'and had no political leanings'. Therefore, anyone who suggested Ireland's independence would have made any difference to Lane 'is grievously in error as far as I can judge'.[26] As the Free State came into being, a suggestion was made by artist Paul Henry that Lane's entire collection, including all the work still housed in Harcourt Street, be given a permanent home in Dublin Castle's State Apartments.[27] Despite widespread support, nothing came of this proposal and in May 1923 W.B. Yeats, by now a senator, proposed a motion in Seanad Éireann that the British government be requested to return the disputed pictures; this was passed, as was a similar motion in the Dáil nine days later. The following year, Sarah Purser founded the Friends of the National Collections of Ireland, the primary purpose of which soon came to be the campaign on behalf of the Lane Bequest.

The campaign in Dublin was matched by similar activity in London. In mid-July 1924 Carson, who had been raised to the peerage three years earlier, brought up the question of the thirty-nine pictures in the House of Lords and was told the government intended to appoint a committee of three 'competent and impartial persons' to investigate the subject. The committee, the membership of which consisted of a Liberal, Labour and Unionist M.P., was to report whether it believed that Lane when he wrote his codicil believed this to be a legal disposition and, if so, 'in view of the international character of the matter', whether the document's legal defect should be remedied by legislation.[28] Two years after being announced and having taken evidence from a wide number of witnesses, the committee presented its report. This declared that at the time of writing his codicil Lane did believe he was making a legal disposition but then concluded that despite his intended wishes being known, it would be improper to give effect to them; accordingly, the report proposed that the codicil should have no validity and the 1913 will be held sacrosanct. Although there were many precedents for the contents of a will being reinterpreted in English courts – such as bequests to the London National Gallery by J.M.W. Turner and Lady Gregory's old friend Sir Henry Layard – this option was not considered.

The reasons given for the report's decision, while many, were uniformly weak. For example, the committee dismissed the 1915 document as 'the momentary wishes of a man who, if still alive, would probably have been the first to deplore the result'.[29] This attempt to imagine what Lane might have thought had he not drowned on the *Lusitania* also underlay another important statement in the committee's report, where it was declared of the deceased that 'had he been spared to witness the growth of the new Gallery at Millbank no doubt could be entertained that he would have destroyed the codicil'.[30] The new Gallery mentioned was an extension to the Tate Gallery, the cost of which was paid for by Joseph Duveen. Since it was officially opened around the same time as the report appeared and since the Lane Bequest was immediately exhibited in the Tate's new rooms, a rumour spread that Duveen's donation was dependent on the presence of the pictures. 'No convincing evidence was ever produced in support of this assertion,' Thomas Bodkin declared later. He insisted not only that Lane often spoke 'in decided dislike of Duveen' but also that if the latter 'thought about the future contents of those galleries at all, he thought hopefully that they would be filled in great part with his own benefactions or, preferably, his own wares'.[31] Duveen had probably not needed to argue for the retention of the Lane pictures. Impressionism, which had enjoyed little favour in Britain outside a small group of *cognoscenti* in the years before the First World War, was now much more widely appreciated. But few examples of it existed in public collections, other than the Lane Bequest. Accordingly this became immensely important because it included representative examples of work by some of the movement's most important artists. Having nothing else, for the moment at least, London was unwilling to surrender Lane's pictures.

The British government committee's conclusions caused enormous pain and offence in Ireland; Lady Gregory, who immediately retaliated by publishing a pamphlet called *Case for the Return of Sir Hugh Lane's Pictures to Dublin*, wrote in her journal that 'we are back to the old story – English interests must have ours sacrificed to them'.[32] This interpretation of the official British report was widespread in Ireland. But the presentation of the Lane Bequest in the Tate Gallery's smart new extension drew attention to the fact that Dublin had made no sustained effort to meet an important condition of the dead man's codicil – that his pictures should go to the city 'providing that a suitable building is provided for them within five years of my death'. Twenty years after its foundation, the Municipal Gallery still occupied what were supposed to have been temporary premises on Harcourt Street, a situation which greatly weakened Ireland's claim on the disputed pictures. In June 1928, yet another public meeting about the Lane Bequest was held in Dublin, and in the same month the Irish government opened a public enquiry into the desirability or otherwise of erecting in Dublin a gallery in which to house the Municipal Gallery's collection as well as the thirty-nine contested works. The enquiry also examined what the costs of this building might be and how these could be met.

Shortly afterwards, the ever-resourceful Sarah Purser suggested to the President, William T. Cosgrave, that the eighteenth-century Charlemont House, which had until recently been used as offices for the Registrar

General, be converted to house the Municipal Gallery. A large garden of some 20,000 square feet lay behind the property and on this space could be built a series of interconnecting rooms to display the entire collection to best advantage. The following year the government handed Charlemont House over to Dublin Corporation, and the city architect Horace O'Rourke, having been allocated a budget of £35,000, began working on schemes for the new gallery. While the main building, originally designed by Sir William Chambers for the first Earl of Charlemont, was left relatively unaltered and served as a Civic Museum, O'Rourke entirely transformed the large site to its rear. Here he placed a series of five top-lit and interconnected rooms, flanked on either side by additional narrower galleries. These elegant spaces have served as Dublin's Municipal Gallery since being officially opened by Eamon de Valera in June 1933. By that date, Lady Gregory – who initially resisted the Charlemont House scheme but eventually agreed 'we must have no public dispute about a site this time'[33] – had died without seeing back in Ireland the pictures for which she had fought. A room for their eventual reception was set aside in the new gallery; this space stood empty except for a marble bust of Lane donated by his old friend Richard Orpen.

With Lady Gregory's death in May 1932, much of the energy that had driven the campaign to regain Lane's pictures for Ireland was lost. True, in the same year the Municipal Gallery's curator John J. Reynolds published his comprehensive *Statement of the Claim for the Return to Dublin of the 39 Lane Bequest Pictures now at the Tate Gallery, London*, and at the request of the Irish government Thomas Bodkin wrote *Hugh Lane and his Pictures*, which eloquently argued Ireland's case for ownership of the thirty-nine works. Dublin Corporation also established its own Lane Bequest Claim Committee, but none of its members felt, or could be expected to feel, quite the sense of personal obligation that had driven Lady Gregory during the seventeen years she lived after Lane's death. And after her passing, the fight for the pictures, while never abandoned, never again claimed as much public attention as had formerly been the case. Ownership of the collection became a matter for argument between two governments which were in dispute over many other matters. Even more than before, the inherent merits of the works became less important than what they represented. But after the publication in 1947 of Lady Gregory's journals, edited by Lennox Robinson with a chapter solely devoted to her battle on behalf of Ireland's right to the thirty-nine paintings, the subject once more came up for discussion on both sides of the Irish Sea. Many British reviewers of the book commented on the Lane Bequest controversy and their country's shameful behaviour in the matter – 'such meanness is almost incredible', remarked Desmond McCarthy in the *Sunday Times*.[34] That year, the question of the Lane pictures' ownership was again debated in the House of Commons where a government speaker dismissively declared that there was no reason to raise the topic.

It would not go away, however, and early in 1949 Thomas Bodkin began a correspondence with Bryan Guinness, Lord Moyne, concerning Ireland's right to the disputed collection. Moyne in turn sought to discuss the pictures in the House of Lords in late 1953 during the reading of the National Gallery and Tate Gallery Bill which proposed to divide the Lane Bequest permanently between the two institutions. On this occasion the government's representative, the Earl of Selkirk, confidently declared: 'My view is that if today Sir Hugh Lane in his grave knew that these pictures were to be removed to Republican Dublin he would turn in his grave.'[35] When the bill came before the House of Commons almost twelve months later, there was widespread discussion, and disapproval, of the decision taken in 1926 to keep the pictures in Britain. Circumstances had changed during the previous decades, and thanks to bequests such as that made by Samuel Courtauld London was no longer dependent on the Lane Bequest for good examples of Impressionism in the national collections. Dublin, on the other hand, had not enjoyed similar good fortune and so Lane's pictures were now proportionately more, rather than less, important if the Irish capital's Municipal Gallery of Modern Art were to live up to its name. But still the works remained in London, even though in 1956 two Irish students, Paul Hogan and William Fogarty, removed one of the Lane Bequest paintings, Berthe Morisot's *Jour d'Été*, from the Tate Gallery where it was on exhibition. After three days and extensive publicity, the picture was restored undamaged to the Irish Embassy in London and thence to the Tate.

By this time, Bodkin was corresponding not only with Moyne but also

Lord Pakenham (later Earl of Longford), who soon came to be known by the prime minister of the time, Harold Macmillan, as 'negotiator between the Irish and British Governments over the Lane pictures'.[36] Thanks to the intervention of Moyne and Pakenham, in 1957 Macmillan requested one of his senior civil servants, David Stephen, to prepare a paper on the bequest. Stephen's document concluded that a negotiated settlement on the dispute would be beneficial for Anglo-Irish relations out of proportion to the cost to Britain and would receive substantial support in the House of Commons. However, he warned, 'It is questionable whether a compromise would ever satisfy the Irish, feeling as strongly as they do. Is it not better to leave the pictures where they belong and where they are valued, and to leave the Irish with their grievance, which they enjoy?'[37]

This advice was ignored and discussions, intermittently acrimonious, continued between the two governments. The outcome was announced in 1959, when Britain agreed to divide the pictures into two lots and to lend one lot at a time to Dublin for five years at a stretch over a twenty-year period. As part of this settlement, Ireland had to guarantee that no legal action would be taken to retain the pictures while they were in Dublin, there would be no official support for any public or private initiative to keep the pictures in Ireland and the works would be housed in proper conditions. Writing to the *Sunday Times* when this news was announced Alec Martin, who had been on the Board of the National Gallery of Ireland since 1959, declared: 'I am certainly not an Irish nationalist. I am only on Lane's side. As an individual, I would infinitely prefer that these masterpieces should remain in London. But I believe that honour has been at stake and that right has been on the side of the Irish people.'[38] Martin, who had already presented Orpen's portrait of Lane's father to the Municipal Gallery in Dublin, now donated his old friend's favourite chair, which he had bought at the contents sale of Lindsey House, to the Crawford Municipal Art Gallery in Cork. The same institution now came to own Gerald Kelly's portrait of Lane just as the latter's sister Ruth finally died. She was followed in 1961 by Thomas Bodkin while Alec Martin, the last member of Lane's intimate circle, lived on until 1971.

And so, at last, the Lane Bequest paintings came back to Ireland, albeit only half at any one time, and were exhibited in the room that had been kept empty for them. It was the compromise suggested by MacColl and rejected by Lady Gregory back in 1917, by no means ideal but at least preferable to an ongoing quarrel. In 1975, to mark the centenary of its founder's birth, the Municipal Gallery was renamed the Hugh Lane Municipal Gallery of Modern Art. Four years later, the 1959 agreement expired and a new one was reached whereby thirty of the Bequest pictures were shown in Dublin while the remaining nine stayed in London. When this second arrangement had reached its time limit in 1993, another was agreed which allowed thirty-one of the pictures to stay in Ireland. The other eight were divided in two, each group to be lent for six years to Dublin. The eight are the most important Impressionist paintings, including work by Manet, Monet, Pissarro, Renoir, Morisot, Vuillard and Degas. The rest of the collection is less kindly judged than would have been the case a century ago; the reputations of Raimundo de Madrazo, Mancini, Narcisse Diaz, Monticelli and Forain – all of them represented in the Lane Bequest – have steadily diminished over the intervening period. London would probably not be troubled were the works by these artists never returned across the Irish Sea. Today, only a fifth of the entire group need be considered valuable, while the rest are of interest primarily for historical rather than artistic reasons. It remains a group, however, because of the nature of Lane's will; to break up the bequest would be to invalidate his will, and this, in turn, would greatly strengthen Dublin's claim to the entire bequest. Officially, therefore, all of the pictures are of equal status. The agreement by which some of them are lent to Ireland runs until 2005; and then, no doubt, a further temporary settlement will be reached. But the essential problem remains unresolved; while one country has legal claim to the Lane Bequest, the other has moral right. There has never yet been consensus on which of these is entitled to precedence.

POSTSCRIPT

In January 1995, Irish newspapers carried extensive reports that a collection of paintings worth up to £50 million had been discovered on the wreck of the *Lusitania*. Polly Tapson, leader of a group of British divers, told reporters that the previous August she and her team, while exploring the vessel off the coast of Cork, had come across three cylinders approximately four feet long and made of lead. She believed these tubes had been sealed to make them watertight because they held valuable pictures.[1] Speculation then arose that if there were works of art inside the containers, they had belonged to Sir Hugh Lane.

Divers had been examining the *Lusitania* for many years. Shortly after these reports first appeared, a case was due to be heard in the American courts over ownership of the wreck, which had been bought in 1969 by a consortium for £1,000 from the Liverpool and War Risks Company. In March 1995, the dispute over rights to the *Lusitania* was resolved when a New Mexico millionaire, F. Gregg Bemis, Jnr, was declared to be its sole owner. During the previous decade, Bemis had organized a number of exploratory dives to the vessel, and in the summer of 1994 he had unsuccessfully attempted to stop Polly Tapson's team from doing the same. Members of her group had attempted to claim salvage rights to the *Lusitania* in American courts later that year but without success. When asked about the paintings Tapson had claimed to have seen, Bemis denied all knowledge of the matter and the leader of his Irish diving team, Des

Quigley, also insisted he had not been asked to look for this material. But he did state his belief that the lead containers existed.[2]

Although Bemis's ownership of the wreck was confirmed in both the United States and Britain, his rights over the *Lusitania*'s cargo were not. In 1988, Irish legislation had extended the country's territorial waters from three nautical miles to twelve, which meant the vessel – previously in international waters – was now within Ireland's jurisdiction. As a result, any artefacts recovered would have to be handed over to the Irish authorities for safekeeping. While the government did not dispute Bemis's claim to own the *Lusitania*, it insisted on retaining rights over the vessel's contents, particularly as reports of the hold containing valuable paintings – and gold bullion – became widespread. Ownership of those contents had already been refused to Bemis in an American court. However, the fear that parties of plundering divers would now attempt to strip the wreck led Ireland's Arts Minister, Michael D. Higgins, to place a Heritage Protection Order on the *Lusitania*.[3] It was the first such order on a vessel less than one hundred years old and meant no further investigation could take place on the ship's remains without governmental permission.

But was there anything much to investigate? Media coverage of the subject tended to depend more heavily on speculation than information. The figure of £50 million given for the pictures supposedly on board was never substantiated by evidence and nor were the names of artists mentioned, such as Rubens, Monet and Titian.[4] An examination of the ship's twenty-eight-page manifest revealed that Lane's luggage contained only '1 case of paintings'. There were no references to lead cylinders and the word 'case' would seem to suggest a box rather than a sealed tube. The likelihood, therefore, is that any paintings would have long since been destroyed. As was pointed out in 1995, even if the 'case' holding art works had been sealed, the relatively primitive methods used for this purpose at the start of the twentieth century were unlikely to have survived more than eighty years of corrosion from salt and other minerals, as well as the constant pressure on the container of thousands of tons of seawater.[5]

In any case, it is highly unlikely that any paintings on board the *Lusitania* were of much value. It was claimed by the writer Colin Simpson in 1995 that Lane was involved in an 'insurance scam' run by Duveen whereby the pictures he had gone to New York to examine on behalf of Lloyds were now being brought back to Europe 'where they could be discreetly sold'. According to Simpson, 'Lane was on Duveen's payroll, as most curators were'.[6] A letter written by Alec Martin to Lady Gregory in August 1926 demonstrates the falsity of this proposition. 'There was little in common and certainly no love between Hugh and Duveen,' he reminded her, before adding bitterly: 'After all, you know that Hugh lost his life in a case against Duveen'.[7] Lane's disapproval of the other dealer's methods was widely known and the possibility of Lane being in the pay of Duveen (admittedly not an uncommon arrangement in the art world) is therefore remote.

Nor did he leave any documentation behind to indicate ownership of valuable pictures at the time of his death. Had Lady Gregory, or the National Gallery of Ireland which was the principal beneficiary of his will, known that he was carrying masterpieces in his luggage, efforts would have been made either to recover the items or to investigate insurance coverage. But among the files of papers dealing with the Lane estate, there is no mention anywhere of items in his possession on the *Lusitania*.

It is also highly improbable that Lane would have wished to bring paintings of any great worth to Britain, where the market had been in serious recession for the previous year. He already had a house full of old master pictures for which he was unable to find buyers. Prices at London auction houses had dropped by almost 50 per cent and his income from dealing had fallen correspondingly. The traffic in art across the Atlantic Ocean since the beginning of the twentieth century had been predominantly in the other direction as American collectors bought pictures from impoverished Europeans. For Lane, who had only just managed to salvage his own finances by selling two paintings to Frick in New York, returning home with more unsellable stock would have been ludicrous.

The likelihood is, therefore, that whatever Lane had with him on board the *Lusitania* was of little value and has since perished. If the lead tubes do exist, there is no direct evidence linking him to them and their contents. The most interesting feature of the 1995 affair is that even eighty years after his death, Lane could still be the cause of disputation and debate.

NOTES

As mentioned in the Introduction, the main sources for information on Lane hitherto have been the books by Lady Gregory (1920) and Thomas Bodkin (1932). Bodkin's papers, now in Trinity College, Dublin, add little to what he included in his Lane biography; even in an essay on his old friend published by Cork University Press in 1961 as part of a *Tribute to Sir Hugh Lane*, he provides no fresh information or insights.

When Lady Gregory wrote her book, she had to rely primarily on her own memory and that of Lane's friends and acquaintances, together with any correspondence in her personal possession. Most of that original material is now held by the Berg Collection in the New York Public Library, where the greater part of Lady Gregory's papers can be found.

Until recently, Lane's own papers have not been so accessible. After his death, they passed to his sister Ruth Shine, who lent them first to D.S. MacColl and then to Martin Wood as each man undertook to write Lane's biography. The papers then returned to her possession until her own death in 1960, when they were left to her cousin, Mrs G. de B. West and her niece Mrs Thistlethwaite. In the early 1960s, the latter gave some items to the bookseller Hodges Figgis in Dublin, where they were offered for sale; the National Library of Ireland bought some 150 letters from this source in 1962. The same institution had already been given Lane material by Mrs G. de B. West almost two years earlier, and her husband added further items to this donation. In 1984, Mrs Thistlethwaite gave the National Library of Ireland another tranche of letters and other documentation. The Library also owns a series of scrapbooks compiled by Ruth Shine in which almost every press reference to her brother and Dublin's Municipal Gallery of Modern Art has been pasted.

Mrs Thistlethwaite's son David had retrieved any unsold Lane material from Hodges Figgis around 1970 and this, together with most of the remaining family papers in his possession, was purchased by the National Library of Ireland in 1996. The new collection (referred to below by its accession number, Acc. 5073) contains much material that has never been seen before. There are, for example, approximately one hundred letters from Lady Gregory, written to her sister (and Lane's mother) Adelaide, to Lane himself and to his sister Ruth. Hundreds of letters, either by or to Lane, refer to various exhibitions he organized in England and Ireland and show the wide range of artists with whom he was in contact, including Jacob Epstein, Auguste Rodin, Augustus John and John Singer Sargent. Other letters provide evidence of Lane's social success and his wide circle of friends, while a series of notebooks he kept while on holidays overseas give an insight into his artistic tastes. Some papers also illuminate his methods as an art dealer.

David Thistlethwaite also provided the National Library of Ireland with a copy of the account book Lane kept during the latter part of his career. This lists all his old master purchases and is obviously of enormous interest, not least to the National Gallery of Ireland which now owns many of these works. The entire collection runs to well over five hundred letters, together with a wealth of related items, and has made it possible to create a much fuller picture of Lane and his world than would previously have been possible. There are still some documents retained by David Thistlethwaite; these are referred to below as 'Thistlethwaite Papers'. The 'Kermode Papers' are a small number of letters written by Lane and kept by his niece Ruth Kermode, who lives in Vancouver where her father Ambrose Lane emigrated before the First World War. Other sources of documentation, such as William Orpen's papers kept by the artist's family, have been consulted by other authors. So too have surviving relevant archives in the Hugh Lane Municipal Gallery of Modern Art and the National Gallery of Ireland.

Lane material continues to surface. In March this year, for example, Whyte's, the Dublin auction house, offered for sale a collection of fifty Lane letters which were bought by the National Library of Ireland. And there may be more: in a letter Ruth Shine wrote to Lady Gregory when the latter was writing Lane's biography, she mentions '12 to 14 cutting books' as well as a 'vast amount' of other papers (Berg, Ruth Shine to Lady Gregory, 12th December 1919). Related documentation is still widely dispersed; for example, an extensive correspondence on the subject of the disputed Lane pictures between Lady Gregory and Leonie, Lady Leslie, is owned by a family who found the papers inside a copy of the former's biography of her nephew.

Note: Full bibliographic data are given in the notes only for items not listed in the Select Bibliography.

ABBREVIATIONS

Acc. 5073: Collection of Lane papers in the National Library of Ireland not catalogued at time of writing

Berg: The Henry W. and Albert B. Berg Collection, New York Public Library

Bodkin: Thomas Bodkin, *Hugh Lane and His Pictures* (The Stationery Office, Dublin, 1956)

Gregory: Lady Gregory, *Hugh Lane's Life and Achievement, with Some Account of the Dublin Galleries* (John Murray, London, 1921)

NLI: National Library of Ireland

Stevenson: Michael Stevenson, *Old Masters and Aspirations: The Randlords, Art and South Africa* (Doctoral Thesis, Department of Art History, University of Cape Town, 1997)

INTRODUCTION

1. Bodkin: Preface to first edition.
2. *The Burlington*, June 1915.
3. *Irish Times*, 28 January 1995.
4. *The Burlington*, June 1915.
5. Berg: Lane to Lady Gregory, 30 December 1914.
6. Acc. 5073: Unsigned document on Lane.
7. George Moore, *Hail and Farewell*, p. 525.
8. Elizabeth, Countess of Fingall, *Seventy Years Young*, p. 197.
9. National Gallery of Ireland, Lane Papers: Lane to Dermod O'Brien, 6 March 1913.

CHAPTER 1: CHILDHOOD

1. Acc. 5073: Elizabeth Coxhead to G. de B. West, 6 February 1961.
2. Gregory, p. 4.
3. *Lake's Falmouth Packet and Cornwall Advertiser*, 17 November 1877.
4. Acc. 5073: Appeal Collecting Book of 1885.
5. Gregory, pp. 1–3.
6. Gregory, p. 6.
7. Bodkin, p. 1.
8. Acc. 5073: Lane to Dermod O'Brien, 6 February 1914.
9. Berg: From Lady Gregory's original manuscript of *Hugh Lane's Life*.
10. William Orpen, *Stories of Old Ireland and Myself* (Williams & Norgate, London, 1924), p. 54.
11. Berg: Ruth Shine to Lady Gregory, undated.
12. James Pethica, ed., *Lady Gregory's Diaries, 1892–1902*: November–December 1893, pp. 21–2.

CHAPTER 2: THE APPRENTICE DEALER

1. Peter Mandler, *The Fall and Rise of the Stately Home*, p. 127.
2. Stevenson, pp. 34–5.
3. Stevenson, p. 286.
4. Anna MacBride White and A. Norman Jeffares, eds, *The Gonne–Yeats Letters 1893–1938: Always Your Friend*: Maud Gonne to W.B. Yeats, 5 September 1913, p. 324.
5. Berg: Lady Gregory to Lane, 16 December 1911.
6. Gregory, pp. 23–4.
7. Acc. 5073: A. Birch to Lady Gregory, 3 January 1898.
8. Gregory, p. 12.
9. *Lady Gregory's Diaries, 1892–1902*, p. 34.
10. Ibid.; also Gregory, p. 16.
11. Acc. 5073: Lady Gregory to Adelaide Lane, May 1894.
12. Acc. 5073: Lane Diary, 3–27 September 1895.
13. Gregory, p. 148.
14. Grant Richards, *Author Hunting: Memories of Years Spent Mainly in Publishing*, p. 97.
15. Bodkin, p. 71.
16. *Lady Gregory's Diaries*, 1892–1902, pp. 83–4.
17. J. M. Solomon, *Hugh Lane: A Memoir*; *Country Life in South Africa*, vol. 1, no. 3, June 1915, p. 11.
18. *Author Hunting*, p. 97.
19. Acc. 5073: B. M. Lawrence to Lane, 5 June 1910.
20. Acc. 5073: Undated typed statement by Lane.
21. Berg: Lane to Lady Gregory, 18 February 1914.
22. Berg: Lady Gregory to Lane, 30 October 1904.
23. Gregory, p. 20.
24. Meryle Secrest, *Being Bernard Berenson*, pp. 139–40.
25. Gregory, pp. 22–4; also Acc. 5073: Document written by Dermod O'Brien in 1918.

CHAPTER 3: SUCCESS

1. Roy Strong, *Tudor and Jacobean Portraits* (HMSO, London, 1969), p. 90.
2. Acc. 5073: Document written by Dermod O'Brien.

3. Gregory, p. 28.

4. Acc. 5073: Copy of Lane's will dated 25 August 1898.

5. Acc. 5073: Receipt from Royal Academy to Lane for loan of paintings, December 1901.

6. Acc. 5073: Address written by Dermod O'Brien for the opening of the Lane pictures exhibition at the National Gallery of Ireland, July 1918.

7. Gregory, pp. 189–90.

8. Ibid., pp. 26–7.

9. Ibid., p. 5.

10. *The Burlington*, June 1915.

11. Hanna Kiel, ed., *The Bernard Berenson Treasury* (Methuen, London, 1962), p.68.

12. Gregory, p. 265.

13. Ibid., p. 73.

14. Acc. 5073: Lane Diary, 24 September–30 October 1899.

15. Gregory, p. 74.

16. Bodkin, p. 69.

17. Gregory, p. 251.

18. Acc. 5073: Humphrey Ward to Lane, 21 October 1900.

19. Ibid.: Lady Gregory to Adelaide Lane, 4 July 1907.

20. *Lady Gregory's Diaries, 1892–1902*, p. 242.

21. Acc. 5073: Lady Gregory to Lane, undated (March 1900).

22. Berg: Lane to Lady Gregory, 7 August 1907.

23. Acc. 5073: Lady Gregory to Lane, 1 February 1910.

24. *Lady Gregory's Diaries, 1892–1902*, p. 284.

25. Ibid.: Introduction, p. XXIV.

26. Ibid.: p. 277.

27. Elizabeth Coxhead, *Lady Gregory: A Literary Portrait*, p. 53.

28. Gregory, p. 31.

29. *Lady Gregory: A Literary Portrait*, p. 73.

30. Gregory, p. 32.

CHAPTER 4: THE DISCOVERY OF IRELAND

1. Gregory, p. 39.

2. NLI, Ms. 13,071: the Earl of Mayo to Lane, 9 June 1904.

3. Acc. 5073: Lutyens to Lane, 12 October 1910.

4. NLI, Ms. 13,071: Hutcheson Pöe to the Earl of Mayo, 10 January 1907.

5. Ibid.: Hutcheson Pöe to Lane enclosing part of letter from Dunraven, 8 July 1905.

6. Ibid.: Earl of Dudley to Earl of Mayo, 23 June 1908.

7. George Russell, *Imaginations and Reveries* (Maunsell & Co, Dublin, 1915), p. 72.

8. *Lady Gregory's Diaries, 1892–1902*, p. 187.

9. Acc. 5073: Jack B. Yeats to Lane, 11 December 1910.

10. Joseph Hone, ed., *J.B. Yeats: Letters to his son W.B. Yeats and Others, 1869–1922*, 31 May 1904.

11. Acc. 5073: John B. Yeats to Lane, 30 November 1903, 13 June 1904, 19 June 1906.

12. Ibid.: Walter Osborne to Lane, 2 March (undated).

13. Ibid.: Sir Gerald Kelly to Ruth Shine, 16 December 1949.

14. Ibid.: Kelly to Lane, 8 November 1907.

15. Gregory, p. 39.

16. Acc. 5073: Walter Sickert to Lane, undated.

17. Ibid.: John Currie to Lane, 17 September 1907.

18. J.M. Solomon, *Hugh Lane: A Memoir*, p. 12.

19. Gregory, p. 35.

20. *The Studio*, 1900, vol. 20, pp. 116–17.
21. *Hermes: An Illustrated University Literary Quarterly*, February 1908, p. 43.
22. *Irish Times*, 24 October 1902.
23. Ibid.
24. *Evening Herald*, 24 October 1902.
25. *Irish Times*, 15 December 1902.
26. Ibid., 7 January 1903.
27. George Moore, *Hail and Farewell*, p. 525.
28. Acc. 5073: Lane to Earl of Dudley, 22 May 1904.
29. NLI, Ms. 13,072: Draft application for directorship of the Walker Art Gallery, Liverpool, 5 October 1903.
30. Acc. 5073: H.S. Tuke to Lane, 29 November 1903.
31. NLI, Ms. 13,072: Robert Ross to Lane, 2 May 1903.
32. Acc. 5073: Lane to Lord Gough, 16 September 1903.

CHAPTER 5: THE IMPACT OF IMPRESSIONISM

1. Acc. 5073: Sir Thomas Drew to Lane, 29 November 1902.
2. Ibid.: Drew to Lane, 13 July 1903.
3. NLI, Ms. 10,201: Lane to Sarah Purser, 13 May 1903.
4. Acc. 5073: Lane to Sir Thomas Drew, 15 July 1903.
5. *Irish Times*, 22 January 1904.
6. Acc. 5073: Horace Plunkett to Lane, 10 February 1904.
7. Ibid.: Buckingham Palace to Lane.
8. Ibid.: Letters from John Lavery to Lane, 4, 14 and 22 February 1904.
9. John Kelly & Ronald Schuchard, eds, *The Collected Letters of W.B. Yeats*, Volume III (Oxford University Press, Oxford, 1994): Yeats to John Quinn, 2 April 1904.
10. *Irish Times*, 15 April 1904.
11. Acc. 5073: Loan Form from Gallery of the Corporation of London, Guildhall to Lane, April 1902.
12. Gregory, p. 60.
13. Acc. 5073: Lane to Earl of Dudley, 22 May 1904.
14. *Catalogue of the Exhibition of Works by Irish Painters*, Art Gallery of the Corporation of London, 1904; Prefatory Notice, p. x.
15. NLI, Ms. 13,071: Note by Lane written on letter from T.K. Williams dated 17 April 1904.
16. NLI, Ms. 13,072: John Lavery to Lane.
17. *The Week's Livery*, unsigned review, 2 July 1904.
18. Acc. 5073: William Orpen to Lane.
19. Orpen Papers: Orpen to Lane, 27 May 1903.
20. Ibid.: Orpen to Lane, 14 July 1904.
21. Sir William Orpen, *Stories of Old Ireland and Myself*, p. 49.
22. Tony Gray, *A Peculiar Man: A Life of George Moore*, p. 87.
23. *Daily Express*, 10 September 1898.
24. *Irish Times*, 1 April 1899.
25. Gregory, p. 56.
26. Ibid., p. 248.
27. *Daily Express*, 30 June 1903.
28. NLI, Ms. 13,071: Signed typescript, November 1906.
29. NLI, Ms. 13,072: Durand-Ruel to Lane, 10 February 1908.
30. *The Saturday Review*, 8 February 1908.
31. Acc. 5073: Theodore Duret to Lane, 29 September 1909.
32. *Irish Times*, 28 November 1912.

33. Orpen Papers: William Orpen to Grace Orpen, 18 September 1904.
34. Ibid.
35. Acc. 5073: Copy of Lane will dated 5 April 1905.
36. Lady Gregory, Berg: *A Note on Causes*, signed and dated 18 May 1916.
37. George Moore, *Hail and Farewell*, p. 525.
38. Gregory, p. 30.
39. Elizabeth Coxhead, *Lady Gregory: A Literary Portrait*, p. 45.
40. Ibid., p. 58.

CHAPTER 6: THE STAATS FORBES COLLECTION

1. Joseph O'Brien, *'Dear, Dirty Dublin': A City in Distress, 1899–1916* (University of California Press, Berkeley, 1982), pp. 126–7 , 131.
2. George Moore, *A Drama in Muslin*, p. 134.
3. NLI, Ms. 13,072: Earl of Mayo to Lane, 18 December 1906.
4. *Irish Times*, 12 January 1907, quoting speech made by Lane the previous afternoon.
5. NLI, Ir. 750841 D3, Volume One: Typed document, *The Collection of Modern Pictures formed by the late Mr J. Staats Forbes*.
6. Ibid.
7. *Irish Times*, 21 November 1904.
8. Ibid.
9. *Daily Express*, 21 November 1904.
10. *Saturday Evening Review*, 3 December 1904.
11. *A Modern Art Gallery for Dublin*, November 1904.
12. George Moore, *Hail and Farewell*, p. 529.
13. Ibid., pp. 647–63.
14. *Daily Express*, 9 December 1904.
15. *Daily Express*, 8 December 1904.
16. *Irish Times*, 21 December 1904.
17. Gregory, p. 49.
18. *Evening Herald*, 2 January 1905.
19. *Irish Times*, 16 January 1905.
20. NLI, Ms. 13,071: Lane to L.W. Livesey, 30 December 1904.
21. *Daily Express*, 5 December 1904.
22. *Daily Express*, 6 December 1904.
23. *Irish Times*, 9 January 1905.
24. RHA Manifesto in the *Daily Express*, 11 January 1905.
25. Bodkin, p. 17.
26. *Illustrated London News*, 25 February 1905.
27. NLI, Ms. 13,071: L.W. Livesey to Lane, 27 February 1905.
28. Ibid.: L.W. Livesey to Lane, 10 March 1905.
29. *Evening Mail*, 3 August 1905.
30. *Daily Express*, 8 June 1905.
31. NLI, Ms. 13,071: Earl of Mayo to Lane, 26 May 1905.
32. *Irish Times*, 11 May 1905.
33. *Daily Express*, 6 June 1905.
34. *Evening Mail*, 5 June 1905.
35. Ibid.
36. See John Hutchinson, 'Sir Hugh Lane and the Gift of the Prince of Wales to the Municipal Gallery of Modern Art, Dublin', pp. 277–87.
37. Bruce Arnold, *Orpen: Mirror to an Age*, p. 149.
38. *Irish Times*, 30 March 1905.

39. *Freeman's Journal*, 28 August 1905.
40. Bruce Arnold, *Orpen*, p. 149.
41. Acc. 5073: John Shawe-Taylor to Lane, 9 February 1906.
42. From the Introduction to *Catalogue of Pictures given to the City of Dublin to form a Nucleus of a Gallery of Modern Art, exhibited at the National Museum*, January 1905.
43. *The Collected Letters of W.B. Yeats*, Vol. III, ed. John Kelly and Ronald Schuchard: Yeats to Clement Shorter, 12 December 1904.
44. Gregory, p. 61.

CHAPTER 7: A MODERN ART GALLERY FOR IRELAND

1. Gregory, p. 9.
2. Ibid., pp. 194–5.
3. NLI, Ms. 13,072: Lane to Lord Balcarres, 21 November 1905.
4. *Irish Times*, 15 January 1903.
5. *Catalogue of the Exhibition of Works by Irish Painters*, Prefatory Notice, p. x.
6. *Hampshire Observer*, 13 March 1911.
7. *Catalogue of the Exhibition of Works by Irish Painters*, Prefatory Notice, p. x.
8. Acc. 5073: *Proposed Gallery of Modern Art*, 7 June 1904.
9. *Irish Times*, 21 November 1904.
10. NLI, Ms. 13,071: Document headed *City of Dublin Gallery*, November 1904.
11. Acc. 5073: *A Modern Art Gallery for Ireland*, 5 December 1904.
12. *Daily Express*, 30 June 1903.
13. *Daily Express*, 2 July 1904.
14. Acc. 5073: Address written by Dermod O'Brien for opening of Lane pictures exhibition at the National Gallery of Ireland, July 1918.
15. *Evening Herald*, 31 December 1904.
16. Gregory, p. 51.
17. *Dublin Evening Telegraph*, 8 December 1906.
18. *The Academy*, 29 January 1908.
19. *The World*, 28 December 1909.
20. Acc. 5073: Harold Begbie to Lane, 3 May (no year given).
21. NGI: Thomas Bodkin to Dermod O'Brien, 29 May 1915.
22. Bodkin, pp. 77–8.
23. Ibid., p. 7.
24. *Irish Times*, 10 February 1906.
25. *Catalogue of Pictures lent to the City of Dublin to form the Nucleus of a Gallery of Modern Art exhibited at the National Museum, Kildare Street*, January 1905: Explanatory Introduction.
26. *Irish Times*, 10 February 1906.
27. *Freeman's Journal*, 11 June 1906.
28. Acc. 5073: Earl of Iveagh to Lane, 28 March 1905.
29. Ibid.: Lady Colin Campbell to Lane, September 1904.
30. Ibid.: letters to Lane from Walter Sickert (no date); Roger Fry (20 November 1904); and William Rothenstein (no date).
31. Ibid.: Giovanni Boldini to Lane, 28 October 1904.
32. Ibid.: Lane to Auguste Rodin, 2 March 1906.
33. Ibid.
34. *Northern Whig*, 9 January 1905.
35. Ibid., 24 December 1904.
36. *First Exhibition of Modern Paintings in the Municipal Art Gallery Belfast, April–May 1906*, Catalogue Preface.

37. *Northern Whig*, 28 April 1906.
38. *The Athenaeum*, 8 June 1907.
39. Acc. 5073: C.H. Brett to Lane, 2 May 1906.
40. Ibid.: Brett to Lane, 18 May 1906.
41. Ibid.: W. J. Gilliland to Lane, 19 May 1906.
42. Ibid.: J.B. Ward to Lane, 6 March 1909.
43. Ibid.: Draft document prepared by Lane, 23 December 1910.
44. Statement issued by Modern Art Gallery sub-committee in January 1906.
45. Ibid.
46. NLI, Ms. 13,071: George Russell to Lane, undated.
47. NLI, IR750841 D3, Volume Two: Copy of citation presented to Lane, 11 January 1907.
48. *Freeman's Journal*, 12 January 1907.
49. *Irish Times*, 12 January 1907.
50. Ibid.

CHAPTER 8: THE GENTLEMAN PATRON

1. George Moore, *Hail and Farewell*, pp. 540–1.
2. Elizabeth Coxhead, *Lady Gregory: A Literary Portrait*, p. 116.
3. NLI, Ms. 13,072: Typed document on The Modern Art Gallery signed by Lane, 22 November 1906.
4. R.F. Foster, *W.B. Yeats: A Life, Volume One: The Apprentice Mage*, p. 327.
5. F.S.L. Lyons, *Ireland since the Famine* (Fontana, London, 1985), p. 242.
6. Ulick O'Connor, *Celtic Dawn: A Portrait of the Irish Literary Renaissance*, p. 314.
7. Acc. 5073: C. Russell to Lane, 22 August 1907.
8. Ibid.: Lane to Ruth Shine, 5 September 1907.
9. Ibid.: Bernard Berenson to Lane, 7 December 1906.
10. *The Scotsman*, 11 August 1907.
11. NLI, Ms. 13,072: Lane to Sir Algernon Coote, 14 May 1902.
12. Gregory, p. 185.
13. Acc. 5073; Alec Martin to Ruth Shine, 3 January 1934.
14. Hugh Lane Municipal Gallery of Modern Art, Dublin, HLG/1/10; Sir Alec Martin to Denis Gwynn, 3 February 1961.
15. Berg: Lane to Lady Gregory, 12 November 1907.
16. Acc. 5073: Durand-Ruel to Lane, 13 November 1907.
17. As told by Sir Alec Martin to David Thistlethwaite: see D.E.H. Thistlethwaite, *Sir Hugh Lane: A Discussion of His Taste and His Achievements* (B.A. Thesis, Cambridge University, 1972), p. 9.
18. *The Burlington*, June 1915.
19. Acc. 5073: Undated typed statement signed by Lane.
20. Acc. 5073: Arthur Willis of Geare & Willis to Lane, 29 May 1906.
21. Ibid: Mary Hunter to Lane, undated.
22. Ibid: Annie Swynnerton to Lane, 11 October 1904.
23. Acc. 5073: Ina Mathias to Lane, undated.
24. Acc. 5073: Mary Hunter to Lane, 30 November 1904.
25. See W.B. Yeats, 'The Municipal Gallery Revisited', in *Selected Poetry*, ed. A. Norman Jeffares (Macmillan, London, 1962).
26. Acc. 5073: Lane to Ruth Shine, 7 January 1908.
27. Ibid.
28. Joseph Hone, ed., *J.B. Yeats: Letters to his son W.B. Yeats and Others*: J.B Yeats to W.B. Yeats, 21 October 1907.
29. *Pall Mall Gazette*, 20 January 1908.

30. Orpen Papers: William Orpen to Lane, undated (1907).
31. Ibid.: William Orpen to Lane, undated (1907).
32. Ibid.: William Orpen to Lane, undated.
33. Ibid.
34. Ibid.
35. Ibid.
36. Orpen Papers: Lane to William Orpen, 19 November 1912.
37. Acc. 5073: William Orpen to Lane, 31 July 1914; Grace Orpen to Lane, undated.
38. Orpen Papers: William Orpen to Lane, undated.
39. Acc. 5073: Lady Foster to Lane, 31 March 1904.
40. Ibid.: Lady Foster to Lane, 2 June 1909.
41. Ibid.: Lady Foster to Lane, 11 March 1909.
42. Ibid.: Lane to unknown recipient, 20 November 1908.
43. Ibid.: Sir Algernon Coote to Lane, 2 March 1914.
44. Ibid.: Lord Castletown to Lane, 26 April (no year).
45. Ibid.: Sir Arthur Vicars to Lane, 2 July 1909.
46. Ibid.: Rose Barton to Lane, 18 June 1909.
47. Ibid.: Lord Fermoy to Lane, 15 July 1913.
48. Ibid.: John Madden, 14 February 1904; Lord Monteagle, (no date); Earl of Granard (no date).
49. Ibid.: Sir Algernon Coote to Lane, 26 December 1913.

CHAPTER 9: THE HARCOURT STREET GALLERY

1. *Irish Times*, 12 January 1907.
2. NLI, Ms. 13,071: Ambrose Lane to Lane, 25 March 1907.
3. *Freeman's Journal*, 8 September 1907.
4. *Irish Times*, 28 November 1907.
5. NLI, Ms. 27,756: Lady Gregory to Lane, 6 December 1907.
6. Acc. 5073: Lane to Ruth Shine, 10 December 1907.
7. *Manchester Guardian*, 6 October 1910.
8. *Daily Express*, 6 May 1912.
9. Catalogue of Municipal Gallery of Modern Art, Dublin, January 1908: Prefatory Notice.
10. Acc. 5073: Tom Robertson to Lane, 28 November 1907.
11. Catalogue of Municipal Gallery of Modern Art, Dublin, January 1908: Prefatory Notice.
12. Ibid.
13. *The Nation*, 5 April 1917.
14. Gregory, p. 50.
15. Catalogue of Municipal Gallery of Modern Art, Dublin, January 1908: Prefatory Notice.
16. Gregory, pp. 50–1.
17. *Irish Times*, 20 January 1908.
18. Viola Barrow, *Hugh Lane*, p. 131.
19. Bodkin Papers, Manuscripts Department, Trinity College, Dublin: William Rothenstein to Lane, 5 February 1908.
20. Ibid.: George Russell to Lane, February 1908.
21. Orpen Papers: William Orpen to Lane, 18 January 1908.
22. *Irish Times*, 21 January 1908.
23. *Freeman's Journal*, 21 January 1908.
24. *Irish Independent*, 21 January 1908.
25. *Le Figaro*, 20 March 1908.
26. *Le Temps*, 26 March 1908.
27. Acc. 5073: John Mulligan and R. Caulfield Orpen of the Municipal Gallery of Modern

Art Committee, Dublin, to British and Irish newspapers, 21 April 1911.

28. Acc. 5073: Lane to Earl of Iveagh, draft, 21 September 1908.
29. Ibid.: Lane to Ruth Shine, 14 September 1908.
30. Ibid.: unidentified artist to Lane, August 1908.
31. Ibid.: Byam Shaw to Lane, 13 August 1908.
32. Ibid.: Beatrice Elvery to Lane, 15 February 1909.
33. *Art Chronicle*, 13 August 1910.
34. Gregory, pp. 138–9.
35. Ibid.: p. 139.
36. Barbara Dawson, 'Hugh Lane and the Origins of the Collection', in *Images and Insights* (Hugh Lane Municipal Gallery of Modern Art, Dublin, 1993), p. 29.
37. Bodkin, p. 70.
38. Acc. 5073: Address written by Dermod O'Brien for opening of Lane pictures exhibition at the National Gallery of Ireland, July 1918.
39. Ibid.: Lane to Ruth Shine, 14 September 1906.
40. Bodkin, p. 70.
41. Ibid.: Lady Mayo to Lane, 3 January 1904.
42. Ibid.: Lady Foster to Lane, 7 September, no year.
43. Elizabeth, Countess of Fingall, *Seventy Years Young*, p. 264.
44. Ibid., p. 264.
45. Ibid., p. 266.
46. Ibid., pp. 266–7.
47. Acc. 5073: Dermod O'Brien Address, July 1918.
48. Gregory, pp. 242, 254.
49. Ibid., p. 247.
50. Ibid., pp. 250–1.
51. Berg: Lane to Lady Gregory, 27 August 1913.
52. Berg: Lane to Lady Gregory, 20 July 1912.
53. R.F. Foster, *W.B. Yeats: A Life*, Volume One, p. 386.
54. Berg: Lane to Lady Gregory, undated.

CHAPTER 10: LINDSEY HOUSE

1. Acc. 5073: Eustace Lane to Lane, 8 February 1909.
2. See Barbara Dawson, 'Hugh Lane and the Origins of the Collection', in *Images and Insights*.
3. Acc. 5073: Lady Gregory to Lane, undated.
4. Bodkin, p. 24.
5. Berg: Lane to Lady Gregory, Saturday (no date).
6. Gregory, p. 158.
7. *The Burlington*, June 1915.
8. Bodkin, p. 69.
9. Gregory, p. 168.
10. Ibid., p. 177.
11. Ibid., pp. 177–8.
12. NLI, Ms. 27,789: Typescript of feature on Lindsey House for *The Connoisseur* by Selwyn Brinton.
13. Acc. 5073: Thomas Bodkin to Lane, 25 August 1913.
14. Royal Institute of British Architects, Lutyens Papers: Lutyens to Lady Emily Lutyens, 14 August 1910.
15. *Country Life*, 26 October 1912.
16. Acc. 5073: Lutyens to Lane, 12 October 1910.

17. Ibid., 20 January 1910.
18. Michael Holroyd, *Augustus John*, p. 305.
19. Ibid.
20. Acc. 5073: Augustus John to Lane, 10 February 1910.
21. Ibid.: Lane to Dermod O'Brien, 31 October 1913.
22. Ibid.: Lane to Miss Newport, draft, 11 November 1913.
23. Michael Holroyd, *Augustus John*, p. 397.
24. Acc. 5073: Augustus John to Lane, 28 March 1915.
25. Ibid.: Richard Orpen to Lane, 29 May 1908.
26. Bodkin, p. 72.
27. Gregory, pp. 91–2.
28. Ibid., p. 58.
29. NLI, Ms. 27,791: Christie's sale catalogue, 27 June 1917.
30. Acc. 5073: Lane to Ruth Shine, undated.
31. Gregory, p. 252.
32. Ibid., p. 185.
33. Berg: Lady Gregory to Lane, May 1912.
34. Gregory, p. 173.
35. Berg: Lady Gregory to Lane, 27 December 1913.
36. Gregory, p. 171.
37. Bodkin, p. 70.
38. Acc. 5073: St John Lucas to Lane, undated
39. Acc. 5073: Lady Meyer to Lane, 10 June [1911].
40. Gregory, p. 180.
41. Angela Lambert, *Unquiet Souls*, p. 79.
42. Acc. 5073: Duchess of Rutland to Lane, 15 June (no year).
43. Ibid., undated.
44. Ibid., undated.
45. Ibid.: Marchioness of Ripon to Lane, Monday (no date).
46. Ibid., undated.
47. Ibid., undated.
48. Ibid., undated.
49. Bodkin, p. 70.
50. Ibid., p. 71.
51. Ibid., p. 73.
52. Acc. 5073: Teresa del Riego to Lane, 26 April 1908.
53. Bodkin Papers, Manuscripts Department, Trinity College, Dublin: Lane to Judy Bodkin, 18 September 1908.
54. *Irish Times*, 12 December 1904.
55. Acc. 5073: Sarah Harrison to Lane, 30 August 1905.
56. NLI, IR750841 D3, Volume Two: Sarah Harrison to Lane, 25 February 1908.

CHAPTER 11: JOHANNESBURG

1. Maryna Fraser and Alan Jeeves, eds, *All That Glittered: Selected Correspondence of Lionel Phillips 1890–1924*, pp. 241–3.
2. NLI, Ms. 13,072: Caroline Grosvenor to Lane, 16 April 1909.
3. Thelma Gutsche, *No Ordinary Woman: The Life and Times of Florence Phillips*, p. 276.
4. Jillian Carman, *Negotiating Museology and the Identity of the Johannesburg Art Gallery in the early Twentieth Century*, pp. 4–5.
5. Ibid., p. 5.
6. *Dublin Evening Telegraph Review*, 1 September 1910.

7. NLI, Ms. 27,775: Otto Beit to Lane, 15 January 1911.

8. Ibid.: Otto Beit to Lane, 3 April 1913.

9. Lady Dorothy Nevill, *Reminiscences* (Chatto & Windus, London, 1906), pp. 99–100.

10. Ibid., p. 105.

11. Stevenson, p. 186.

12. Ibid.

13. Gutsche, *No Ordinary Woman*, p. 235.

14. Gregory, p. 143.

15. Ibid., pp. 143–4.

16. *All that Glittered*, p. 224.

17. MLI, Ms. 13,072: Julius Wernher to Lane, 30 August 1910.

18. Ibid., Undated.

19. Stevenson, p. 201.

20. Illustrated Catalogue, Municipal Gallery of Modern Art, Johannesburg, Prefatory Notice by Lane, 29 November 1910.

21. Ibid.

22. Stevenson, p. 197.

23. *The Burlington*, 19 July 1911.

24. *The Morning Post*, 12 May 1910.

25. Acc. 5073: Lane to Ruth Shine, 4 June [1911?].

26. Ibid.: Lane to Ruth Shine, 7 May [1911?].

27. RIBA, Lutyens Papers: Lutyens to Lady Emily Lutyens, 9 September 1910.

28. Bodkin, p. 27.

29. Jillian Carman, *Negotiating Museology*, p. 7.

30. Johannesburg Art Gallery, South Africa, Ross Papers: Florence Phillips to Robert Ross, undated.

31. Acc. 5073: Florence Phillips to Lane, 27 December 1910.

32. RIBA, Lutyens Papers: Lutyens to Lady Emily Lutyens, 31 April 1911.

33. Ibid.: Lutyens to Herbert Baker, 27 March 1912.

34. Johannesburg Art Gallery, Ross Papers: Florence Phillips to Robert Ross, 6 December 1912.

CHAPTER 12: THE ONSET OF UNHAPPINESS

1. Anna Gruetzner Robins, *Modern Art in Britain 1910–1914* (Barbican Art Gallery, London, 1997), p. 16.

2. Acc. 5073: Henry Tonks to Lane, 8 April 1911.

3. *Morning Post*, 7 November 1910.

4. *The Athenaeum*, 12 November 1910.

5. *Hampshire Observer*, 18 March 1911.

6. *Irish Times*, 26 January 1911.

7. *Freeman's Journal*, 26 January 1911.

8. *Irish Times*, 29 March 1912.

9. Acc. 5073: Dermod O'Brien to Lane, 7 February 1911.

10. Bodkin, p. 73.

11. B.L. Reid, *The Man from New York: John Quinn and His Friends* (Oxford University Press, New York, 1968), pp. 213–14.

12. Acc. 5073: Frank Rutter to Lane, 25 February 1914.

13. Orpen Papers: William Orpen to Lane, undated (March 1906?).

14. Acc. 5073: Max Beerbohm to Lane, Saturday (undated).

15. Ibid.: Max Beerbohm to Lane, 7 May 1911.

16. Gregory, p. 183.

17. Elizabeth, Countess of Fingall, *Seventy Years Young*, p. 72.
18. Acc. 5073: Lady Annesley to Lane, 4 November (no year).
19. Berg: Lane to Lady Gregory, 25 July 1911.
20. Lane's will, 11 October 1913.
21. Gregory, p. 81.
22. Ibid., p. 147.
23. Berg: Lady Gregory to Lane, 27 July 1911.
24. Gregory, p. 184.
25. Ibid.
26. Bodkin, p. 73.
27. Gregory, pp. 166–7.
28. Acc. 5073: Unsigned and undated document of reminiscences of Lane.
29. NLI, Ms. 13,071: Lord Ronald Sutherland to Lane, 15 May 1900.
30. Acc. 5073: Lord Ronald Sutherland to Lane, 9 July 1907.
31. Gregory, p. 172.
32. Acc. 5073: Unsigned and undated document of reminiscences of Lane.
33. Bruce Arnold, *Orpen: Mirror to an Age*, pp. 243–4.
34. Orpen Papers: William Orpen to Lane, undated.
35. NLI, Ms. 27,781: Joseph Solomon to Lane, 13 May 1913.
36. Ibid.
37. Acc. 5073: Joseph Solomon to Lane, 7 July 1914.
38. Gregory, p. 253.
39. Acc. 5073: Joseph Solomon to Lane, 27 August 1914.
40. J.M. Solomon, 'Sir Hugh Lane: A Memoir', *Country Life in South Africa*, June 1915.
41. Ibid.
42. Berg: Lane to Lady Gregory, 13 November 1912.
43. Gregory, p. 252.
44. Acc. 5073: Part of Lane's horoscope by Mrs Newton-Deakin, undated.
45. Gregory, pp. 21–2.
46. Ibid., p. 33.
47. Ibid., p. 110.
48. Acc. 5073: Unsigned and undated document of reminiscences of Lane.
49. Ibid.: Lady Gregory to Ruth Lane, 8 October 1911.
50. Berg: Lane to Lady Gregory, 25 August 1911.
51. Ibid.: Lady Gregory to Lane, 10 September 1911.
52. Gregory, p. 184.
53. Grant Richards, *Caviare* (Grant Richards, London, 1912), pp. 73–7.
54. NLI, Ms. 27,766: Gerald Kelly to Lane, 11 September 1912.
55. Acc. 5073: Grant Richards to Lane, 6 September 1906.
56. Ibid.: Grant Richards to H. Harris Brown, 26 August 1911.
57. Ibid.: Sarah Purser to Grant Richards, 30 August 1911.

CHAPTER 13: MAX MICHAELIS AND CAPE TOWN

1. Stevenson, p. 223.
2. Gregory, p. 151.
3. Bodkin, p. 27.
4. *The Studio*, May 1913.
5. Thelma Gutsche, *No Ordinary Woman: The Life and Times of Florence Phillips*, p. 288.
6. Ross Papers, Johannesburg Art Gallery, Florence Phillips to Robert Ross, November 1912.
7. Gregory, p. 150.

8. Stevenson, p. 235.

9. Acc. 5073: Max Michaelis to Lane, 18 October 1912.

10. Ibid.: Lane to Max Michaelis, 19 October 1912.

11. Ibid.: Lane to Max Michaelis, 27 October 1912.

12. Ibid.: Max Michaelis to Lane, 1 November 1912.

13. Stevenson, p. 122.

14. Acc. 5073: Wilhelm von Bode to Lane, 15 December 1906.

15. Ibid.: Max Michaelis to Lane, 23 November 1912.

16. Ibid.: Wilhelm von Bode to Lane, 3 December 1912.

17. Ibid.: Lane to Wilhelm von Bode, draft, 8 December 1912.

18. Ibid.: Wilhelm von Bode to Lane, 18 March 1913.

19. *The Burlington*, 22 January 1913.

20. Stevenson, p. 244.

21. Gregory, p. 151.

22. Stevenson, p. 254.

23. Ibid.

24. Acc. 5073: Max Michaelis to Lane, 11 May 1913.

25. *Daily Telegraph*, 27 May 1913.

26. Homan Potterton, *Dutch Seventeenth and Eighteenth Century Paintings in the National Gallery of Ireland: A Complete Catalogue*, p. 125.

27. *Daily Telegraph*, 27 May 1913.

28. *The Times*, 12 February 1914.

29. Acc. 5073: Max Michaelis to Lane, 29 May 1913.

30. Ibid.: Lane to Max Michaelis, 30 May 1913.

31. Stevenson, p. 249.

32. Ibid., p. 250.

33. Acc. 5073: Wilhelm von Bode to Lane, 28 July 1913.

34. Ibid.: Alois Hauser to Lane, 13 August 1913.

35. Ibid.

36. *The Times*, 13 February 1914.

37. *The Times*, 19 February 1914.

38. Acc. 5073: Copy of Lane to Wilhelm von Bode, 19 February 1914.

39. Stevenson, p. 253.

40. Ross Papers: Robert Ross to Florence Phillips, 7 March 1917.

41. Acc. 5073: Edward Roworth to Lane, 20 May 1913.

42. NLI, Ms. 27,780: Florence Phillips to Lane, 7 May 1913.

43. NLI, Ms. 27,781: Joseph Solomon to Ruth Shine, 22 June 1913.

44. NLI, Ms. 27,781: Joseph Solomon to Lane, 18 September 1913.

45. NLI, Ms. 27,781: Joseph Solomon to Lane, 18 September 1913.

46. Acc. 5073: Joseph Solomon to Ruth Shine, 3 December 1915.

47. Ibid.: Joseph Solomon to Ruth Shine, 28 January 1916.

CHAPTER 14: CONTROVERSY

1. Ross Papers, Johannesburg Art Gallery: William Orpen to Robert Ross, 9 June 1913.

2. *Irish Times*, 25 July 1912.

3. Kermode Papers: Lane to Ruth Shine, 11 July 1912.

4. *Irish Times*, 20 July 1912.

5. Catalogue of the Municipal Gallery of Modern Art, Dublin, January 1908: Prefatory Notice.

6. Kermode Papers: Lane to Ruth Shine, 11 July 1912.

7. *Irish Times*, 13 July 1912.

8. Ibid.: 30 July 1912.
9. Gregory, p. 106.
10. Acc. 5073: Edwin Lutyens to Lane, 12 October 1912.
11. *Irish Times,* 2 December 1912.
12. Berg: Lane to Lady Gregory, 13 November 1912.
13. *Freeman's Journal,* 19 November 1912.
14. *Sunday Independent*, 17 November 1912.
15. *Irish Times,* 30 November 1912.
16. NLI, Ms. 13,071: Earl of Iveagh to Countess of Mayo, 14 September 1912.
17. NLI, Ms. 13,071: Countess of Mayo to Lady Gregory, 17 September 1912.
18. *Irish Times,* 30 November 1912.
19. Berg: Lady Gregory to Lane, 11 December 1912.
20. Berg: Lane to Lady Gregory, 15 February 1913.
21. Ibid.: W.B. Yeats to Lady Gregory, 8 January 1913.
22. *Irish Times,* 11 January 1913.
23. Ibid., 24 March 1913.
24. *Irish Catholic*, 21 December 1912.
25. Ibid., 18 January 1913.
26. *Irish Times,* 13 January 1913.
27. *Daily Express*, 18 January 1913.
28. *Irish Times,* 20 January 1913.
29. *Irish Times,* 11 February 1913.
30. Ibid.
31. Berg: Lane to Lady Gregory, 1 July 1913.
32. *Freeman's Journal*, 29 November 1912.
33. *Irish Times,* 11 February 1913.
34. Ibid., 19 February 1913.
35. Ibid., 20 March 1913.
36. Ibid., 19 March 1913.
37. Gregory, p. 110.
38. *Irish Times,* 6 December 1912.
39. P.L. Dickinson, *The Dublin of Yesterday*, p. 38.
40. Gregory, p. 131.
41. *Irish Independent*, 20 August 1913.
42. *Dublin Daily Express*, 21 April 1913.
43. *Dublin Evening Mail*, 31 July 1913.
44. Gregory, p. 141.
45. *Irish Independent*, 14 July 1913.
46. *Manchester Guardian*, 15 July 1913.
47. See Gregory, pp. 119–20.
48. *Irish Times,* 19 July 1913.
49. Berg: Lane to Lady Gregory, 13 August 1913.
50. NLI, Ms. 27,756: Lady Gregory to Lane, 25 August 1913.
51. Berg: Lane to Lady Gregory, 27 August 1913.
52. P.L. Dickinson, *The Dublin of Yesterday*, pp. 38–9.
53. Berg: Lane to Lady Gregory, 31 July 1913.
54. Acc. 5073: Lady Gregory to Lane, 3 August 1913.
55. *Irish Times,* 22 August 1913.
56. Berg: Lady Gregory to Lane, 16 September 1913.
57. Berg: Lane to Lady Gregory, 19 September 1913.
58. *Manchester Guardian*, 9 September 1913.
59. *Dublin Saturday Herald*, 13 September 1913.

CHAPTER 15: TWO NATIONAL GALLERIES BECKON

1. Acc. 5073: Lane to Charles Holroyd, draft, 17 January 1907.
2. S.C. Harrison, *Inquiry concerning the Continental Pictures of Sir Hugh Lane, 1926* (Hodgson & Son, London, 1927), p. 4.
3. Ibid.
4. Acc. 5073: Robert Ross to Lane, 24 July 1913.
5. Acc. 5073: Charles Holroyd to Lane, 28 July 1913.
6. Berg: Lane to Lady Gregory, 31 July 1913.
7. Acc. 5073: Lane to Lord Curzon, draft, 8 August 1913.
8. Ibid.: Hawes Turner to Lane, 12 August 1913.
9. Ibid.: Lord Curzon to Lane, 30 August 1913.
10. *Northern Whig*, 30 August 1913.
11. Ibid., 20 September 1913.
12. Ibid.
13. NLI, Ms. 13,071: Lord Mayor of Belfast to Lane, 19 September 1913.
13. *Freeman's Journal*, 15 January 1914.
14. Berg: Lane to Lady Gregory, 21 November 1913.
15. *Irish Times*, 22 September 1913.
16. Berg: Lane to Lady Gregory, 27 September 1913.
17. National Gallery of Ireland, Lane Papers: Copy of Lane's will, 11 October 1913.
18. Gregory, p. 220.
19. Berg: Lane to Lady Gregory, 12 November 1913.
20. Gregory, p. 218.
21. NLI, Ms. 27,773: F. Derwent Wood to Lane (undated).
22. Berg: Lane to Lady Gregory, September 1913–23. Bodkin, p. 74.
24. Theodore Dreiser, *A Traveller at Forty*, p. 136.
25. Ibid., p. 280.
26. Ibid., p. 278.
27. Ibid., p. 297.
28. Acc. 5073: Lane to Ruth Shine, 20 March (no year).
29. Ibid.: Lady Gregory to Ruth Shine (undated).
30. Kermode Papers: Lane to Ruth Shine, 10 November 1913.
31. *Daily Mail*, 22 December 1913.
32. Trinity College, Dublin, Bodkin Papers: Lane to Arabella Bodkin, December 1913.
33. Acc. 5073: Lady Gregory to Lane, [late 1909].
34. Berg: Lane to Lady Gregory, 8 August 1912.
35. Acc. 5073: Lane to Mrs Newport, draft, 11 November 1913.
36. Berg: Lane to Lady Gregory, 21 November 1913.
37. Berg: Lane to Lady Gregory, 13 February 1914.
38. George Moore, *Hail and Farewell*, p. 546.
39. Berg: George Moore to Lady Gregory, 9 January 1914.
40. George Moore, *Hail and Farewell*, p. 527.
41. Ibid.
42. Ibid., p. 526.
43. Berg: Lane to Lady Gregory, 13 February 1914.
44. Berg: Lane to Lady Gregory, 9 March 1914.
45. Ibid.: Lane to Lady Gregory, 8 April 1912.
46. Ibid.
47. William Orpen, *Stories of Old Ireland and Myself*, p. 54.
48. National Gallery of Ireland, Lane Papers: Lane to Dermod O'Brien, 6 April 1913.
49. NLI, Ms. 27,781: Joseph Solomon to Lane, 13 May 1913.
50. Berg: Lane to Lady Gregory, 31 July 1913.

51. Ibid.: Lane to Dermod O'Brien, 31 October 1913.
52. National Gallery of Ireland, Lane Papers: Lane to Sarah Purser, 1 December 1913.
53. Ibid.: Sir Walter Armstrong to Lane, 30 December 1913.
54. NLI, Ms. 13,071: Lane to J.P. Mahaffy, 31 December 1913.
55. Gregory, p. 200.
56. Berg: Lady Gregory to Lane, 23 January 1914.
57. NLI, Ms. 13,071: J.P. Mahaffy to Lane, 5 January 1914.
58. National Gallery of Ireland, Lane Papers: Lane to Sir Walter Armstrong, 28 February 1914.
59. NLI, Ms. 27,784: Telegrams from Thomas Bodkin, Sarah Harrison and Lady Gregory to Lane, 26 February 1914.
60. Gregory, pp. 201–2.
61. NLI, Ms. 27,785: E. Trevelyan Turner to Lane, 27 February 1914.

CHAPTER 16: AN OFFICIAL POSITION

1. Gregory, p. 202.
2. Ibid.
3. Acc. 5073: Edwin Lutyens to Lane, 22 May 1914.
4. National Gallery of Ireland Catalogue, 1914, p. 47.
5. Kermode Papers: Lane to Ruth Shine, 5 June 1914.
6. *Illustrated Summary Catalogue of Paintings*, National Gallery of Ireland, 1981: Introduction, p. xxvii.
7. National Gallery of Ireland, Lane Papers: Lane to Sarah Purser, 1 December 1913.
8. NLI, Ms. 13,071: Lane to J.P. Mahaffy, 31 December 1913.
9. Berg: Lady Gregory to Lane, 13 December 1905.
10. Ibid.: Lane to Lady Gregory, 11 November 1911.
11. Gregory, p. 187.
12. Kermode Papers: Lane to Ruth Shine, 10 November 1913.
13. Kermode Papers: Lane to Ruth Shine, 27 December 1915.
14. Gregory, p. 250.
15. Acc. 5073: the Countess of Warwick to Lane, 5 June 1912.
16. Ibid.
17. NLI, Ms. 13,071: Lane to J.P. Mahaffy, 31 December 1913.
18. National Gallery of Ireland, Lane Papers: the Treasury to the NGI, 11 April 1914.
19. Ibid.: NGI to the Tresaury, 24 April 1914.
20. Ibid.: W.F. Bailey to the Treasury, 14 July 1914.
21. Ibid.: the Treasury to John Boland, 18 January 1915.
22. Ibid.: Lane to the Treasury, 20 January 1915.
23. Acc. 5073: Draft Lane to Alfred Beit, 29 May 1906.
24. Gregory, p. 213.
25. Thistlethwaite Papers: Copy of Lane's business account book.
26. Acc. 5073: Caroline Grosvenor to Lane, 4 March 1911.
27. Thistlethwaite Papers: Copy of Lane's business account book.
28. Bodkin, p. 42.
29. Acc. 5073: Raymon Wyer to Lane, 1 October 1914.
30. Berg: Lane to Lady Gregory, 30 December 1914.
31. National Gallery of Ireland, Lane Papers: Copy of Lane's codicil, 3 February 1915.
32. Acc. 5073: Diary of Ruth Shine, entry for 20 February 1915.
33. Gregory, p. 211.
34. Private Collection: Copy of National Gallery of Ireland catalogue, 1914.
35. Berg: R. Freeman Smith to Lady Gregory, 30 May 1921.

36. *Irish Times*, 10 May 1915.
37. Berg: Alec Martin to Lady Gregory, 3 September 1924.
38. Ibid.: Lane to Lady Gregory, 28 April 1915.
39. Kermode Papers: Postcard from Lane to Ruth Shine, 11 April 1915.
40. New York Public Library, Quinn Papers: John Quinn to Lady Gregory, 11 May 1915.
41. Ibid.: John Quinn to Lady Gregory, 7 May 1915.
42. Ibid.: John Quinn to Lady Gregory, 27 April 1915.
43. NLI, Ms. 27,786: Charles Henry Brady to Ruth Shine, 28 May 1915.
44. Acc. 5073: Alec Martin to Ruth Shine, 27 April 1915.
45. *Manchester Guardian*, 28 April 1915.
46. Berg: Lane to Lady Gregory, 28 April 1915.
47. NLI, Ms. 27,756: Lady Gregory to Lane, 30 April 1915.
48. New York Public Library, Quinn Papers: Lane to John Quinn, 30 April 1915.

CHAPTER 17: AFTERMATH

1. Acc. 5073: Alec Martin to Ruth Shine, 7 May 1915.
2. Gregory, p. 216.
3. Acc. 5073: Diary of Ruth Shine, 9 May 1915.
4. Acc. 5073: Public Notice: *Lost on the Lusitania*.
5. Gregory, p. 216.
6. Acc. 5073: Cicely Loftus to Ruth Shine, 12 May 1915.
7. Gregory, p.217.
8. New York Public Library, Quinn Papers: John Quinn to Lady Gregory, 11 May 1915.
9. NLI, Ms. 10,929: W.F. Bailey to Lady Gregory, 25 May 1915.
10. Elizabeth Coxhead, *Daughters of Erin*, p. 155.
11. NLI, Ms. 10,929: Priscilla Annesley to Ruth Shine, 12 May 1915.
12. Ibid.: Margaret Grosvenor to Ruth Shine, 19 May 1915.
13. *Freeman's Journal*, 10 May 1915.
14. *Sunday Times*, 16 May 1915.
15. *Daily Chronicle*, 20 May 1915.
16. *Irish Times*, 8 May 1915.
17. Ibid.: 10 May 1915.
18. *Irish Times*, 20 May 1915.
19. *Irish Times*, 4 September 1916.
20. National Gallery of Ireland, Lane Papers: Thomas Bodkin to Dermod O'Brien, 29 May 1915.
21. Ibid.: Thomas Bodkin to Dermod O'Brien (undated).
22. Ibid.: Dermod O'Brien to J.P. Mahaffy, 1 June 1915.
23. Ibid.: Earl of Mayo to W.F. Bailey, 28 May 1915.
24. National Gallery of Ireland, Douglas Papers: R. Langton Douglas to the Chief Crown Solicitor, 23 November 1917.
25. Ibid.
26. Ibid.: R. Langton Douglas to Dermod O'Brien, 24 June 1917.
27. Introduction to catalogue of *Old Master Paintings Given and Bequeathed to the National Gallery of Ireland by Sir Hugh Lane*, National Gallery of Ireland, 1918.
28. NLI, Ms. 10,929: John Quinn to Lady Gregory, 26 January 1918.
29. Acc. 5073: Lady Gregory to Ruth Shine, 30 March 1916.
30. Berg: D.S. MacColl to Lady Gregory, 24 June 1916.
31. *Observer*, 24 December 1916.
32. Berg: D.S. MacColl to Lady Gregory, 28 December 1916.
33. *Observer*, 14 January 1917.

34. Acc. 5073: Alec Martin to Ruth Shine, 4 May 1917.
35. Ibid.: Alec Martin to Ruth Shine, 26 August 1917.
36. Ibid.: Martin Wood to Lady Gregory, 19 August 1917.
37. Ibid.: Alec Martin to Lady Gregory, 21 May 1919.
38. Ibid.: Lady Gregory to Alec Martin, 25 August 1919.
39. Ibid.: Lady Gregory to Ruth Shine, 19 November 1919.
40. Ibid.
41. Berg: Lady Gregory to Alec Martin, 25 August 1919.
42. Acc. 5073: Lady Gregory to Ruth Shine, 19 November 1919.
43. NLI, Ms. 27,756: Lady Gregory to W.B. Yeats, 15 December 1919.
44. Ibid.: Lady Gregory to Ruth Shine, 8 June 1919.
45. Acc. 5073: Lady Gregory to Alec Martin, 25 August 1919.
46. Berg: Lane to Lady Gregory, 31 July 1913.
47. Kermode Papers: Lane to Ruth Shine, 10 November 1913.
48. NLI, Ms. 13,071: Letters from Sarah Cecilia Harrison to Lane, June to September 1913.
48. Berg: Ruth Shine to Lady Gregory, 9 December 1918.
49. Ibid.: Lady Gregory to Sarah Harrison, 12 March 1923.
50. Lennox Robinson, ed., *Lady Gregory's Journals, 1916–1930*, p. 301.
51. Acc. 5073: Typed document: *Statement of Miss S.C. Harrison prepared for the Municipal Council of Dublin, 19 May 1924.*
52. Ibid.: Lady Gregory to Ruth Shine, 1 June [1924?].
53. Ibid.: Thomas Bodkin to Lady Gregory, 18 January 1932.
54. Ibid.: W. Meagher to Ruth Shine, 14 January 1932.

CHAPTER 18: THE CONTESTED GIFT

1. *Catalogue of the Municipal Gallery of Modern Art, Dublin*, January 1908: Prefatory Notice.
2. National Gallery of Ireland, Douglas Papers: R. Langton Douglas to the Treasury Solicitor, 13 November 1917.
3. Acc. 5073: Draft Lane to Lord Curzon, 8 August 1913.
4. Ibid.: Lord Curzon to Lane, 10 August 1913.
5. Ibid.: Hawes Turner to Lane, 15 January 1914.
6. Ibid.
7. Acc. 5073: Lane to the National Gallery, 12 February 1914.
8. Ibid.
9. Berg: Lady Gregory to Lane, 15 February 1914.
10. Ibid.: Lane to Lady Gregory, 18 February 1914.
11. Acc. 5073: Hawes Turner to Lane, 28 February 1914.
12. Ibid.: C.H. Collins Baker to Lane, 11 October 1914.
13. Ibid.: Lane to C.H. Collins Baker, 12 October 1914.
14. National Gallery of Ireland, Lane Papers: Thomas Bodkin to Dermod O'Brien, 29 May 1915.
15. Acc. 5073: D.S. MacColl to Lady Gregory, 7 January 1917.
16. *Irish Times*, 30 November 1922.
17. Gregory, p. 218.
18. Lennox Robinson, ed., *Lady Gregory's Journals*, p. 286.
19. Berg: Robert Ross to Lady Gregory, 29 October 1916.
20. *The Times*, 5 December 1916.
21. Hugh Lane Municipal Gallery of Modern Art, Dublin, Lane Papers: Copy of the Trustees and Director of the National Gallery, London to Lady Gregory, 1 December 1916.
22. *Irish Times*, 17 July 1924.

23. Bodkin, p. 46.
24. Lennox Robinson, ed., *Lady Gregory's Journals*, p. 291.
25. *The Nation and Athenaeum*, 10 February 1923.
26. Trinity College, Dublin, Bodkin Papers: Hermione Lecture given by Thomas Bodkin at Alexandra College, Dublin in February 1948.
27. *Freeman's Journal*, 4 October 1922.
28. *Statement of the Claim for the Return to Dublin of the 39 Lane Bequest Pictures now at the Tate Gallery, London* compiled and edited by John J. Reynolds (Dublin Corporation, 1932), p. 37.
29. Bodkin, p. 53.
30. Ibid.
31. Ibid., p. 93.
32. Lennox Robinson, ed., *Lady Gregory's Journals*, p. 310
33. Ibid., p. 316.
34. *Sunday Times*, 2 February 1947.
35. Bodkin, p. 86.
36. *Irish Times*, 2 January 1990.
37. Ibid.
38. *Sunday Times*, 22 November 1959.

POSTSCRIPT

1. *Sunday Press*, 22 January 1995.
2. Ibid.
3. *Cork Examiner*, 30 January 1995.
4. *Sunday Press*, 22 January 1995.
5. *Irish Times*, 28 January 1995.
6. *Guardian*, 29 April 1995.
7. Berg: Alec Martin to Lady Gregory, 15 August 1926.

SELECT BIBLIOGRAPHY

CATALOGUES

Catalogue of the Exhibition of Old Master Paintings at the Royal Hibernian Academy, December 1902.
Catalogue of the Exhibition of Works by Irish Painters, Art Gallery of the Corporation of London, Guildhall, May 1904.
Catalogue of the Exhibition of J. Staats Forbes Collection, Royal Hibernian Academy, November 1904.
Catalogue of Pictures Lent to the City of Dublin to Form the Nucleus of a Gallery of Modern Art exhibited at the National Museum, Kildare Street, January 1905.
Illustrated Catalogue with Biographical and Critical Notes, Municipal Gallery of Modern Art, Dublin, January 1908.
Illustrated Catalogue of Municipal Gallery of Modern Art, Johannesburg, November 1910.
Illustrated Catalogue of the National Gallery of Ireland, Dublin 1914.
Catalogue of the Exhibition of Pictures of Old Masters Bequeathed to the National Gallery of Ireland by Sir Hugh Lane, Dublin, 1918.
Catalogue of the Municipal Gallery of Modern Art and Civic Museum, Dublin, 1933.

BOOKS AND ARTICLES

Arnold, Bruce. *Jack Yeats* (Yale University Press, London, 1998).
Arnold, Bruce. *Orpen: Mirror to an Age* (Jonathan Cape, London, 1981).
Barrow, Viola. 'Hugh Lane' (*Dublin Historical Record*, Vol. XXVIII, No. 4, September 1975).
Behrman, S.N. *Duveen* (Vintage Books, New York, 1952).
Bence-Jones, Mark. *Life in an Irish Country House* (Constable, London, 1996).
Bence-Jones, Mark. *Twilight of the Ascendancy* (Constable, London, 1987).
Bodkin, Thomas. *Hugh Lane and His Pictures* (The Arts Council, Dublin, 1956).
Borland, Maureen. *D.S. MacColl: Painter, Poet, Art Critic* (Lennard Publishing, Herts, 1995).
Borland, Maureen. *Wilde's Devoted Friend: A Life of Robert Ross 1869–1918* (Lennard Publishing, Oxford, 1990).
Bowe, Nicola Gordon, and Elizabeth Cumming. *The Arts & Crafts Movements in Dublin & Edinburgh, 1885–1925* (Irish Academic Press, Dublin, 1998).
Boylan, Patricia. *All Cultivated People* (Colin Smythe, Gerrards Cross, 1988).

Select Bibliography

Boylan, Patricia. 'Mrs Duncan's Vocation' (*Irish Arts Review*, Volume 12, 1996).

Brown, Jane. *Lutyens and the Edwardians: An English Architect and His Clients* (Viking, London, 1996).

Campbell, Julian. *The Irish Impressionists: Irish Artists in France and Belgium, 1850–1914* (National Gallery of Ireland, Dublin, 1984).

Campbell, Julian. *Frank O'Meara and his Contemporaries* (Hugh Lane Municipal Gallery of Modern Art, Dublin, 1989).

Cannadine, David. *The Decline and Fall of the British Aristocracy* (Yale University Press, London, 1990).

Carman, Jillian. *Negotiating Museology and the Identity of the Johannesburg Art Gallery in the Early Twentieth Century* (paper delivered at the 14th annual conference of the South African Association of Art Historians, July 1998).

Carman, Jillian. *The Foundation of the Johannesburg Art Gallery and Culture in the Service of Empire* (paper delivered at the 15th annual conference of the South African Association of Art Historians, September 1999).

Clarke, Harold & Aidan O'Flanagan, eds. *75 Years of Giving: The Friends of the National Collections of Ireland* (Friends of the National Collections of Ireland, Dublin, 1999).

Collis, Maurice. *Somerville & Ross* (Faber & Faber, London, 1968).

Colson, Percy. *A Story of Christie's* (Sampson & Low, London, 1950).

Coxhead, Elizabeth. *Daughters of Erin* (Secker & Warburg, London, 1965).

Coxhead, Elizabeth. *Lady Gregory: A Literary Portrait* (Secker & Warburg, London, 1966).

Crook, J. Mordaunt. *The Rise of the Nouveaux Riches* (John Murray, London, 1999).

Crookshank, Anne, and the Knight of Glin. *The Painters of Ireland, c.1660–1920* (Barrie & Jenkins, London, 1978).

Daly, Mary. *Dublin – The Deposed Capital: A Social and Economic History 1860–1914* (Cork University Press, Cork, 1984).

Dickinson, P.L. *The Dublin of Yesterday* (Methuen, London, 1929).

Duncan, Ellen. 'Sir Hugh Lane and His Work' (text of a lecture delivered to the National Literary Society, Dublin, 5 March 1917).

Dreiser, Theodore. *A Traveller at Forty* (Grant Richards, London, 1914).

Fingall, Elizabeth, Countess of. *Seventy Years Young* (Lilliput Press, Dublin, 1991).

Foster, R.F. *W.B. Yeats, A Life: Volume 1: The Apprentice Mage* (Oxford University Press, Oxford, 1997).

Fransen, Hans. *Michaelis Collection, The Old Town House, Cape Town* (Michaelis Collection, Cape Town, 1997).

Fraser, Maryna, and Alan Jeeves, eds. *All that Glittered: Selected Correspondence of Lionel Phillips* (Oxford University Press, Cape Town, 1977).

Frazier, Adrian. *George Moore 1852–1933* (Yale University Press, London, 2000).

Gray, Tony. *A Peculiar Man: A Life of George Moore* (Sinclair-Stevenson, London, 1996).

Green, Christopher, ed. *Art Made Modern: Roger Fry's Vision of Art* (Courtauld Institute of Art, London, 1999).

Gregory, Lady. *Hugh Lane's Life and Achievement, with Some Account of the Dublin Galleries* (John Murray, London, 1921).

Gwynn, Denis, ed. *A Tribute to Sir Hugh Lane* (Cork University Press, Cork, 1961).

Gutsche, Thelma. *No Ordinary Woman: The Life and Times of Florence Phillips* (Howard Timmins, Cape Town, 1966).

Harrison, S.C. *Inquiry concerning the Continental Pictures of Sir Hugh Lane: The Next Step* (Hodgson & Son, London, 1927).

Holroyd, Michael. *Augustus John* (Chatto & Windus, London, 1996).

Hone, Joseph, ed. *J.B. Hone: Letters to his son W.B. Yeats and Others, 1869–1922* (Secker & Warburg, London, 1983).

Hutchinson, John. 'Sir Hugh Lane and the Gift of the Prince of Wales to the Municipal Gallery of Modern Art, Dublin' (*Studies*, Winter 1979, No. 272, Volume LXVIII).

Select Bibliography

Keane, Maureen: *Ishbel: Lady Aberdeen in Ireland* (Colourpoint, Dublin, 1999).

Kelly, John, and Ronald Schuchard, eds. *Collected Letters of W.B. Yeats, Vol. III 1901–1904* (Oxford University Press, Oxford, 1994).

Kelly, Thomas. 'Pallace Row' (*Dublin Historical Record*, Vol. IV, No. 1, September–November 1941).

Kennedy, S.B. *Irish Art & Modernism, 1880–1950* (Hugh Lane Municipal Gallery of Modern Art, Dublin, 1991).

Kynaston, David. *The City of London, Volume II: Golden Years 1890–1914* (Chatto & Windus, London, 1995).

Lambert, Angela. *Unquiet Souls* (Harper & Row, New York, 1984).

Larmour, Paul. *The Arts & Crafts Movement in Ireland* (Friar's Bush Press, Belfast, 1992).

McConkey, Kenneth. *A Free Spirit: Irish Art 1860–1960* (Antique Collectors Club, London, 1990).

McConkey, Kenneth. *Sir John Lavery* (Canongate Press, Edinburgh, 1993).

McCoole, Sinead. *Hazel: A Life of Lady Lavery, 1880–1935* (Lilliput Press, Dublin, 1996).

Mandler, Peter. *The Fall and Rise of the Stately Home* (Yale University Press, London, 1997).

Mayes, Elizabeth, and Paula Murphy, eds. *Images and Insights* (Hugh Lane Municipal Gallery of Modern Art, Dublin, 1993).

Moore, George. *A Drama in Muslin* (Appletree Press, Belfast, 1992).

Moore, George. *Hail and Farewell* (Colin Smythe, Gerrards Cross, 1985).

Morrissey, Thomas. *William Martin Murphy* (Historical Association of Ireland, Dublin, 1997).

Mulcahy, Rosemarie. *Spanish Paintings in the National Gallery of Ireland* (National Gallery of Ireland, Dublin, 1988).

Murphy, William M. *Prodigal Father: The Life of John Butler Yeats 1839–1922* (Cornell University Press, London, 1978).

O'Connor, Ulick. *Celtic Dawn: A Portrait of the Irish Literary Renaissance* (Hamish Hamilton, London, 1984).

O'Grady, John. *The Life and Work of Sarah Purser* (Four Courts Press, Dublin, 1996).

O'Neill, Marie. 'Sarah Cecilia Harrison: Artist and City Councillor' (*Dublin Historical Record*, Vol. XLII, No. 2, March 1989).

Orpen, William. *Stories of Old Ireland and Myself* (Williams & Norgate, London, 1924).

Pethica, James, ed. *Lady Gregory's Diaries, 1892–1902* (Oxford University Press, New York, 1996).

Potterton, Homan. *Dutch Seventeenth and Eighteenth Century Paintings in the National Gallery of Ireland* (National Gallery of Ireland, Dublin, 1986).

Potterton, Homan, ed. *National Gallery of Ireland, Illustrated Summary Catalogue of Paintings* (National Gallery of Ireland, Dublin, 1981).

Reid, B.L. *The Man from New York: John Quinn and His Friends* (Oxford University Press, New York, 1968).

Reynolds, John J. *Statement of the Claim for the Return of the 39 Lane Bequest Pictures now at the Tate Gallery, London* (Dublin Corporation, 1932).

Richards, Grant. *Author Hunting: Memoirs of Years Spent Mainly in Publishing* (Unicorn Press, London, 1960).

Richards, Grant. *Caviare* (Grant Richards, London, 1912).

Robins, Anna Gruetzner. *Modern Art in Britain, 1910–1914* (Barbican Arts Centre, London, 1997).

Robinson, Lennox, ed. *Lady Gregory's Journals 1916–1930* (Macmillan, New York, 1947).

Rosenblum, Robert, Maryanne Stevens and Ann Dumas, eds. *1900: Art at the Crossroads* (Royal Academy of Arts, London, 2000).

Ryan-Smolin, Wanda, Elizabeth Mayes and Jenni Rogers, eds. *Irish Women Artists from the Eighteenth Century to the Present Day* (National Gallery of Ireland and the Douglas Hyde Gallery, Dublin, 1987).

[267]

Select Bibliography

Secrest, Meryle. *Being Bernard Berenson: A Biography* (Holt, Rinehart & Winston, New York, 1979).

Sheehy, Jeanne. *Walter Osborne* (National Gallery of Ireland, Dublin, 1983).

Simpson, John. *The Artful Partners: The Secret Partnership between Bernard Berenson and Joseph Duveen* (Unwin, London, 1988).

Smith, Janet Adam. *John Buchan* (Rupert Hart-Davis, London, 1965).

Snoddy, Theo. *Dictionary of Irish Artists – 20th Century* (Wolfhound Press, Dublin, 1996).

Somerville-Large, Peter. *The Irish Country House. A Social History* (Sinclair-Stevenson, London, 1995).

Stevenson, Michael. *Old Masters and Aspirations: The Randlords, Art and South Africa* (PhD Thesis, Department of Art History, University of Cape Town, September 1997).

Sutton, Denys. 'Robert Langton Douglas' (*Apollo*, No. 109, April–July 1979).

West, Trevor. Horace Plunkett, *Co-operation and Politics* (Colin Smythe, Gerrards Cross, 1982).

White, Anna MacBride, and A. Norman Jeffares. *Always Your Friend: The Gonne–Yeats Letters 1893–1938* (Hutchinson, London, 1992).

White, James. Introduction to Lady Gregory, *Sir Hugh Lane: His Life and Work* (Colin Smythe, Gerrards Cross, 1973).

White, James. 'Sir Hugh Lane as a Collector' (*Apollo*, Vol. XCIV, No. 144, February 1974).

INDEX

Index

Index